John Andrew Doyle

The American Colonies Previous to the Declaration of Independence

The Arnold prize essay, read in the theatre at Oxford, June 9, 1869

John Andrew Doyle

The American Colonies Previous to the Declaration of Independence
The Arnold prize essay, read in the theatre at Oxford, June 9, 1869

ISBN/EAN: 9783337152888

Printed in Europe, USA, Canada, Australia, Japan

Cover: Foto ©ninafisch / pixelio.de

More available books at **www.hansebooks.com**

THE AMERICAN COLONIES

PREVIOUS TO THE

DECLARATION OF INDEPENDENCE

THE AMERICAN COLONIES

PREVIOUS TO THE

DECLARATION OF INDEPENDENCE

(THE ARNOLD PRIZE ESSAY, READ IN THE THEATRE AT OXFORD, JUNE 9, 1869)

BY

JOHN ANDREW DOYLE, B.A. OF BALLIOL COLLEGE.

"*Westward the course of empire takes its way.*"

RIVINGTONS
London, Oxford, and Cambridge
1869

TABLE OF CONTENTS.

	PAGE
INTRODUCTION	vii

CHAPTER I.

ENGLISH DISCOVERIES IN AMERICA DURING THE SIXTEENTH CENTURY.

	PAGE		PAGE
English Navigation at the end of the Fifteenth Century,	1, 2	Frobisher's Voyages,	7-9
Sebastian Cabot,	2-4	Sir Humphrey Gilbert,	9-12
Other Early Discoverers,	4-6	Raleigh sends out Amidas and Barlow,	12, 13
Commencement of a new Epoch under Elizabeth,	6, 7	Settlement under Granville and Lane,	13-16
		White's Voyage,	16, 17
		Concluding Remarks,	18

CHAPTER II.

FORMATION OF THE THIRTEEN COLONIES.

	PAGE		PAGE
Formation of the Virginia Company,	10	Colonisation of New Haven,	69
Captain John Smith,	19, 20	Difficulties between New England and the Home Government,	69, 70
Colonisation of Virginia in 1606,	21-23	Acquisition of New Netherlands,	70, 71
The Second Colony,	23, 24	James II. attempts to consolidate the New England Colonies,	71
Growth of the Colony,	24-26	Government of Andros,	71
Story of Pocahontas,	26, 27	His Defeat,	71, 72
The Indian Massacre,	27, 28	State of New England from 1640 to 1675,	72
Early Legislation of Virginia,	28-30	The Pequod War,	72-74
Emigration to Virginia,	30	Laws of the New England Colonies,	74, 75
The Virginia Company dissolved,	30, 31	Peculiarly Religious Character of New England,	75-77
First Independent Legislation,	31, 32	Its Intolerance,	77-79
History of Virginia from 1630 to 1659,	32-34	Provision for Education	79
Slavery in Virginia,	34, 35	Contrast between New England and Virginia,	79, 80
Social and Economical State of the Colony,	35-38	Early Attempts to colonise Carolina,	80, 81
Intolerant Laws,	38, 39	Locke's Constitution for Carolina,	81, 82
Constitution of Virginia,	39-41	Formation of a Settlement at Albermarle,	82
Laws regulating the cultivation of Tobacco,	41, 42	Colonisation and Early History of South Carolina,	82, 83
Laws concerning the Indians,	42-44	North Carolina,	83, 84
Bacon's Insurrection,	44-48	Quakerism,	84, 85
Government of Culpepper and Effingham,	48, 49	William Penn,	85
Early History of Maryland,	49, 50	His Colony in West New Jersey,	85, 86
Attempt to colonise New England in 1607,	51, 52	Establishment of a Quaker Colony in Pennsylvania,	87, 88
Gorges's Attempts at Colonisation,	52, 53	Penn's Relations with the Indians,	88, 89
The Leyden Puritans,	53-55	Early History of Pennsylvania,	89, 90
Their Project of Colonisation,	55, 56	General James Oglethorpe	90, 91
The Colonisation of Plymouth,	57, 58	Colonisation and Early History of Georgia,	91-95
Positin of the New England Company,	58-61	General Survey of the Thirteen Colonies,	95, 96
Weston's Colony,	62		
Colonisation of New Hampshire,	62		
Colonisation of Massachusetts,	62-64		
Roger Williams,	64-67		
Colonisation of Connecticut	67, 68		
Gorges colonises Maine,	68, 69		

CHAPTER III.

GENERAL VIEW OF THE COLONIES FROM 1688 TO 1760.

	PAGE		PAGE
Ethnology of the Indians,	97, 98	His Scheme for Confederation,	110, 111
Their Character, Religion, and Political System,	98-101	Braddock's Defeat,	111, 112
		Defeat of the French near Fort Edward,	112
Failure of all Attempts to civilise them,	101-103	The French Inhabitants of Acadia,	112, 113
King Philip's War,	103-105	Their Eviction by the British Government,	113
Early American Slavery,	105, 106	Conclusion of the War,	114, 115
The Witch Persecutions in New England,	106-108	Discussion whether England shall keep Canada or Guadaloupe,	114, 115
French Aggressions in the Ohio Valley,	108, 109		
Benjamin Franklin,	109, 110	Canada becomes British Territory,	115

CHAPTER IV.

THE CONTEST FOR INDEPENDENCE

Position of the Colonies at the Conclusion of the French War,	116-118	The Boston Tea-riot.	163, 164
		The Boston Port-bill,	165, 166
State of England at the Accession of George III.,	118-120	How received by Boston,	166, 167
		And the other Colonies,	167, 168
Influence of that event,	120, 121	Preparations for Resistance,	168, 169
Character of the Ministers Granville and Townshend,	121	Proceedings of the Congress at Philadelphia,	169-171
Project of an American Revenue,	121, 122	The British Parliament of 1775,	171-174
How received by the Americans,	122, 123	Chatham's Policy of Conciliation,	174-176
Attempt to subvert the Independence of the Judiciary,	123	The Newfoundland Fishery Bill,	176, 177
		Lord North's Scheme of Conciliation,	177, 178
Townshend's American Policy,	123, 124	Burke's Policy,	178-180
Carried out by George Granville,	124-126	Address presented by the Citizens of London,	180
The Stamp Act,	126, 127		
General Attitude of England towards the Colonies,	127-133	Proceedings of the British Soldiers at Boston,	180-182
News of the Stamp Act received in America,	133-135	The Virginian Convention	182
		Patrick Henry's Speech	182, 183
Granville's Scheme discussed in Parliament,	135, 136	Preparations for Resistance in Virginia,	183, 184
		General Survey of the Position of both Countries at the Commencement of the War,	184-187
The Stamp Act becomes Law,	136, 137		
Patrick Henry,	137, 138		
His Resolutions denouncing the Stamp Act passed by Legislature of Virginia,	138, 139	Concord Bridge and Lexington,	187, 188
		Siege of Boston,	188, 189
Massachusetts proposes a Congress,	139, 140	Capture of Ticonderoga and Crown Point,	189
Nine Colonies meet in Congress,	140	Military Daring of the Americans,	189
Proceedings of Massachusetts Assembly,	140, 141	The Philadelphia Congress	190
Reception of the Stamp Act,	141, 142	Its Proceedings,	190-192
Ministerial Changes in England,	142, 143	Washington elected General,	192
Pitt opposes the Taxation of America,	143, 144	His Character,	192
Trecothick and Franklin examined,	144, 145	Bunker's Hill,	193-195
Rockingham's Ministry repeal the Stamp Act,	145	Proceedings of Congress,	195, 196
		Weakness of the Colonial Army,	196, 197
Rejoicings in England and America,	146	The Americans resolve to attack Canada,	197
Disputes in Massachusetts Assembly,	146, 147	Montgomery appointed General	198
Chatham's Ministry,	147	Operations in Canada,	198-200
Townshend introduces a Scheme for Taxing America,	147-149	Siege of Quebec,	200, 201
		Death of Montgomery,	201
Further Resistance in America,	149	Quebec is relieved	201, 202
Policy of Massachusetts,	150-153	Proceedings of Dunmore in Virginia	202, 203
Proceedings in England,	153, 154	State of things in England,	203-205
The Southern Colonies pass Non-importation Resolves,	154, 155	Examination of Penn before the Lords,	205, 206
		Proceedings of Parliament,	206-209
Departure of Bernard from Boston,	155, 156	Washington raises the Siege of Boston,	209-210
The Boston Massacre,	156, 157	Victory of the Americans in North Carolina,	210, 211
Lord North's Policy,	158, 159		
The Non-importation Agreements fail,	159	Battle of Fort Moultrie,	211, 212
Disputes between Hutchinson and the Assembly,	159-162	Proceedings of Congress,	212, 213
		South Carolina and Virginia construct Governments,	213, 214
The Slavery Question in Virginia,	162, 163		
Virginia resolves on Committees of Correspondence,	163	Congress resolves on Independence,	214, 215
		The Declaration of Independence,	215, 216
Hutchinson's Letters,	163	Conclusion	216-219

INTRODUCTION.

I PROPOSE in this Essay to examine a few of the most remarkable in that course of events by which a wilderness, inhabited only by savages and wild beasts, was changed in less than two hundred years into the home of one of the greatest of the civilised powers of the world. For this purpose I propose, *first*, to glance briefly and in outline at that movement which changed the sober, homely Englishman of the earlier Tudor reigns into the enterprising versatile Elizabethan Englishman, and which moulded the gentry, yeomanry, and merchants of the sixteenth century into a race of navigators and explorers, the boldest and most adventurous that the world has ever seen. I propose then to trace somewhat more fully the growth of the several colonies, to illustrate their social and political life, their manners, religion, and laws; to pass in review the most striking incidents, and the most eminent characters in their history; to consider their relations to the savage inhabitants whom they drove out, and to the colonists of other civilised nations with whom they came in contact; *lastly*, to examine the principal causes which gradually alienated, and finally rent them asunder, from their mother country, and bound them together in one independent empire.

THE AMERICAN COLONIES

PREVIOUS TO

THE DECLARATION OF INDEPENDENCE.

CHAPTER I.

ENGLISH DISCOVERIES IN AMERICA DURING THE SIXTEENTH CENTURY.

IN 1488 an obscure Genoese, one Bartholomew Columbus, was sailing to England with an offer from his brother, an unsuccessful projector at the Court of Castille, to Henry VII.[1] That offer, if accepted in time, might have enabled England to anticipate Spain in the New World, and to become the great gold-power of Europe. England was saved from that lot by the unconscious agency of a pirate ship. Bartholomew Columbus escaped from captivity and completed his mission at the English Court, but, before he could return, the eyes of the Spanish sovereign had been in some measure opened to the importance of his brother's designs, and the destiny of Spain and South America was sealed. Even had Columbus' offer come in time, it is hardly likely that the English king would have committed himself to the adventure, or that the English people would have followed it up. The English of that

[1] Knight's "History of England," vol. iii., p. 776.

day were a thriving, industrious race, content with the resources of a moderately populated soil and a stationary commerce. "The wine brigs made their annual voyages to Bordeaux and Cadiz; the hoys plied with such regularity as the winds allowed them between the Scheldt and Thames; summer after summer the Iceland fleet went north for the cod and ling, which were the food of the winter fasting days; the boats of Yarmouth and Rye, Southampton, Pool, Brixham, Dartmouth, Plymouth, and Fowie fished the channel."[1] The spirit of Drake and Gilbert and Raleigh yet slept. Even eight years later, when Columbus had already sailed on his second voyage, it was left for foreign enterprise, albeit helped by English seamanship, to take the first step towards founding a British Empire in the New World. In 1496 John Cabot, a Venetian, and his two sons, obtained a patent from Henry VII. for the discovery of hitherto unknown lands.[2] In

---

[1] Froude's "History of England," vol. viii., chap. xiii., p. 423.

[2] The History of Sebastian Cabot and his voyages from 1496 to 1498, is somewhat obscure. I have throughout followed Biddle's "Memorial of Sebastian Cabot." The principal points in question are—1. The birthplace of Sebastian Cabot; 2. The distinctness of the two voyages; 3. Whether it was John or Sebastian Cabot that undertook, or at all events commanded, the first voyage? 4. What was the land discovered?

1. Stow says, " One Sebastian Gabatto, a Genoa's son, borne in Bristow." Stow's "Annals," p. 481. Eden, " Sebastian Cabot tould me that he was born in Bristow." Eden and Wylles Decades of the New World of Indies, published, London, 1555, by William Powell. An old Bristol chronicle, " Sebastian Cabot borne in Bristol." Quoted by Mr Seyers, in his Memoirs, Historical and Topographical, of Bristol.

Best says in the dedication of his account of Sir Martin Frobisher's three voyages, published 1578, to Sir Christopher Hutton, " Sebastian Cabota being an Englishman and born in Bristowe." Hakluyt, [Ed. 1589], p. 680. " Sebastian his sonne an Englishman borne."

2. That Cabot made a voyage in 1497, is proved by an extract from a MS. in "The History and Antiquities of Bristol." " In the year 1497, 24th of June, on St John's Day, was Newfoundland found by Bristol men in a ship called the Matthew," and by extracts from the Privy Purse expenses of Henry VII. for 1497, " to Lym that found the new Isle £10," and " to John Carter going to the newe Isle, a reward £2." Moreover, from the passage quoted above, Stow says, " This yeere [1498] one Sebastian Gabatto, a Genoa's son borne in Bristow, professing himselfe to be expert in knowledge of the circuit of the world and islands of the same, as by his charts and other reasonable demonstrations he shewed, caused the king to man and victual a ship at Bristol, to search for an island which he knew to be replenished with rich commodities." This evidently implies a previous knowledge of the land

the next year the eldest son, Sebastian Cabot, set sail in pursuit of the philosopher's stone of the mariners of that day, a north-

to be traded with. Besides, the second patent [given by Biddle, p. 76] refers to "the land and isle of late found by the said John in oure name and by oure commandment." Bacon too, in his life of Henry VII., speaks like Stow of a voyage in 1498, in terms which evidently refer to a voyage of commerce, and imply a previous discovery. That a voyage was made in 1498 from England to trade with the "New Island," is proved by entries in the King's Privy Purse Accounts "to Lanslot Thirkell of London, upon a prest for his ship going towards the New Island, £2, 22d of March, 1498."

"Delivered to Lanslot Thirkell going towards the new Isle, a prest. £20.

"To Thomas Bradley and Lanslot Thirkell going to the New Isle, £30, April 1st 1498."

3. With the exception of Hakluyt in his later edition, all the early writers, including Stow, attribute the voyage of 1497 to Sebastian, not to John, Cabot. It is clear, too, that it was attributed to Sebastian in the authority from which Hakluyt took his statement, and that he must himself have changed the name to John. His account is taken from Stow, and is headed, "A Note of Sebastian Cabot's First Discovery of Part of the Indies, taken out of the latter part of Robert Fabyan's Chronicle, not hitherto printed, which is in the custody of Mr John Stow, a diligent preserver of antiquities." In the original edition of Hakluyt, 1582, the name of Sebastian was left to stand not only in the heading, but in the narrative. It is clear that when Hakluyt compiled this edition, he had not read the patents of 1496 and 1498. It is probable that, after reading them, he substituted the name of John for that of Sebastian in the narrative, though he omitted to do so in the heading. The statement in the second patent, that the land and isles were found by John Cabot, may mean that the expedition went out at his expense; nor does the fact of the first patent being made out in his favour necessarily imply that he went on the voyage. That the father should undertake the expense of the voyage, and send out his son, a man in the prime of life, is in itself reasonable and probable, while the testimony of contemporary writers is strongly in favour of the claims of the younger Cabot.

4. *The extent of Cabot's Voyages.*—The authorities for the statement that he sailed as far as 67½ degrees of north latitude [in all probability into Hudson's Bay] are,—1. Cabot's own statement in "Peter Martyr's Decades," iii. lib. 6. 2. In the prayse and report of Master Martyn Forboisere's voyage to Meta incognita, published in Hakluyt, the author says, "In reading Belle Forest, in the second tome, and other authors, I find that Gabotha was the first in King Henry VII.'s daies that discovered this frozen land or seas, from sixtie-seven degrees towards the north, and from thence towards the south along the Coast of America to thirtie-six degrees and a half, as it is affirmed in the sixth book of the Decade."

The land which Cabot discovered, was in all probability not Newfoundland, but Labrador. The character of the country, the elks, the white bears, fishing, and the appearance of the inhabitants, [Peter Martyr], all correspond with the character of Labrador. The mention of the Island of St John, as off the coast discovered by Cabot, has given rise to some confusion, but this is cleared up by reference to Ortelius, who, in his "Theatrum orbis terrarum," in a map, dated 1587, calls a small island just off the coast of Labrador St Joan.

west passage to "Cataia." Baffled by the increasing icebergs when he had reached sixty-seven and a half degrees of north latitude, he turned south, and on St John's Day discovered the coast of Labrador. Still sailing south he explored the coast of Florida as far as thirty-six and a half degrees of north latitude. On his return he obtained a second patent, and again sailed in 1498 with several ships laden with "grosse and sleighte wares" for trafficking with the natives.[1] With so little attention, however, did his successes meet, that after this we hear no more of him in England for nineteen years.

There may have been various causes beside lack of enterprise which may have made Henry VII. and his subjects disinclined for maritime discoveries in the direction of America. The bull of Alexander VI. could not but have some effect with a still Roman Catholic nation, and the hope of a Spanish alliance may have made the king chary of encroaching on the treasures of the New World. Still he did not altogether neglect American discoveries. For the next seven or eight years we have scattered intimations that voyages were made, though of their circumstances and results we know nothing. We find a patent granted to three Englishmen, Thomas Ashurst, Richard Warde, and John Thomas, and three Portuguese, John Gonsalo, and John and Francis Fernando, bearing date, March 1501,[2] and another patent in December of the same year, in favour of Hugh Eliot and Thomas Ashurst, merchants of Bristol, and John Gonsalo and Francis Fernando, Esquires.[3] Both these patents reserve the rights of the king of Portugal, and expressly forbid the offering of any violence to the persons of the natives,[4] a condition which speaks well for the humanity of the king, if not for the morality of the early navigators. It is also stated in Purchas that Robert Thorne

---

[1] Stow, p. 481.   [2] Biddle. Appendix D.

[3] Rymer, vol. xiii., pp. 37, 42. Rymer places the date of the first patent the 10th of May, sixteenth year of Henry VII. Biddle, however, shows that this is wrong.

[4] "Sive aliquas mulieres insularum seu patriarum predictarum rapuerint et violaverint, juxta leges ac statuta per ipsos in hac parte ordinata castigandi et puniendi."

and Hugh Eliot "discovered the Newfoundland," and that had they followed their pilot's mind the lands of the West Indies had been ours."[1] Traces also are to be found of such voyages in the existing records of the time. We read in the King's Privy Purse Accounts such entries as these—

"*17th November* 1503.—To one that brought hawkes from the new founded isle, £1."

"*8th April* 1504.—To a preste that goeth to the islande, £2."

"*25th August* 1505.—To Clays going to Richmond with wylde catts and popyngays of the new found islande for his costs, 13s. 4d."

"To Portugales that brought popyngais and catts of the mountayne, with the stuff to the king's grace, £5."

It was probably in one of these voyages that the savages were brought over, who, Stow says, were seen in London in 1502.[2]

After the accession of Henry VIII. we hear of no more voyages till the nineteenth year of his reign. In that year two ships were sent out in search of the North-west Passage, under Thorne and Eliot, of which the larger was lost on the coast of Newfoundland. The other returned safe to England. Nine years later Hore sailed from London with two ships, and encountered the horrors of the north seas in their worst form.[3] That some definite progress had been made by the year 1541 is proved by an Act of Parliament, in which special provision is made for the Newfoundland Fisheries.[4] In 1549, the third year of Edward

---

[1] Purchas, [Ed. 1626], p. 810. Biddle identifies this with the voyage of 1527, mentioned below, but the expression, "discovered the Newfoundland," and the reference to the West Indies would seem to refer to an earlier date.

[2] Stow, p. 485. "This yeere [1502] were brought into the king taken in ye Newfound Ilands by Sebastian Gabote, before named, in anno 1498. These men were clothed in beasts' skins, and eate raw flesh, but spake such a language as no man could understand, of the which three men, two of them were seene in the king's court at Westminster two yeeres after. They were clothed like Englishmen, and could not be discerned from Englishmen." It is exceedingly improbable that if these men had been brought over by Cabot in 1498, as Stow supposes, and still retained their native customs and language four years later, that two years could afterwards have made so great a change in them.

[3] Purchas, p. 822.   [4] Bancroft's "History of America," vol. i., p. 77.

VI., Cabot's services at last met with a portion of the reward they had deserved, and he was made Grand Pilot of England, with a pension of £166, 13s. 4d.[1] Age had not lessened his energy for discovery, but America was no longer the field of his labours. He, like most of the navigators of his age, attached more value to the visionary project of a north-west or a north-east passage to Asia, than to the substantial advantages which the American trade and fisheries placed within their grasp. He became president of a merchant company, which included Willoughby, Chancellor, and Burroughs, and whose object was the discovery of a north-east passage to China.[2] The voyage in 1553 was in its main object unsuccessful, and resulted in the loss of Willoughby and his ship, but the failure was compensated for by the discovery of a passage to Archangel.[3]

After this Cabot disappears from the history of discovery; but the seed which he had sown was in a few years to bear fruit that would have far surpassed his most fervent anticipations. In the words of an old writer, " it pleased Almighty God, of His infinite mercy, at length to awake some of our worthy countrymen out of their drowsy dreame wherein we have all so long slumbered."[4] The seventy years preceding the reign of Elizabeth had not only changed English modes of thought and life; they had begotten a new race of Englishmen. Various tendencies had combined to bring about this growth. The movement which in theology had produced the Reformation, and in philosophy contained the teaching of Bacon, and of the seventeenth century in its womb, had changed the social and mercantile, as well as the political life of the nation. Henry VIII., when he made England independent of the Papacy, foresaw that growing struggle between the two great principles of the age which culminated in the fight with the Armada, and he provided for it by making England an independent military and naval power. There were special reasons

---

[1] Purchas, p. 810.   [2] Ibid.   [3] Bancroft, vol. i., p. 79.
[4] "A True Report of the Late Discoveries and Possession taken in the Right of the Crown of England in the Newfoundland," in Hakluyt, [Ed. 1589], p. 704.

why the newly awakened life of the nation should show itself on the seas. The theoretical discoveries of Galileo, the practical discoveries of Columbus, shed a halo of science and romance over seamanship. Spain was no longer an ally to be respected, but a dangerous and hated rival. The spectacle of Philip and his Spanish courtiers riding into London decked in the spoils of Mexico and Peru must have been at once dazzling, enraging, animating. Might not England fight Spain on her own ground, and with her own weapons? Might not the treasures of the New World be used to support England and Protestantism, not Spain and the Inquisition? Even the thirst for gold was ennobled when thus linked with love of national greatness and religious freedom. Another motive ought not in justice to be overlooked. As in the search for gold, so, in the conversion of the Indians, Spain was at once a pattern and a rival. To carry out the gospel to wild races dwelling in distant lands was a task peculiarly suited to the temper of an adventurous generation that had just passed through a great religious crisis. Such was the combination of influences under which England entered upon her career in the New World. The reign of Mary had repressed, but in nowise destroyed, the new-born spirit of the nation. When that evil time was passed, and a popular, ambitious, and enterprising monarch sat on the throne, the torrent burst forth in full strength. Privateers harassed the Spanish commerce on the coast of South America, and from thirty to fifty ships went every year to the Newfoundland fisheries.[1] In 1576, Frobisher, afterwards Sir Martin Frobisher, a west country sea captain, hitherto only known as having been implicated in a charge of piracy,[2] conceived a design of discovering the North-west Passage. Encouraged by the example of Cabot, with whose voyage he was acquainted,[3] on

---

[1] Bancroft, vol. i., p. 80.   [2] Catalogue of State Papers, vol. xl., 7.
[3] George Gascoyne says, in the preface to Sir Humphrey Gilbert's Account of a North-west Passage, with reference to an account of Sebastian Cabot, "The which, as well because it was not long, as also because I understoode that Mr Fourboiser [a kinsman of mine] did pretend to travaile in the same discoverie, I craved at the saide Sir Humfreye's hands for two or three days to reade and to peruse."

the 15th of June he set sail from Blackwell. He sailed into Frobisher's Straits, landed on the coast of Labrador, captured a native and returned, having lost five men.[1] He brought back not the report of a North-west Passage, but hopes as chimerical and more dangerous. A stone which he had found was reported to contain gold. England was already gold-mad,[2] and the prospect of a northern Peru instantly awakened the enthusiasm of those who had been unmoved by the project of a North-west Passage. The Company of "Kathai," or Cathay, was formed, of which Michael Lok was to be governor, and "Furbisher" high admiral of all the newly discovered lands.[3] In 1577, Frobisher sailed with three ships on his search for ore.[4] He returned, after a severe voyage, with a cargo of earth to be deposited in the mint.[5] The next year, at the desire of the Queen,[6] a third voyage was undertaken on a larger scale, and a colony projected.[7] Colony and voyage alike were failures. Beset by fogs and icebergs one vessel was crushed, and the rest lost their course. The sailors almost mutinied, one of the ships with provisions for the colony deserted, and the settlers became disheartened. The fleet was freighted with two thousand tons of ore, and returned home.[8] The ore proved worthless, and all that we ever hear further of the Cathay Company is a succession of squabbles between Lok and the adventurers.[9] But the chapter

[1] Purchas, p. 811.

[2] The public records of the time are full of references to the gold brought back by Frobisher. In the Catalogue of State Papers, vol. cxlvii. 69, we find an offer from Lok to work the ore brought from the north-west voyage by "Captain Furbisher." So also in vol. cxviii. 36, 39, 40, 41, 42, 43; vol. cxix. 8, 9, 10, 12, 14, 15; vol. cxxii. 3, it is stated in a note that some of the gold still remains attached by wax to a paper.

[3] State Papers, vol. cx. 21.

[4] State Papers, vol. cxi. 48, 49. Purchas, p. 811.

[5] State Papers, vol. cxvi. 25.

[6] State Papers, vol. cxxiii. 5. Letters from Walsingham to the Lord Treasurer and Lord Chamberlain, March 11, 1578.

[7] Bancroft, vol. i., p. 84.

[8] Catalogue of State Papers, vol. cxxvi. 20. Bancroft, vol. i., p. 85.

[9] Frobisher's gold discoveries seem to have been prolific in disputes. We find Lok repeatedly applying to the Council for orders to be given to the adventurers to

of British maritime discovery was not yet closed. Regardless of Frobisher's failure, Davies and Hudson essayed once more to discover the North-west Passage. It was not granted to the Elizabethan seamen to win that goal for which they had so persistently striven, or to share in the colonisation of America. But though they left no permanent memorial of their triumphs, they stamped their impress on the generation that followed them. They were worthy to be the fathers of those puritan settlers, who left their English villages and farms to sail across three thousand miles of ocean with no home awaiting them but a bleak wilderness. Nothing in modern seamanship can give us an idea of the hardships and sufferings of the early navigators. In vessels little bigger than fishing smacks they ventured through fogs and icebergs into unknown seas, or landed on frozen shores, where they were reduced by hunger to eat the bodies of their companions,[1] or to live on sea-weed, when they scarce had strength to steer their boat.[2]

But their spirit of adventure, heroic as it was, was essentially that of explorers, not of colonists. Gilbert and Raleigh alone were conspicuous exceptions. Gilbert was, as far as we know, the first in that age to whom the idea of founding a great transatlantic empire had suggested itself. Even with him it is probable that the main idea was that of a great commercial power to counteract and cripple Spain, rather than an agricultural community in a great measure independent of the mother country.[3]

pay their shares. Catalogue of State Papers, vol. cxvi. 24; vol. cxxii. 9; vol. cxxvii. 8, 9, 10, 16, 20; vol. cxxix. 4, 12. Nor do they seem profitable to the adventurers, as we find Thomas Renham claiming allowance from the Council in consideration of his losses in "Furbisher's" voyage, vol. cxxvi. 33; vol. cxlix. 12. We find Lok complaining in 1581 "that Furbisher and others had slandered him, and Captain Furbisher had endangered the Company by his evil service and prodigality," and about the same time [vol. cli. 17] we find Captain Frobisher's wife, Isabel Frobisher, petitioning the Queen, and setting forth "that Captain Frobisher [whom God forgive] had spent all our money, and she was starving and her children's children."

[1] Account of Hore's voyage in 1536. Purchas, p. 822.
[2] Account of Hudson's third voyage. Purchas, p. 818.
[3] There is among the State Papers a document bearing date November 6, 1577,

In 1578 he took his first step towards the project of forming "a Christian plantation and regiment,"[1] by obtaining a general patent bearing date June 11, 1578, and giving him "free power and liberty" to discover and colonise all "remote heathen and barbarous lands" not already occupied by any Christian prince or people. At the same time the patent prohibited any colonisation within two hundred leagues of the territory occupied by Gilbert, reserved certain rights to the crown, and was to expire if the colony should not be founded in six years.[2] On the 23d of September 1578 he sailed from Dartmouth with a fleet of eleven ships victualled for a year.[3] The expedition, however, was unprosperous from the outset. One of the ships leaked and had to be left behind, and shortly after seven more deserted. From what we know of the habits of the sailors of that day it is not unlikely that they preferred piracy to colonisation. The expedition was a complete failure, and left Gilbert too crippled in means to go on with his project.[4] In 1580 he transferred his patent to Sir Thomas Gerrard and Sir George Peckham.[5] They either did nothing in the matter, or failed so completely that all trace of their attempt is lost. In 1583, Gilbert himself, rather than allow the patent to expire, made one more effort.[6] On Tuesday, June 14, he set sail with five ships, the largest of two hundred tons, the smallest ten tons, and with two hundred and sixty men. No

[the year before Gilbert got his patent], entitled "A Discourse how her Majestie may annoy the King of Spayne by fitting out a fleet of shippes of war under pretence of a voyage of discovery, and so fall upon the enemies' shippes, and destroy his trade in Newfoundland and the West Indies, and possess their countrie." The signature is obliterated, but it is supposed to be "H. Gylberte."

[1] A Report of the Voyage, and the Success thereof, attempted in the yeere of our Lord 1583 by Sir H. Gilbert, knt., written by Mr Edward Haies, gent., in Hakluyt, [Ed. 1589], p. 679.
[2] The patent is given in Stith's "History of Virginia," book i., p. 4, and in Hakluyt, pp. 677-679.
[3] Letter from J. Gilbert to Walsingham, December 20, 1578. State Papers, vol. cxxvi. 20.
[4] Haies, pp. 681, 682.   [5] State Papers, vol. cxlvii. 40.
[6] The whole of the following account is taken from Haies' account. Hakluyt, pp. 679-697, and from "A True Report of the Late Discoveries," &c. Hakluyt, pp. 702, 714.

cost seems to have been spared on this attempt, and everything was arranged with the view to a permanent settlement, and to the establishing friendly relations with the natives, and carrying on trade with them. There were men "of every faculty, good choice, as shipwrights, masons, carpenters, smiths, and such like requisite to such an action; also mineral men and refiners. Beside, for solace of our people, and allurement for the savages, we were provided of music in good variety, not omitting the least toyes, as morris dancers, hobby-horsse, and maylike conceits, to delight the savage people, whom we intended to winne by all fayre means possible. And to that end we were indifferently furnished of all petty haberdashery wares to barter with those simple people." At the outset the voyage was unfortunate. Two days after they left Plymouth the largest ship deserted. The sailors were, with difficulty, restrained from piracy. On the 5th of August they landed in Newfoundland, and Gilbert took possession in the queen's name. A pillar was erected with the royal arms on it. Three laws were passed, interesting as being the earliest specimen of British legislation in America, and as illustrating the spirit of those times. The first provided for religion, "which, in public exercise, should be according to the Church of England." The second for the maintenance of her Majesty's right and possession of those territories. Should anything be attempted against these, it should be treated as high treason against the laws of England. The third provided that if any one uttered words dishonourable to her Majesty, he should lose his ears, and his goods and ships should be confiscated.

Nevertheless, no settlement was effected. The soil was barren and the climate harsh, while the colonists were an unruly mob of adventurers, ill-fitted to be the fathers of an infant state. They were more congenially employed in collecting silver ore, and in attempts at piracy. Finally, another of the ships deserted, reducing the fleet to three. With these Gilbert set sail to investigate the coast further south. Soon, however, the largest of the three remaining ships was wrecked, and the silver ore all lost, an event which seems to have troubled Gilbert more than any of the other mischances of the voyage. The two remaining ships, *The Squirrel* and *The Golden Hind*, then turned homewards. Storms arose. Gilbert, with characteristic heroism, persisted in sailing in the *Squirrel*. At twelve o'clock on a September night his lights disappeared, and the father of New England colonisation went to his rest. His last words were, "We are as near heaven by sea as by land," "a speech well beseeming a soldier resolute in Jesus Christ, as I can testify he was."[1]

The task in which Gilbert had failed was to be undertaken by one better qualified to carry it out. If any man in that age was fitted to be the founder of a colonial empire, Raleigh was that man. Like Gilbert, he had studied books; like Drake, he could rule men. The pupil of Coligny, the friend of Spencer, traveller, soldier, scholar, courtier, statesman, Raleigh, with all his varied graces and powers, rises before us, the type and personification of the age in which he lived. Nothing daunted by Gilbert's failure, by which he himself had been a loser, in 1584 he obtained a patent from Elizabeth in precisely the same terms as Gilbert's,[2] and sent out two vessels under the command of Philip Amidas and Arthur Barlow.[3] They reached the coast of Virginia, then called Florida, on the 15th of July, took possession in the name of the queen, and anchored off a small island.[4] On the third day, a native came across from the mainland and approached them, "never making any showe of feare or doubt."[5] They received him on board, gave him food and clothes, and showed him the interior of the ship. The next day, the king's brother, Granganimeo, came over with a number of Indians, the king himself being prevented from coming by a wound which he had received in a recent fight. The natives carried on some friendly intercourse with them, did "some small traffic, and eat and drank very merrily with them;" and Granganimeo sent them game and

---

[1] Haies, p. 695. [2] Stith, book i. pp. 7, 8. [3] Purchas, p. 829; Hakluyt, p. 728.
[4] Hakluyt, p. 729; Stith, book i., p. 9. [5] Hakluyt, p. 729.

fruit.[1] Nor did the soil please them less than the people. The natives reported that it produced three grain crops a-year,[2] and the English tested its fertility for themselves by sowing peas, which grew fourteen inches in ten days.[3] Emboldened by the friendliness of the natives, they explored further. They ventured up Pamptico Sound,[4] and the next day sailed to the island of Roanoke. On landing there, they were received by the wife of Granganimeo "with wonderful courtesy and kindness." She carefully guarded their property, entertained them in her own house, and took away her men's bows and arrows to disarm all suspicion. When the English at dusk retired for safety to their ships, she sent them down their supper, and appointed guards to watch by the shore all night; "in short, she omitted nothing that the most generous hospitality and hearty desire of pleasing could do to entertain them." About the middle of September, Amidas and Barlow returned to England, bringing with them two natives, Wanchese and Manteo.[5] Their tidings were received at court with delight, and the queen bestowed on the country the name of Virginia, either to commemorate herself, or as being "not yet polluted with Spanish lusts."[6]

The next year, Sir Richard Grenville sailed in the spring with seven ships for the purpose of founding a colony.[7] The spot selected for the settlement was Roanoke. A hundred and eight colonists were left under the government of Mr, afterwards Sir Ralph, Lane. Amidas also stayed with them, and Herriot, a man of eminent scientific attainments, who acted as the historian of the expedition.[8] On the 25th of August, Grenville left the colony,

[1] Stith, book i., pp. 9, 10.   [2] Hakluyt, p. 731.
[3] Stith, book i., p. 10. Hakluyt, p. 731. This seems to have been a common practice among the early explorers. We find Sebastian Cabot doing the same thing. Eden and Wylles, fol. 297.
[4] Stith, book i., p. 10.   [5] Stith, book i., p. 11.   [6] Purchas, p. 828.
[7] Hakluyt, p. 732 ; Purchas, p. 829 ; Stith, book i., p. 12.
[8] "An Account of the Particularities of the Employment of the Englishmen left in Virginia by Sir Richard Greuvill under the charge of Master Ralfe Lane, Generall of the same, from the 17th of August 1585 until the 18th of June 1586, at which time they departed the countrie;" "sent and directed to Sir Walter Raleigh in Hakluyt," p. 738. Stith, book i., p. 13.

unfortunately not before he had marred the harmony which had hitherto subsisted between the colonists and the natives. During his journey of exploration among the Indian villages, a silver cup was stolen by a native. In retaliation, the English burnt their village,[1] and from that time we perceive a difference in the temper of the Indians. After Grenville's departure, Lane went on an exploring journey, and penetrated the country for a hundred and thirty miles as far as the territory of the Chawonocks.[2] Their king Menatonon, "impotent in his limbs, but otherwise for a savage a very grave and wise man, and of very singular good discourse in matters touching the state,"[3] seems to have perceived and worked upon the colonists' weaknesses, by holding out to them the extravagant hopes of pearl fisheries and mines where was to be found a wonderful mineral called Wassader.[4] Stimulated by these hopes, Lane and his party journeyed inland, and would not give up the hopeless undertaking until they had been reduced to eating their mastiffs. On their return to Roanoke, they found that Grenville's severity had already borne fruit. Their friend Granganimeo was dead, and his brother Wingina, or, as he was now called, Pemissapan, was plotting against the colonists.[5] He had already prejudiced the tribes, through whose territory Lane had been travelling, against the intruders. When, however, they returned safe, bringing with them the son of Menatonon, and when their Indian guide testified how little any danger or hardship had deterred them, Pemissapan deferred his hostile purpose. The death of his father, Ensenore, who was friendly to the English, at once removed an obstacle to his hostile designs, and furnished him with an opportunity for executing them. On the pretext of celebrating the funeral, he collected about sixteen hundred men, and prepared a wholesale massacre of the English. The plot, however, was revealed to Lane by Skico, the son of Menatonon, in time to save the colonists, and hostilities ensued, in which Pemissapan

[1] Stith, book i., p. 12.   [2] Stith, book i., p. 13.   [3] Hakluyt, p. 738.
[4] Hakluyt, pp. 739-741 ; Stith, book i., p. 13.   [5] Stith, book i., p. 14.

and fifteen of his men were killed.[1] But though the colonists had escaped from the immediate danger of a massacre, their prospects were very gloomy. They were suffering from lack of food;[2] their hopes of mines and pearl fisheries, their main object, had failed; the Indians were no longer their friends, and there seemed little hopes of Grenville's return. At this crisis Drake's fleet, just sailing back from a raid on the Spanish Coast, appeared off Roanoke. He got ready a ship for the settlers, with a hundred men, and provisions for six months, but just as it was ready a storm arose, and it was driven out to sea.[3] Another attempt was made to send a ship to their relief, but the harbourage was insufficient, and the design had to be abandoned. Finally, the colonists despairing of maintaining their position, resolved to embark in Drake's fleet, and at the end of July 1586, they arrived at Portsmouth.[4] The colonists had only sailed a few days before a ship arrived, sent out by Raleigh, with provisions. After an ineffectual search for the colony it returned to England.[5] About a fortnight later, Grenville arrived with three ships well provisioned.[6] Having spent some time in searching for the colony, he landed fifteen men with provisions for two years, to keep possession, and sailed home.[7] In the next year, Raleigh, undeterred by his previous failures, prepared three ships under the command of John White, who was appointed governor of the colony, with twelve assistants as a council. To these, Raleigh gave a charter, and incorporated them by the name of the City of Raleigh in Virginia.[8] On the 25th of April, the colonists sailed from Plymouth. In spite of the attempted treachery of their shipmaster, they arrived safely and landed on the 22d of July. They found no trace of Lane's colony or of the fifteen men left by Grenville, save one skeleton. Afterwards

[1] Hakluyt, pp. 742-746; Stith, book i., p. 15. [2] Stith, book i., p. 15.
[3] Hakluyt, p. 747. [4] Stith, book i., p. 16.
[5] Hakluyt, p. 747; Stith, book i., pp. 21, 22.
[6] Hakluyt, p. 748; Stith, book i., p. 22, says that Grenville left fifty men; but Purchas, p. 829, confirms Hakluyt.
[7] Hakluyt, p. 764. [8] Hakluyt, pp. 766-768; Stith, book i., pp. 22-24.

they learnt from the Indians that Grenville's men had been attacked and one slain; the rest had disappeared and were no more heard of. Before the settlers had landed three days, the Indians commenced hostilities, and one of the assistants, Howe, was killed. In retaliation for this the settlers fell upon a party of Indians and killed one, but found when it was too late, that they were of a friendly tribe. The 13th of this month was signalised by the baptism of Manteo, who, as a reward of his fidelity, was created Lord of Roanoke and Dasamonpeake. A few days after, the ships returned to England with White. He brought home tidings that a child of English parents had been born on American soil. On the 18th of August a girl had been born to his daughter, the wife of Ananias Dare, and as the first fruits of the colony, had been christened Virginia.[1] After White's return, Raleigh fitted out a fleet under the command of Grenville.[2] Before that fleet could sail, Raleigh and Grenville were called off to a more pressing task than even the relief of the Viginian plantation. But notwithstanding the prospect of the Armada, White persuaded Raleigh to send out two small vessels, with which he sailed from Bideford on the 22d of April 1588.[3] The sailors, however, fell into the snare so often fatal to the explorers of that age, and "being more intent on a gainful voyage than the relief of the colony, ran in chase of prizes; till at last, one of them, meeting with two ships of war, was, after a bloody fight, overcome, boarded, and rifled. In this maimed, ransacked, and ragged condition, she returned to England in a month's time; and in about three weeks after, the other also returned, having perhaps tasted of the same fare, at least, without performing her intended voyage, to the distress, and as it proved, the utter destruction of the colony in Virginia, and to the great displeasure of their patron at home."[4] Raleigh had now spent £40,000 on the colonisation of Virginia, with absolutely no return. Moreover,

---

[1] Hakluyt, p. 767; Stith, book i., p. 24.
[2] Hakluyt, pp. 771, 772; Stith, book i., p. 25.
[3] Hakluyt, p. 772; Stith, book i., p. 25.   [4] Stith, book i., p. 25.

he had a large grant of land in Ireland, the proper management of which would require all his attention and capital. Accordingly, in March 1589, he made an assignment by indenture granting to Sir Thomas Smith, White, and others, the privilege of planting and trading in Virginia, while he proved at the same time that he had not relinquished his interest in the undertaking by a gift of £100 for the conversion of the natives. Delay pervaded the plans of the new company. No relief was sent for a whole year, and when at length White sailed with three ships, they preferred buccaneering among the Spaniards in the West Indies to conveying immediate aid to the colony. When at length they arrived, nothing was to be seen of the settlers. After some search, the name Croaton was seen carved on a post, according to an arrangement made with White before his departure, by which they were thus to indicate the course they had taken. Remnants of their goods were found, but of the colonists themselves nothing was ever heard.[1] The ships returned, and the colonisation of Virginia was for the time at an end. Even Raleigh's indomitable spirit gave way, and he seems henceforth to have abandoned all hopes of plantation. Yet five times did he send out at his own expense in the vain hope of recovering the colonists.[2] Before he died, the great work of his life had been accomplished, but by other hands. In spite of the intrigues of Gondomar and the scoffs of playwrights,[3] Virginia had been settled, and had become a flourishing colony. A ship had sailed into London laden with Virginian goods,[4] and an Indian princess, the wife of an English gentleman, had been received at

---

[1] Stith, book i., pp. 25-28.   [2] Purchas, p. 829 ; Stith, book i., p. 30.
[3] "The New Life of Virginea," Dedication. "Massachusett's Historical Society's Collection," second series, vol. viii., p. 200.—"The malitious and looser sort [being accompanied with the licentious vaine of stage poets] have whet their tongues with scornful taunts against the action it selfe." The reference is probably to Fletcher's "The Noble Gentleman," Act i. sec. i., where a husband being asked to bring his wife to court says,—
"Sir, I had rather send her to Virginia
To help to propagate the English nation."
[4] A letter from John Chamberlain to Sir Dudley Carleton, July 7, 1608, in "The Court and Times" of James I., p. 76.

court, and had shone for a season the delight and admiration of the fashionable world.

England, under the Tudors, had done great things, but the settlement of America was not to be among them. The yeomen and citizens of England had to undergo other training ere they were fit to be the founders of a great empire across the Atlantic. They were to go through trials which should beget in them a sternness of spirit and a steadfastness of purpose, to which the age of Elizabeth was a stranger. Raleigh was in his life the embodiment of his age, and in his death it passed away; the curtain fell on that splendid drama, in which Drake and Hawkins, Grenville and Howard had played their parts so well, when Raleigh came back from the Guiana voyage to linger in prison palsied and broken-hearted, till summoned to the scaffold by a traitor king. We cannot take leave better than in the words of an old writer, of "those merchants and mariners which, to the glory of our nation, spare no costs and feare no danger in these their attempts: resolute, gallant, glorious attempts! by which they seeke to tame nature where she is most unbridled, in those northeasterly, north-westerly, and northerly borders, (where she shewes herself any border, indeed), and to subdue her to that government and subjection which God over all blessed for ever hath imposed on all sensible creatures to the nature of man. How shall I admire your heroike courage, yee marine worthies, beyond all names of worthinesse, that neither dread so long eyther presence or absence of the sunne nor these foggie mists, tempestuous winds, cold blasts, snowes, and hailes in the aire. Great God, I beseech thee to prosper in this and like attempts of this nation of ours, that the virgin truth by Virginia plantation and northerly discovery may triumph in her conquest of Indian infidelity, maugre the brags of that adulteresse, that vaunteth herselfe to be the only darling of God and nature."[1]

[1] Purchas, p 820.

CHAPTER II.

FORMATION OF THE THIRTEEN COLONIES.

AFTER 1590, the project of colonising Virginia slept for sixteen years. Voyages of exploration had been sent out to the coast of America. In 1602, Gosnold had discovered the coast of New England.[1] In 1603, Hakluyt had persuaded the merchants of Bristol to raise a stock of £1000, and to send out two ships under Pring.[2] In 1605, Lord Southampton had sent Weymouth on an exploring voyage to the coast of America, who discovered St George's River, and brought home five natives, one of whom was a Sagamore.[3] In 1606, a number of enterprising London merchants and west country gentlemen resolved to make another attempt at planting the fertile territories of which Gosnold had brought back a glowing account. They obtained a patent from James I. for two colonies one hundred miles distant from one another. Two councils were nominated, to be under the control of one general council in England, and a code of laws drawn up. On the 19th of December 1606, the colonists, one hundred and five in number, sailed, and on the 26th of April they reached the coast of America.[4] The spot which they selected for their settlement was an island in the river, of which the backwater at once formed a harbour and protected them against the Indians, while it had the additional recommendation of being free from the salt-worm which infested the lower parts of the river.[5] The

[1] Purchas, p. 829; Stith, book i., p. 31.
[2] Stith, book i., p. 32.
[3] Purchas, p. 819; Stith, book i., p. 33.
[4] Stith, book ii., pp. 44, 45.
[5] Beverley's "History of Virginia," p. 19.

settlement was called, in honour of the king, Jamestown. At first it seemed as if the colony would be no more successful than its predecessors. The settlers quarrelled. Wingfield, the governor, stole the stores for his own use, and lived "in elegance and luxury" on sack and beef, while the other colonists had to subsist on crabs and rotten grain. Had it not been for the humanity of the Indians, who brought them food, they might have perished.[1] There were but four carpenters and twelve husbandmen to provide for the mutual wants of the whole colony.[2] Fortunately there was one man equal to the occasion. Captain John Smith was one of the soldiers of fortune with whom the growth of standing armies, the curse of the sixteenth century, had filled Europe. The son of a Lincolnshire gentleman, he had learnt the art of war on the battle ground of Europe, the low countries. Disgusted by those scenes of bloodshed, he had embarked at Marseilles to seek adventures in the East. Thrown into the sea by French pilgrims as a Huguenot Jonah, he had been saved by a pirate, and retrieved his fortunes by a successful voyage in the Mediterranean. In Hungary he had fought in single combat with a Turkish champion, and had borne off his enemy's head in the sight of the whole Christian army. He had been left for dead on the field of Rottenton, and sold into slavery. Rescued by a Turkish beauty, he was again enslaved by a jealous pasha, and after beating out his rival's brains with a club, had fled in disguise through the wilds of Circassia. His travels had led him through every civilised country in Europe, and to the court of Morocco. England, under a king who dreaded the sight of a drawn sword, was no place for such a spirit, and having exhausted the field of enterprise in Europe, he had eagerly seized the opportunity of seeking fresh adventures in the New World. The hero of so romantic a career was far superior in character to the ordinary mercenary of the age. "He fought not for gain, or empty praise, but for his country's honour and the publick good." The ordinary soldier of fortune with whom the armies of

---

[1] Stith, book ii., pp. 48, 49.   [2] Bancroft, vol. i., p. 124.

the great continental powers then abounded, was sordid, brutal, and licentious. Smith was high-minded, humane, and temperate. To the courage of a tried soldier, he united a degree of versatility and tact that made his services invaluable to an infant colony among savages.[1]

He had already been attacked by Wingfield, who had brought an absurd charge of sedition against him during the voyage. He had completely cleared his character, and had obtained £200 damages, which he generously cast into the common store. He was now the life of the colony. Wingfield was deposed in consequence of his continued misconduct. His successor, Ratcliffe, was equally inefficient, and the whole power devolved on Smith. His task was no easy one. He had to superintend the building, working with his own hands harder than any one, to forage for food among the Indian villages, and to prevent Ratcliffe from deserting the colony. In one of his expeditions among the Indians he was overtaken when separated from his party. He made a gallant resistance, and for a time kept his enemies at bay, but in his endeavours to escape, he suddenly fell into a quagmire and was taken. But the good fortune which had saved him in so many perils did not desert him. He even contrived to send a message by his captors to warn the colonists at Jamestown that an attack was meditated. He was taken round the country and shown in triumph, and "conjured for three days with frightful shoutings and many strange and hellish ceremonies." At length, after a long consultation, his death was decided on, and he would have perished, but for the courageous interference of Pocahontas, the daughter of Powhatan, the Indian king. After seven weeks captivity he was set free, and returned to Jamestown, where he arrived just in time to prevent some of the settlers from embarking for England.[2]

Smith's next exploit was the investigation of Chesapeake Bay. For seven weeks he cruised about, taking observations of the coast, landing among the Indians, and exploring their country.

---

[1] Stith, book iii., pp. 108-112. [2] Stith, book ii., pp. 44-56.

When the strangers first appeared, the Indians generally prepared for an attack, but in every case Smith either terrified them into good behaviour, or won them with presents, and in no case were the colonists obliged to resort to arms.[1] In his absence, as usual, the colony fell into confusion. The president had "riotously consumed the store, and greatly harassed and fatigued the people in building an unnecessary house of pleasure for himself in the woods." Smith, on his return, deposed him and became nominally, as he had hitherto been in reality from the first, governor of the colony.[2] Meanwhile little had been done towards effecting the main object of the settlement, no mines had been found, and there seemed little hope of a permanent commercial settlement. The folly of the settlers had ruined the Indian trade. By not keeping to the fixed regulations, necessary in an infant community, the price of Indian goods had so risen that what was at first bought for an ounce of copper could not now be had for a pound. Newport, too, had been needlessly lavish in his generosity to Powhatan.[3] The sailors sent out by the company set up a floating tavern, and extravagance and rioting followed. The sailors stayed longer than was necessary, and consumed the colonists' stores. They even stole their goods to traffic with the Indians. The colonists were afraid to offend them lest they should carry home bad reports. The colonists themselves, too, were dissolute and idle. Rather than work to earn their bread they would sell their implements to the Indians.[4] Smith at length, by a threat of banishment, succeeded in enforcing some degree of industry, but so repugnant was it to the settlers that some of them ran away to the Indians rather than work. So great, however, was Smith's influence with the Indians, that all the fugitives were brought back by force. A variety of circumstances had contributed to inspire the Indians with a reverence for Smith. The extraordinary courage and energy which he had

---

[1] Stith, book ii., pp. 62-66.   [2] Stith, book ii., p. 66.
[3] Stith, book ii., p. 57. A True Declaration of the State of the Colonies in Virginia, p. 17. Purchas, p. 831.   [4] Stith, book ii., pp. 57-60, 94.

shown throughout his dealings with them, the ill success of all the attempts on his life, his restoration of an Indian who appeared to be dead, and an accidental discharge of gunpowder, which had wounded several of them, produced a belief that the English generally, and Captain Smith in particular, were superior beings. If they wanted rain they would send to Smith to pray to his God for it: they returned stolen goods unasked, and even sent the criminals to Jamestown for punishment. In fact "the whole country became as absolutely free and safe to the English as to the natives."[1]

In England the company was not unnaturally dissatisfied with the results of the colony. The only return they had yet had was two shiploads of timber.[2] Accordingly they determined to get a new charter, and to send out a fresh colony of five hundred settlers in nine ships. The character of the new settlers was not such as to give much hope for the future welfare of the colony. A great part of them "were unruly sparks, packed off by their friends to escape worse destinies at home," or "poor gentlemen, broken tradesmen, rakes and libertines, footmen and such others as were much fitter to spoil and ruin a commonwealth than to help to raise or maintain one."[3] The injury to the plantation did not end with their dissoluteness and idleness. The evil reports which they brought back prejudiced men in England against the colony.[4] The colonists sailed from England in the latter end of May, but the admiral's ship, with one hundred and fifty men, and three governors on board, was cast away on the Bermudas.[5] Before they had been out three months

[1] Stith, book ii., pp. 90, 91.
[2] Stith, book ii., p. 81. Letter from John Chamberlain to Sir Dudley Careton, July 7, 1608. "There is a ship lately come from Virginia. . . . She hath brought nothing more than sweet wood." Court and Times of James I., p. 76.
[3] Stith, book iii., pp. 101-103. New Life of Virginia, pp. 9, 10.
[4] The prejudices thus excited against Virginia seem to have prevailed to a late period, for in 1722 we find Beverley complaining that the colony had been so misrepresented to the common people in England that they believed that in Virginia servants were used as beasts of draught in carts and ploughs, and that the climate turned the inhabitants black.
[5] Stith, book iii., p. 102.

they had conducted themselves so factiously that Smith was compelled to cast several of the ringleaders into prison, and finding it impossible to govern the colony satisfactorily as it was, he determined to separate it into three parts. Accordingly he planted one hundred and twenty men under Martin at Nansemond, and the same number under West near the falls of James River. Martin soon quarrelled with the Indians; after losing several of his men, returned to Jamestown, leaving the settlement to its fate. West, too, had selected his site for a plantation so ill, that as Smith was on his way to the falls to visit them, he met them returning, driven away by inundations. He then settled them on a tract called Powhatan, probably after the chief from whom it was bought. They remonstrated against Smith's interference, but soon after his departure they embroiled themselves with the Indians, and were glad to fall back on his help. They did not stay at Powhatan, but returned to their original settlement at the falls.[1] Shortly after this, Smith met with an accident which necessitated his return to England.[2] After his departure, everything went wrong. The settlement seemed to be a mere repetition of White's and Lane's failures. The Indians were no longer kept in check. The settlers bartered their weapons and necessaries for food, and left themselves without means of defence. Their indolence was such that they ate their food raw rather than be at the trouble of cooking it. The animals that ought to have been kept to stock the colony were killed and eaten, and at last the settlers were reduced to subsisting on roots and wild fruit, eked out by a little fish.[3] While the colony was in this state, Gates and Somers arrived from the Bermudas. They saw that the condition of the colony was hopeless, and resolved to sail for England. Fortunately, however, just at the moment of their leaving the river, Lord Delaware appeared with three ships well supplied. The colony was re-settled. Lord Delaware

---

[1] Stith, book ii., pp. 104-106.   [2] Stith, book ii., pp. 106-108.
[3] Stith, book iii., pp. 107, 115-117. "A True Declaration of the State of Virginia," published in Force, vol. iii., p. 15.

infused a new spirit into both the government and the colonists. Vines were planted, and the soil cultivated; corn was brought from Powhatan, and forts were built in spots selected for their healthiness, to receive and acclimatise new-comers.[1] From that time, under the government of Dale and Gates, the colony prospered. Even the weakness of Yeardley and the violence of Argall had no permanently injurious influence. Great improvement resulted from the substitution of private holdings for the tenure of land in common. The period for this had been by the the original constitution limited to five years, and at the expiration of that time Dale allotted to each man three acres of cleared ground.[2] The effect of private possession on industry soon made itself felt. In 1616, the condition of the colony was so improved that the shares of land were reduced from one hundred to fifty acres. These shares were valued at L.12, 10s. each, and one allotted to each colonist, at a nominal quit-rent. Emigrants of special value, such as "divines, ministers of state and justice, knights, gentlemen, physitians, were allowed extra shares according to a fixed rating." When colonists were sent out by private adventure, the produce of the land was divided between the colonists and the shareholder.[3] In 1618, Argall, the governor, wrote home to complain of the want of skilled labourers,[4] and of agricultural implements, and in the next year we find husbandmen from Devonshire, and iron workers from Sussex and the midland counties mentioned among the emigrants.[5] The country still continued to be cursed with "jail-birds,"[6] but juster ideas as to the merits of Virginia began to prevail in England. In 1611, Dale had written home that "four of the best kingdoms in Christendom altogether may in no way compare with this country, either for commodities or goodness of soil."[7] In 1620, a com-

---

[1] Stith, book iii., pp. 117, 118, 120. "True Declaration of the Colony in Virginia," Force, vol. iii., p. 20.   [2] Stith, book iii., pp. 131, 132.
[3] "Nova Britania," Force, vol. i., p. 23. Stith, book iii., pp. 139, 140.
[4] Stith, book iii., p. 148.
[5] "A Declaration of the State of Virginia," Force, vol. iii., p. 5.
[6] Stith, book iii., p. 168.   [7] New Life of Virginia, p. 21.

mission was sent out to report on the soil of Virginia, and a pamphlet was drawn up by order of the company, setting forth the merits of the country.[1]

In 1612, an event occurred which at first seemed likely to embroil the settlers with the Indians, but which ultimately proved a strong bond of union between them. Argall had gone on a trading expedition up the Potomac, and had formed friendly relations with one Japazaus, who had known Smith. Pocahontas was at that time staying near, and Argall conceived the design of capturing and detaining her as a hostage for Powhatan's good behaviour. To effect this, he entered into diplomatic negotiations with Japazaus. The king of Potomac was won by the splendour of a bright copper kettle; Pocahontas was lured on board Argall's ship, and taken as a prisoner to Jamestown. A message was sent to Powhatan, demanding the English prisoners' guns and tools as ransom for his daughter. The news troubled the chief, and he was divided between his love for his daughter and for the English commodities. At last he sent back seven Englishmen, each with an unserviceable musket, and promised five hundred bushels of corn on the restoration of his daughter. The English refused his terms, and Pocahontas remained a prisoner. She soon became a Christian, and by the next year she had won the heart of John Rolfe, a young Englishman. In 1613, this singular marriage was celebrated, with the approbation of Powhatan, who from that time lived on friendly terms with the English. In 1616, Pocahontas and her husband sailed for England. Her intelligence, grace, and courtesy won her universal admiration; she was received at court, and the friendship which she showed for the English promised to be a bond of unity between the two races. But the heroine of this strange career, who had been reared in an Indian wigwam, and entertained in the drawing-rooms of English peeresses, never revisited Virginia. On the eve of her departure in 1617, she died at Gravesend, leaving one son,

---

[1] Published in Force, vol. iii., and referred to above.

from whom many of the best families in Virginia afterwards claimed descent.[1]

Another circumstance served to strengthen the friendship between Powhatan and the English. He dreaded their allying themselves with his brother Opechancanough, of whom, as virtually the next successor, he stood in perpetual fear. Another tribe, the Chickahominies, once subjects of Powhatan, but who had now set up a sort of republic, also feared that Powhatan might employ the English to reconquer them, and, to guard against this danger, offered to place themselves under the government of Sir Thomas Dale. A formal treaty was made in which they were received as English subjects.[2]

In 1618 Powhatan died, and was succeeded, nominally, by his brother Opitchapan. He, however, being feeble both in mind and body, left the whole power in the hands of his brother Opechancanough.[3] In the year of Powhatan's death events occurred which excited suspicions of Opechancanough's fidelity, but no open rupture ensued.[4] For four years the friendly relations continued. A college was established to train up the Indian children in Christianity.[5] No violence was used in conversion, and a perfect trust in the good intentions of the Indians was shown. The English lived in plantations widely separated from one another, alone and unarmed. The natives were "kindly received into their houses, fed at their tables, were lodged in their bedchambers; they seemed entirely to have coalesced, and to live together as one people."[6] This harmony was not to last. In 1622 an Indian chief, Nemattanow, or, as he was called by the English, "Jack of the Feather," one of the most noted warriors of his tribe, treacherously murdered an English trader. He was apprehended, and afterwards, in attempting to escape, killed. Opechancanough had previously shown an unfriendly

---

[1] Stith, book iii., pp. 127-130, 42-46. Pocahontas is more than once referred to in the correspondence of Chamberlain and Sir Dudley Carleton.
[2] Stith, book iii., pp. 130, 131.
[3] Stith, book iii., p. 129.
[4] Stith, book iii., p. 169.
[5] Stith, book iii., pp. 162, 163.
[6] Stith, book iv., p. 210.

spirit to Nemattanow, and it is unlikely that he was moved by any spirit of revenge, but the pretext was a good one, and a general massacre was determined on. Fortunately, a warning was given by a converted Indian, and the colony escaped with the loss of three hundred and forty-seven lives.[1] The next year an order was issued by the assembly "that the inhabitants of every corporation should fall upon their adjoyning salvages, as we did the last yeere." Other precautions were enjoined. Houses were to be palisaded, and no one was to go to church unarmed.[2]

The original code of laws for the settlement was drawn up by the king, and sent out with the first colonists. It provided that the colony should be governed by a council who should elect a president from among themselves; that the doctrines of the Church of England should be observed by the colonists, and promulgated among the natives; that the land tenures should be the same as in England; that tumults, rebellion, conspiracy, mutiny, and sedition, together with murder, manslaughter, incest, rape, and adultery, should be capital crimes; that such offences should be tried by jury, and that the right of pardon should be vested in the crown; that all other cases should be tried by the president and council; that the president and council should have full power to make laws, orders, or ordinances subject to the approval of the king, and provided they were not contrary to the laws of England. Such a constitution evidently contained within it none of the elements of a representative government, nor did it even provide the security of trial by jury, except for capital offences.[3] The condition was, however, added that, as the colony increased, the king, his heirs and successors, should have power to ordain and give such laws, constitutions, and ordinances as they should think fit; and at first, while the colony was more like a family than a state, the form of its constitution was not very important. In 1611 Sir Thomas Smith, the treasurer of the company, sent over a printed book of articles and laws chiefly

---

[1] Stith, book iv., pp. 210-214. [2] Henings, vol. i., pp. 127, 128.
[3] Stith, book ii., pp. 37-41.

translated from the martial laws of the low countries, and drawn up probably by Edward Strachey.[1] These laws, if carried out rigorously, would have established a civil and spiritual tyranny of the most unendurable kind. Blasphemy against God, or any article of the Christian faith, or any words or acts tending to the derision or dispute of God's Holy Word, were capital crimes. Divine service was to be attended twice a-day; the first omission was to be punished by the loss of the day's allowance of food, the second by whipping, and the third by six months in the galleys. Gambling on Sunday, or neglecting Sunday worship, was severely punished, and, if persisted in, the offender was put to death. To slander the council by seditious speeches or writing, was on the third offence a capital crime. The laws for the regulation of trade, and the like were in themselves judicious, but the penalties imposed terribly severe. Plundering the Indians, trading with them without leave, or showing favouritism in the distribution of provisions, were all capital offences. Dale at first caused these laws to be executed rigorously,[2] and the demoralised state of the colony, when he succeeded to the governorship, no doubt made strong measures necessary; but we can hardly suppose that the code was long maintained in its integrity. In 1619, the settlers were "again restored to their birthright, the enjoyment of British liberty,"[3] and the colony was granted a constitution. Yeardley, the new governor, brought out "commissions and instructions from the company for the better establishinge a commonwealth," and made proclamation "that those cruell lawes by which the ancient planters had soe longe been governed were now abrogated." The colony was divided into boroughs, and each had two burgesses. The assembly was to be held once a year, and was to consist of the governor, the council, and the burgesses. The governor and council were to be elected by the

[1] Stith, book iii., p. 122. The laws are published in Force, vol. iii., under the title "For the Colony of Virginea Britania, Laws Divine, Morall, and Martiall." For the probability of their being by Strachey, see the preface to Strachey's "Travayle into Virginia," published by the Hakluyt Society.
[2] Stith, book iii., p. 123.   [3] Stith, book iii., p. 160.

council of the colony in England, who were also to distribute lands in Virginia, and to settle matters of trade. The officers were to hold office for three years at least, and afterwards during pleasure, except the governor, who was to hold office for six years at least. At the same time, a committee was appointed from among the members of the company to establish a constitution for the colony; the design, however, was not carried out, and Virginia was from that time governed by laws made by its own representatives.[1]

In the same year no less than twelve hundred and sixty-six persons were sent out, making up the whole number to more than eight thousand.[2] A few years later, sixty young women "handsome and well recommended for their virtues, education, and demeanour," were sent out with written characters, at the fixed price of one hundred and twenty pounds of tobacco. It was also specified that they should be married, not to servants, but to "freemen and tenants capable of supporting them handsomely," while at the same time the colonists were bribed into matrimony by a number of boys being sent out to be apprenticed to those who married.[3] In other respects the colony was, in spite of the massacre, prosperous. The cattle had multiplied, manufactures had been set up, the numbers of adventurers had greatly increased, and forty-two ships were employed every year in the Virginian trade.[4]

In England, Virginian affairs were not so flourishing. The misconduct of Sir Thomas Smith, the treasurer, and Wrote, a member of the council, had given rise to considerable strife. Hitherto, the king had taken but little active interest in the colony. From one point of view, indeed, Virginia was interesting; it produced tobacco, and to tax tobacco was, to the author

---

[1] Bancroft, vol. i., pp. 163, 164.
[2] Declaration of the State of Virginia, pp. 5-10.
[3] Stith, book iv., p. 197. The sixty maids seem to have abused their matrimonial monopoly, for in 1624 it was made an offence punishable either by corporal chastisement, or a fine for any one, male or female, to contract him or herself to two persons at once. [4] Stith, book iv., pp. 254, 264, 266.

of "The Counterblast," both pleasant and profitable.[1] Moreover, he had, as we have seen, drawn up a code of laws which were almost immediately superseded, and he had expressed a great desire to possess a Virginian flying squirrel;[2] but his services to the colony had been confined to a donation of condemned arms at the time of the massacre.[3] Gradually, however, the disputes among the company began to assume a political character. The members of the country party in the Virginian Council opposed the interference of the Privy Council in the affairs of Virginia.[4] Gondomar, whose Spanish gold, it was openly alleged, had already influenced many of our leading statesmen against Virginia, advised the king that the Virginian Court was but a seminary to a seditious parliament.[5] The taxation of tobacco soon afforded the king a ground for attack. After a long and complicated dispute, an order was issued by the Privy Council establishing a new constitution for Virginia. The company resisted, but in vain. A commission was sent out to Virginia, which, as might be expected, brought back a report unfavourable to the company. The council carefully and successfully answered the charges brought against them, but their fate was predetermined, and in June 1624 their patents were cancelled.[6] This proceeding was beyond all doubt an unjust one, but the colony was probably the gainer. A constitutional king was a better, because a less jealous and exacting ruler than a commercial corporation.

In the meantime, the Virginian legislature had been asserting itself independent alike of king and company. They had constructed the first code ever framed for itself by an Anglo-American state. The laws consisted of thirty-nine articles. They provided for the observance of religion by ordering a maintenance for a ministry, and by enforcing attendance at public worship.

---

[1] Stith, book iv., pp. 243, 244.
[2] Letter from Lord Southampton to Lord Salisbury, Catalogue of State Papers, i. 65.
[3] Bancroft, vol. i., p. 183.   [4] Bancroft, vol. i., p. 186.
[5] A New Description of Virginia. Massachusetts Historical Collection, 1st Series, vol. ix., p. 111.   [6] Stith, book v., p. 323.

The liberty of the subject was maintained in two most important particulars, by restricting the right of taxation to the assembly, and by forbidding the governor to employ the inhabitants on any service without consent, if possible, of the assembly; if a sudden emergency should arise, of the council. From that time, the colony commenced its existence as (in fact, though not in theory) an independent and self-governed state.[1] The first assembly had met in 1619.[2] It was, as we have seen, composed of the representatives of boroughs. In 1629 plantations were substituted, and in 1632 counties.

Under Charles I. little worthy of notice occurred in the political history of Virginia. Sir John Harvey, during his governorship, involved himself in a conflict with the assembly. It is, however, manifest that no very substantial grievances existed, since, in 1642, two months after Harvey's retirement, the assembly refer to the happy state of the colony under the royal government.[3] Attempts were made to raise a revenue on tobacco, and subsequently to establish a royal monopoly of the tobacco trade. The attempts were averted, and the king contented himself with the pre-emption of the Virginian tobacco, and with enacting that no foreign vessel should be allowed to trade with Virginia, or to carry Virginian goods.[4] In 1639 an attempt was made to re-establish the authority of the company, but was strenuously and successfully opposed by the assembly.[5] That the royal government sat lightly on Virginia may be inferred from the loyal tone which had thus early become a characteristic of the colony. After the establishment of the commonwealth, "Virginia was whole for monarchy and the last country belonging to England that submitted to obedience of the commonwealth of England,"[6] and under Berkeley's government

---

[1] Stith, book iv., pp. 318-323.
[2] Stith, book iii., p. 110.
[3] Hening's Statutes of Virginia, vol. i., p. 231.
[4] Bancroft, vol. i., pp. 194, 195, 221.
[5] Extract from MSS. relating to Virginia. Force, vol. ii.
[6] Rachel and Leah; or, The Two Fruitful Sisters. Force, vol. iii., p. 22.

the plantation was a safe refuge for the defeated cavaliers.[1] In October 1649, the assembly passed an Act premising " that there were some who, out of ignorance or malice, schism and faction— in pursuance of some design of innovation—cast blemishes of dishonour upon the late most excellent and now undoubtedly sainted, king," and "to those close ends vindicating and attesting the late proceedings against the said blessed king, and who, by such arguments, press and persuade the power of the commission to be null and void, and all magistracy and office depending thereon, to have lost their vigour and efficacy, by such means assuredly expecting advantages for the accomplishment of their lawless and tyrannous intentions," and enacting "that any person that shall go about to defend and maintain the late traitorous proceedings against the aforesaid king of most happy memory, under any notions of law and justice, such persons using any reasoning, discourse, or argument, or uttering any words or speech to that purpose or effect, to be an accessory *post factum*, and to be proceeded against as such. Or whoever should go about, by unreverent or scandalous words or language, to blast the memory and honour of that late most pious king (deserving of altars and monuments in the hearts of all good men) shall be punished at the discretion of the governor and council." To question Charles II.'s right of succession, or to propose a change of government, was made high treason.[2] The hopes of the royalists in England were raised, and in spite of the surrender of all the other colonists, they trusted that Virginia would hold out. But as soon as two or three parliamentary ships appeared all thoughts of resistance were laid aside.[3] Yet, whether from lenity or caution, the parliament was satisfied with moderate terms. The submission of the colonists was accepted as free and voluntary; they obtained an act of indemnity for all things said or done against the parliament. They stipulated that Virginia should be free from all taxes and impositions except those imposed by the assembly, and that

---

[1] Col. Norwood's Account of a Voyage to Virginia, 1649. Force, vol. iii., p. 50.
[2] Hening, vol. i., pp. 358-361. [3] Clarendon, book xiii., pp. 466, 467; ed. 1706.

neither governor nor council should be obliged to take any oath or engagement to the commonwealth for one whole year, nor should they be censured for praying for the king, or speaking well of him, during the same space of time, in their own houses or "neighbouring conferences." They agreed for free trade with the Dutch and all other nations at peace with England. In conjunction with the parliamentary commissioners the assembly elected a governor and council, and during the commonwealth no attempt was made to impose governors on Virginia.[1] In 1659 a message was sent out announcing Cromwell's death and the frustration of his plans for the benefit of the colony, approving of their conduct hitherto, and requiring them to acknowledge Richard Cromwell, an injunction which the assembly obeyed."[2] When the news of restoration arrived the assembly passed a resolution taking the government into their own hands, "until such a council and commission of Virginia come out from England as shall be by the assembly adjudged lawfull." They then appointed Berkeley governor, premising that he should govern according to the written laws of England and the established laws of this country, and that all writs be issued in the name of the Grand Assembly.[3] When the restoration of the Stuart dynasty was confirmed the Virginians acquiesced in it as peaceably as they had in its overthrow; a proof that the imperial legislature did not materially affect them.

All doubts were now at an end as to the stability and prosperity of the colony. In 1649 there were fifteen thousand white inhabitants,[4] and by 1671, they had increased to forty thousand.[5] The evils resulting from the transportation of criminals was kept in check by a humane system of slavery, itself in time to be the parent of greater evils than those which it cured. The whole question of American slavery will be considered more

---

[1] Hening, vol. ii., pp. 363-369.   [2] Hening, vol. ii., pp. 509, 510.
[3] Hening, vol. ii., p. 530.
[4] A Perfect Description of Virginia, p. 3.
[5] Berkeley's Report of the State of Virginia. Hening, vol. i., p. 5-15.

fully hereafter. But it will not be amiss in this place to notice a few of its principal features as they appeared in Virginian society. In 1649 there were only three hundred negroes in the colony.[1] In 1671, the number of Christian servants was eight thousand; that of black slaves, two thousand.[2] Of these white servants, the majority were convicts, many of them condemned for political offences. Others were kidnapped and sent off, either because there was a motive for getting them out of the way, or because their friendless condition made them safe objects to the slave merchant. The earliest restriction we find imposed on the slaves, was an act punishing them for secret marriages.[3] At the same time, we find enactments guarding against their running away. In 1670, we find it made no felony to kill slaves if they resisted their master. A difference arose very early between the condition of the white servants and the negroes. The whites were emancipated after a certain time; the negro was a slave for life. In the white race, slavery did not descend from parent to child. The negro was born a bondman. As the practice of transporting to the plantations ceased, the white servants became gradually absorbed into the free population, and slave and negro became synonymous terms. Hence, a strong caste feeling soon grew up. The union of the races was strictly prohibited. In 1637, we find that Robert Sweet was condemned to do penance, according to the laws of England, for getting a negro woman with child, and the woman was sentenced to be whipped,[4] and in 1691, a law was passed, that a white woman having a child by a negro, should be fined £15, or in default of payment, be sold for five years.[5]

With settled government and increased material prosperity,

[1] A Perfect Description of Virginia, p. 4.
[2] Berkeley's Report. Hening, vol. i., p. 515.
[3] Hening, vol. i., pp. 252, 253, 458.
[4] Hening, vol. i., p. 552. Subsequently, we find one Hugh Davies sentenced "to be soundly whipped before an assembly of negroes and others, for abusing himself to the dishonour of God and shame of Christians, by defiling his body in lying with a negro." Hening, vol. ii., p. 265.
[5] Hening, vol. ii., p. 87.

crime disappeared. Theft was almost unknown. Houses were left open all night, and clothes suffered to hang on hedges in perfect safety. A neighbourly and social spirit prevailed. If a man was sick, his neighbours would see that his crops took no hurt.[1] Travellers were entertained in private houses, and inns throughout the country were unknown.[2] Poverty scarcely existed, and unless due to improvidence or indolence, was hardly possible.[3] The labour of a single man could produce in a year two hundred and fifty bushels of maize.[4] Wheat yielded from thirty to fifty fold, maize from a hundred to three hundred fold, and the latter was ready to gather in three months after sowing.[5] Servants were allowed a plot of land for the cultivation of tobacco.[6] Much land was found cleared ready to hand by the Indians.[7] The prevalence of wolves made sheep farming difficult, but horned cattle and swine needed no care, and were ready for the butcher when driven out of the woods.[8] Wild fowl abounded. An indifferent sportsman, Beverley tells us, could kill twenty at a shot.[9] Wild turkeys grew to fifty pounds weight. The rivers swarmed with fish, of which five thousand had been taken at a single draught, none less than two feet long. The aspect of the country was "so delectable, that the melanchollyest eye in the world could not look upon it without contentment, or content himself without admiration." "Purling streams and wanton rivers everywhere kissed the happy soyle into perpetuall verdure and unto an unwearied fertility."[10] Few who once visited it ever wished to return.[11]

---

[1] Rachel and Leah, pp. 16, 19.

[2] Norwood's Voyage, Virginia, p. 48. Rachel and Leah, p. 15.

[3] Beverley, p. 233.

[4] A True Relation of Virginia and Maryland. By Nathaniel Shrigley. Force, vol. iii., p. 5.

[5] Virginia Richly and Truly Valued. By Edward Williams, gent. London, 1650. Force, vol. iii., p. 12.

[6] Rachel and Leah, p. 14.   [7] Virginia Richly and Truly Valued, p. 13.

[8] A True Relation, &c., p. 5.   [9] Beverley, p. 123.

[10] Virginia Richly and Truly Valued, pp. 11, 21, 27, 28.

[11] Rachel and Leah, p. 12.

The want of skilled labour, and the great distance between the plantations, were two of the chief drawbacks to the welfare of the plantation. The latter was due partly to the character of the country, which fitted it for a patriarchal mode of life and also made communication difficult; partly to the provisions of the original charter, which had enabled the early adventurers to claim fifty acres of land for every colonist whom they sent out, and which thus gave rise to a system of *latifundia*.[1] The lack of skilled labour was due, no doubt, to the character of the early colonists, and was perpetuated by the fertility of the soil, which made no demand on the energy or invention of the farmer. Much of the best land was allowed to lie waste through ignorance of draining. Tobacco excluded all other crops. Attempts were made to introduce the cultivation of the vine and of silk grass, but to no purpose.[2] Of the attempts made by the legislature to check the over-production of tobacco, I shall have occasion to speak hereafter. The most serious evil of all was the want of education. In 1671, Berkeley, in the true spirit of his party, thanked God "that there were no free schools nor printing, and I hope we shall not have these hundred years; for learning has brought disobedience and heresy and sects into the world, and printing has divulged libels against the best government. God keep us from both."[3] "The greater number of Christian children" were, through this, "unserviceable in Church and State."[4] The clergy did nothing to make amends for this. From the first, Virginia seems to have been unfortunate in her ministers. "Many came of such as wore black coats and could babble in a pulpit, roare in a tavern, exact from their parishes, and rather by their dissoluteness destroy than feed their flock." They "paddled in factious and state matters."[5] Berkeley complained "that as of all other commodities, so of these the worst are sent us."[6] Gross religious in-

---

[1] Virginia's Cure. London, 1661. Force, vol. iii., p. 8. Beverley, p. 45.
[2] Clayton's Account of Virginia, 1688. Force, vol. iii., pp. 20, 21. Virginia Richly and Truly Valued, p. 25.
[3] Berkeley's Report. Hening, vol. ii., p. 517.   [4] Virginia's Cure, p. 6.
[5] Rachel and Leah, pp. 7-20.   [6] Hening, vol. ii., p. 517.

tolerance prevailed. We have already seen how rigorous were the early laws, both those of King James, and those afterwards sent out by Sir Thomas Smith, in their provisions for religion. Yet they seem either to have suited the temper of the colonists, or to have infected them with bigotry, for their own laws, though less severe, were not more tolerant. To be absent from church was to incur a penalty of a hogshead of tobacco, and a month's absence was punished by a fine of £50. The civil magistrates were ordered "to see that the Sabbath-day was not profaned by working or any employments, or journeying from place to place." These acts were passed in 1623, and renewed in 1629.[1] In 1642 an oath was administered to the churchwardens, binding them to make a true presentment of all such as "prophane God's name and his holy Sabbath, abuse His holy word and commandments, contemn His holy sacrament, or anything belonging to His service and worship."[2] In 1657, the use of boats or guns or any other act tending to the profanation of the Sabbath, was forbidden under a penalty of one hundred pounds of tobacco.[3] In 1659, an edict was issued against "an unreasonable and turbulent sort of people commonly called Quakers." A penalty of £100 was imposed on any master of a ship who should bring in Quakers, and orders were given that all Quakers should be apprehended and kept in custody till they gave security to leave the colony.[4] In 1661 it was enacted that Quakers and Nonconformists who absented themselves from church, should be fined for every offence, £20 sterling, and if they continued to absent themselves for a year, they were to find securities for good behaviour. Conventicles of Quakers were to be fined two hundred pounds of tobacco each individual, and if any of them were insolvent, the more able were to pay for them.[5] Even to sympathise with Quakers was a crime. In 1663, Mr John Porter, a member of the assembly, being suspected of being "loving" to the Quakers and leaning to

[1] Hening, vol. i., p. 144.
[2] Hening, vol. i., p. 240.
[3] Hening, vol. i., p. 433.
[4] Hening, vol. i., p. 532.
[5] Hening, vol. ii., p. 166.

anabaptism, was ordered to take the oath of allegiance and supremacy, and, refusing, was expelled the assembly.[1] About 1650, a congregation of Independents established themselves. It was determined to suppress them. Their pastors and other teachers were banished; some of them were imprisoned, and the rest disarmed, till at length they fled to Maryland, where the upright and pious Lord Baltimore had shown that, in the New World at least, Romanism was not incompatible with toleration.[2]

Laws equally stringent were enacted on behalf of morality. Whoredom, fornication, and the "loathsome sin of drunkenness," were all the subject of severe penal laws, and the enforcement of these laws was the special province of the churchwardens.[3] But in spite of these manifestations of the protective spirit in religion and morals, politically Virginia enjoyed a high degree of freedom. Under the original constitution of 1619, every freeman had a vote. In 1655, the suffrage was limited to householders, and any attempt on the part of an unqualified person to vote was punishable by a fine of one hundred pounds of tobacco. In the next year this act was repealed on the ground that it was "something hard and unagreeable to reason that any persons should pay equal taxes and yet have no votes in elections." In 1670, the franchise was again restricted, and an act passed setting forth that, "Whereas the lawes of England grant a voyce in such election only to such as by their estates, real or personal, have interest enough to tye them to the endeavour of the publique good;" none but freeholders and householders should be allowed to retain the privilege of voting.[4]

The government of the colony consisted, as we have already seen, of a governor, a council, and a body of burgesses. The governor was elected by the council, except during the more Liberal Government which Virginia enjoyed under the commonwealth. His office was, in theory, to represent the king. In addition to this, he had the supreme naval and military authority.

---

[1] Hening, vol. ii., p. 198. [2] Rachel and Leah, p. 23.
[3] Hening, vol. i., p. 240. [4] Hening, vol. i., pp. 403, 412; vol. ii., p. 280.

His salary was, until 1677, £1000 a year. In that year the assembly voted Berkeley an addition of £200.[1] The council consisted of twelve members, nominated by the king. Under certain circumstances, the governor had power to fill up vacancies.[2] The whole deliberative and legislative power of the state was in the hands of the burgesses—limited only by the governor's veto. Originally the governor, the council, and the burgesses, had all sat together. But in progress of time, the burgesses sat apart and constituted by themselves the assembly.[3] All laws passed by them and approved by the governor were sent over to England for the royal sanction, but remained in force provisionally from the time they were passed.[4] The expenses of the burgesses, which the scattered state of the population made considerable, were paid by the constituencies, and to guard against candidates purchasing votes by offering to serve for little or no remuneration, a fixed rate was established.[5] Under the commonwealth, a dispute arose between the governor and the burgesses—each claiming the right of dissolving the assembly. The dispute was settled in favour of the burgesses, but it may be doubted whether they retained the right after the restoration.[6] That there was but little state in the meetings of these colonial legislators, we may judge from some records in Hening. In 1663, it was deliberated "whether it were not more profitable to purchase, than continue for ever at the expense, accompanied by the dishonour of all our laws being made, and our judgments given, in an ale-house." At the same time, fines were imposed for various acts of disorder, and amongst other offences, "piping it" was prohibited.[7]

The judiciary was almost irresponsible. The governor and the council formed the chief court both for civil and criminal cases,—subject to no appeal, except in civil cases in which

---

[1] Beverley, p. 188. Account of Virginia in the Massachusetts' Historical Collection. 1st series, vol. v., p. 142.
[2] Beverley, p. 189.   [3] Beverley, p. 187.   [4] Beverley, p. 190.
[5] Hening, vol. ii., pp. 73, 106, 109.   [6] Hening, vol. i., pp. 498-500.
[7] Hening, vol. ii., p. 204.

the matter at issue was over £300 in value.[1] Besides this, there were county courts, presided over by justices appointed by the governor, in which cases of less than £15 value were tried.[2]

The special legislation on the subject of tobacco is too important a feature in the early history of Virginia to be passed over. As I have said before, the cultivation of tobacco was unduly practised, to the exclusion of other branches of agriculture. This was due, no doubt, to want of skill in the labourers employed, many of whom were, as we have seen, slaves. It has often been observed, that a rotation of crops requires greater intelligence and versatility than is found among slave labourers, and that consequently the slave-driver is compelled to exhaust his land by repeating the same crop year after year, and then to fall back upon fresh tracts of virgin soil. As early as 1619 Yeardley had endeavoured to legislate against the over-production of tobacco.[3] In 1623, it had become an established custom among the inhabitants to make their contracts and to keep their accounts in tobacco instead of money. This was found to be inconvenient, and a law was passed to provide that all such dealings should thereafter be transacted in money. Notwithstanding this attempt, tobacco became ultimately the recognised currency of Virginia.[4] Various other attempts were made to limit tobacco planting among the early Virginian settlers. Vine dressers were introduced from France.[5] Efforts were made to cultivate silk, and it was supposed that it would afford a branch of industry for which the Indian women and children would be peculiarly fitted.[6] But none of these attempts seem to have attained any permanent success. So great was the evil, that it was thought necessary, very early in the history of the colony, to have recourse to direct legislation. In 1629, an act was passed to limit the production, by which

---

[1] Berkeley's Account of Virginia. Hening, vol. i., p. 511.
[2] Stith, book iv., p. 207. Hening, vol. i., p. 511.
[3] Stith, book iii., pp. 163-165. [4] Hening, vol. i., p. 216.
[5] Virginia Richly and Truly Valued, p. 17. Hening, vol. i., p. 161.
[6] Virginia Richly and Truly Valued, p. 38.

new-comers were forbidden to grow tobacco, while every planter was definitely limited to two thousand plants. Inspectors were appointed, and delinquents debarred from future cultivation. The growing of slips or seconds was also prohibited, a prohibition which was renewed in 1658 under the heavy penalty of ten thousand pounds of tobacco. In 1631, the price was limited to sixpence a pound. In 1633, the quantity was further limited to fifteen hundred plants, and the cultivation of certain sorts was forbidden. A public warehouse was appointed, where all the tobacco was to be lodged and examined by an inspector. In the autumn of the same year seven warehouses were established, and the price raised to ninepence. In 1639, it was determined to take further measures to limit the supply, and a law was passed that half the tobacco which was passed by the inspector should be burnt along with the condemned. In 1662, it was enacted that no tobacco should be planted after July 10th, a limitation which was afterwards made more stringent by substituting June 1st. These attempts to limit artificially the supply of tobacco were, however, for the most part nullified by the refusal of Maryland to co-operate. In 1682, the tobacco difficulty gave rise to serious troubles. A number of individuals took the law into their own hands, and limited the tobacco supply forcibly by destroying the plants. So serious did the matter become, that in 1684 an act was passed "for the better preservation of the peace in Virginia, and preventing unlawful and treasonable associations," providing "that, if more than eight persons assemble to cut tobacco, and do not disperse within four hours, they should be deemed guilty of high treason, and put to death." [1]

Another prolific subject of legislation was the relation of the colonists to the Indians. We have already seen that in 1624 special enactments were made for an offensive and defensive warfare with them. In 1631, we find an order issued, containing the words, "because wee hold the neighbouring Indians oure irrecon-

---

[1] For these tobacco laws, see Hening, vol. i., pp. 141, 152, 161, 162, 164, 206, 209, 224, 399, 478; and vol. ii., pp. 106, 119, 190, 209, 222, 562.

cilable enemies."[1] In 1632, an order was passed, forbidding all trade or intercourse with the Indians.[2] Two years later, a similar order was re-imposed, with severe penalties. In 1643, another massacre was perpetrated, in which three hundred white men were cut off. But Opechancanough was now long past his prime, and the attack was conducted feebly. War was declared, and in 1646 Opechancanough was captured, and put to death under circumstances of peculiar brutality.[3] In the same year, we find the declaration of war repealed, and a treaty made with Necotowance, Opechancanough's successor, which was renewed in 1658.[4] From that time, for nearly thirty years, the red men and the colonists remained at peace. So utterly were the dangers of Indian warfare forgotten, that in 1650 Williams wrote that "one man that was master but of a heart and pitchforke hath been known to stave off and affright ten of them; nor were any that had the generosity to oppose, or the discretion to kepe good their houses, massacred by them;"[5] and in 1661 Berkeley reported that "the Indians our neighbours are absolutely subjected, so that there is no fear of them."[6] So little was danger apprehended, that all precautions against the Indians bearing arms were omitted. In 1655, an attempt was made to improve their condition by educating their children, by giving them cows as rewards for the destruction of wolves, and by incapacitating them from alienating their lands.[7] In 1658, they were allowed to carry arms, and all restrictions on Indian commerce were removed on the ground that the restrictions were futile, and prejudicial to the beaver trade.[8] Indeed, the whole tone of the Virginian laws in reference to the Indians during the period of peace from 1646 to 1674 is singularly humane. Berkeley's conduct in this respect goes far to atone for his arbitrary and even brutal policy at other times. In 1653, a law was passed, prohibiting the enslaving of Indians. In 1654, another law protected their lives when they

[1] Hening, vol. i., p. 193.
[2] Hening, vol. i., p. 173.
[3] Beverley, pp. 49, 50.
[4] Hening, vol. i., p. 323.
[5] Virginia Richly and Truly Valued, p. 58.
[6] Hening, vol. i., p. 515.
[7] Hening, vol. i., p. 393.
[8] Hening, vol. i., p. 525.

came on to the lands of the settlers. In 1657, the settlers were prohibited from squatting on the lands of the Indians. The legislature of 1659 enacted that no debts should be recoverable from Indians, and that no merchants should take Indian children to England without the consent of their parents. In 1660, to guard against encroachments on the Indian territory, certain lands were settled inalienably on the Indians of Accomack.[1] In 1666, an act was passed containing a sort of digest of all the laws then in force with respect to the Indians. Alienation of Indian lands was forbidden, and those who had encroached on their territory were to be ejected, and their houses pulled down. No Indian chief was to be imprisoned, and no Indian whatever to be held as a slave for a longer period than was allowed in the case of a white man. Badges were granted as passports to the friendly Indians coming on the English lands. In the same session, we find that Colonel Yorke was fined ten thousand pounds of tobacco for allowing the murderer of an Indian to escape, and that Captains Brent and Hawk should pay fifteen thousand pounds of tobacco, and be disqualified from holding any civil or military office for the illegal imprisonment of an Indian, and that Colonel Moore Fauntleroy was similarly disqualified for extorting Roanoke from the Indians, under the pretence that it was ransom.[2] In 1665, a law was passed, that in the case of a white man being murdered by the Indians, the nearest town should be responsible, but in the next year it was repealed.[3]

In spite of this amity and tranquillity, events were at hand which were to recall the horrors of the massacre, followed by the still worse horrors of civil war. A variety of circumstances had combined to disaffect the minds of the settlers. In 1669, Charles II. granted to Lords Culpepper and Arlington the whole of Virginia, giving at the same time the power of nominating sheriffs and surveyors, of presenting to churches, of dividing the colonies into counties and parishes, of granting lands, and of

[1] Hening, vol. i., pp. 396, 401, 476, 541, 546 ; and vol. ii., p. 13.
[2] Hening, vol. ii., pp. 138-150.   [3] Hening, vol. ii., pp. 208, 237.

nullifying previous grants.[1] The colonists instantly took alarm; Morryson, Smith, and Ludwell were sent over as agents. Of the result of their agency I shall have to speak again : its immediate effect was to necessitate considerable expense, and compel the assembly to impose a poll-tax of fifty pounds of tobacco. This, added to the low price of tobacco, and the severe restrictions imposed on trade, had caused considerable distress.[2] Moreover, corruption had become rife in the government offices, and in the management of elections.[3] The Virginians were, as we have seen, a loyal people, and Berkeley was popular. But their lack of education, and their mode of life, had developed in them what a modern writer has well called " that peculiar taint of barbarism which makes men prefer occasional disobedience to systematic liberty."[4] Moreover, the treatment they had met with from the king whom they befriended must have contrasted singularly with the liberality of the parliament which they had resisted. Events were soon to fire the train thus prepared. In 1675, troubles arose with the Susquehannah Indians on the Potomac, and one thousand men had been raised for purposes of defence in Virginia, and a similar number in Maryland. During the course of their disturbances, six Susquehannah chiefs, who had come to treat of peace, were treacherously murdered. In retaliation, their countrymen ranged through the colony, and killed sixty white men. The necessity of taking prompt measures for defence was represented to Berkeley, who, however, was content to send vague promises of assistance. The Virginians were not of a temper to suffer the country to be ravaged, and the inhabitants murdered for want of legal authority to take up arms. Almost every colonist was a skilful marksman, and fitted by his habits for a backwoods warfare, and all they needed was a head. The leader they wanted was found in Nathaniel Bacon, "the most accomplished gentleman in Virginia, to serve his king and

---

[1] Hening, vol. ii., p. 247.   [2] Beverley, pp. 61, 62.
[3] Evidence of this is to be seen in Bacon's law, of which I shall speak hereafter.
[4] Buckle (History of Civilisation in England) uses these words of the Spaniards.

country at the councill table, or to put a stop to the insolences of the heathen."[1] He was the son of a member of the council; and it is clear from subsequent events, that he possessed the confidence of the country, and was eminently fitted to be the leader in a guerilla warfare. Berkeley, however, refused him a commission. Upon this he declared that as soon as another white man was killed, he would take up arms. Immediately afterwards news arrived that Bacon's plantation had been attacked, and his overseer, a favourite servant, killed. Bacon immediately carried out his threat, and five hundred men soon gathered to his standard. Berkeley thereupon proclaimed him a rebel, arranged with the friendly Indians to cut off his supplies, and marched against him. A civil war was now added to that with the Indians; but before Berkeley could overtake Bacon, Jamestown was up in arms. A fresh assembly was summoned, and Bacon elected member for Henrico county. Through the influence of his father, Bacon was granted a free pardon upon his submission. The proceedings which immediately followed are somewhat obscure. At the opening of the session Bacon appears as a pardoned rebel; almost immediately afterwards he is an influential leader instituting great political reforms. It is at least certain that on the 5th of June the assembly passed measures which sufficiently show how much ground there was for disaffection. An act was passed setting forth that abuses had crept into government offices, and ordering that the sheriffs' and under-sheriffs' tenure of office should be limited to a year. No officer was to hold more than one office of profit at the same time, or to take more than their legal fees. The secretary and his clerk had been in the practice of levying a duty of eighty hogsheads of tobacco on every parcel of land granted; for the future they were ordered to levy this duty only on each patent, (one patent frequently including several parcels.) Another act was passed enabling freemen to vote for burgesses, and preventing false returns. Taxation was transferred from the county magistrates

[1] Private letter, written at the time, given in Force.

to the assembly. At the same time measures were taken to guard against the immediate danger from the Indians. An act was passed " for carrying on a warre against the barbarous Indians." One thousand men were to be raised, of whom one-eighth were to be horse, and Nathaniel Bacon was appointed commander-in-chief. Yet it is clear that Bacon's position was by no means safe. Being warned that Berkeley meditated treachery, he left Jamestown, on the pretext of visiting his wife, who was sick, and returned in a few days with four hundred men. Berkeley yielded. An act of indemnity was passed for all offences done between March 1st and June 24th, those only excepted who had traded with the Indians, and Berkeley was compelled to sign a report approving of Bacon's conduct. Berkeley was scrupulously honest in his dealings with the hostile Indians, but he appears to have thought that rebels were entitled to no such consideration. In spite of the act just passed, he again declared Bacon a rebel. For a time the insurgents' cause seemed completely triumphant. Bacon had the whole colony with him. Berkeley's retreat from Jamestown was considered tantamount to abdication, and a provisional government was appointed. Gloucester, the most populous and loyal country in Virginia, refused to take the governor's part. At length, he succeeded in raising a force in Accomack. He bribed servants by the hope of liberty, others by promises of the insurgents' estates, and of immunities from taxation. A civil war ensued, in which, as might be expected, the insurgents had the best of it. They obtained possession of Jamestown, the only city in the colony, and burnt it, lest the enemy should find shelter there. But on the 1st of October they were deprived of their leader. Bacon died, whether by sickness or " Paracelsian art " seems uncertain, and the rebel force having lost its head fell to pieces in less than two months. The ringleaders were most of them taken and put to death by Berkeley under circumstances of peculiar brutality. At length the assembly interfered, and passed an act of indemnity pardoning all treasons, murders, &c., committed since

April 1st, with certain exceptions. At the same time they passed an act of attainder against Bacon and others, and declared all Bacon's acts null and void. To obliterate, as far as possible, all recollection of past grievances, they enacted that no private compensation was to be made for injuries inflicted during the rebellion, and that no abusive terms were to be used having reference to it. In the next year the king sent out instructions to Berkeley to pardon all except Bacon. He was to be captured by "all waies of force or design," if he refused to surrender; an order which had already been rendered unnecessary, perhaps by having been too faithfully anticipated. These instructions were confirmed by an act sent out two years later by Culpepper, and passed by the assembly. The ease with which Bacon's party was overthrown after his death proves how little of the material for a revolution the country contained within itself; but his reforms did not wholly die with him. Many of his laws were re-enacted, and we do not find any complaint afterwards of such abuses as those which he had remedied.[1]

The history of Virginia, under the two last Stuarts, continues to present to us a policy of petty tyranny and irregular resistance. In 1680, as we have seen, Lord Culpepper was sent out as governor. He brought two acts with him, beside that of indemnity. One of these made the naturalisation of aliens a prerogative of the governor, not as hitherto a privilege of the assembly. The other imposed a perpetual export duty on tobacco, the proceeds of which were to be accounted for not to the assembly, but to the king.[2] At the same time, Lord Culpepper obtained from the assembly a doubled salary on the ground of his being a peer, with an addition of house rent.[3] On the other hand, the colonists had, by their agents in London, obtained an important advantage. A charter had been pro-

---

[1] I have taken this account of Bacon's proceedings from three pamphlets written by contemporaries, and published in Force, and from Hening, vol. ii., pp. 341-365, 408, 409, and 423. I have occasionally referred to Bancroft, who quotes, in addition to the above authorities, some Richmond Records.

[2] Hening, vol. ii., pp. 458, 466.   [3] Beverley, p. 188.

mised, granting them immunity from taxation, but it was allowed to fall through. A second attempt was more successful. After much resistance, Culpepper and Arlington gave up their grant, reserving only escheats and quit-rents. Beside this, the agents drew up a new charter, to which they obtained the king's assent. This charter provided that the crown should have no power to transfer its authority, as in the case of Culpepper, that the present grants should be confirmed, and that no taxes should be imposed but by consent of the assembly.[1]

Culpepper was succeeded in 1683 by Lord Howard of Effingham. A century of corruption was then beginning to assert its sway over English politics, and in Effingham's government, Virginia had a foretaste of it. He established a chancery court with an arbitrary table of fees, and constituted himself Lord Chancellor. Other despotic measures followed. The printing press was prohibited. The franchise was restricted. The assembly, on the other hand, questioned the royal veto, and was accordingly dissolved, and one of its members kept in irons for using treasonable language.[2] But the governor was too weak and ill supported to take any decisive measures, and Virginia was allowed to grow up a stronghold of liberty, with institutions which inadequately expressed the needs of her citizens.

In Virginia, we have seen a colony growing up in the spirit of the old world, and with many of its faults and failings. In New England, we shall see hereafter a community throwing off the yoke of the old world, flying into a wilderness for freedom, and with too faithful imitation, establishing a spiritual tyranny different only in form from that which it had escaped from in the old world, and scarcely less irksome. In Maryland, we see the stranger spectacle of that Church, whose name is in Europe associated with intolerance, setting a continent the example of toleration. In 1629, Lord Baltimore had visited Virginia, but the bigotry of the legislature had made it impossible for him to remain there.[3] But there was a country to the north of Virginia,

[1] Hening, vol. i., p. 520.   [2] Beverley, pp. 128-131.   [3] Beverley, pp. 46, 47.

another "fruitful sister," in which he might find a home for himself and those who held his faith. In fertility, Maryland equalled Virginia, while in climate it was superior. Wild cattle, deer, and swine abounded. Delaware Bay afforded rich fisheries, and the Potomac swarmed with beaver.[1] In 1632, Lord Baltimore obtained a proprietary grant of Maryland, modified by provisions for the protection of the colonists against the proprietary. It was provided that the statutes of the province should be established with the advice and approbation of the majority of the freemen and their deputies, and that the authority of the proprietary should not extend to the life or estate of any emigrant. Before the patent was completed, Lord Baltimore died, but it was renewed in the name of his son. On the 2d of November 1633, Leonard Calvert, the brother of Lord Baltimore, and two hundred colonists sailed.[2] The conditions of the adventure were, that every share of £100 entitled the holder to two hundred acres of land, beside a distribution in proportion to personal services.[3] On the 27th of March, they landed at the Indian town of Yoacomoco. As if by "a miracle, the savages trusted themselves like lambs" to the colonists, and "surrendered to them themselves and their property."[4] The early history of Maryland is a scene of unruffled peace and prosperity. The relations with the Indians, which had opened so favourably, were kept up by the agency of the Roman Catholic missionaries. The solitary priest, with his interpreter and servant, his little stock of provisions, his baptismal water and sacramental wine, and a few small presents for the natives, wandered through the Indian villages, carrying his tent with him, and "enjoying his humble fare and hard couch, with no less enjoyment than more luxurious provisions in Europe."[5] In 1642, the Indians, provoked by the rapacity of white traders, commenced a war of

---

[1] "A Relation of the Colony of the Lord Baron of Baltimore in Maryland, copied from the Archives of the Jesuits' College at Rome," pp. 5-7. Force, vol. ii.
[2] Bancroft, vol. i., pp. 240-246.   [3] A Relation, &c., p. 4.
[4] A Relation, &c., p. 25.   [5] A Relation, &c., pp. 39, 40.

retaliation. Friendship, however, was soon restored, and laws were passed, giving the pre-emption of the soil to Lord Baltimore, making the kidnapping of Indians a capital offence, and the selling arms to them a felony.[1]

All the troubles that beset the youthful state resulted from the intrigues of a Virginian—Clayborne, who claimed a right over the territory, under an old license granted for commercial purposes in 1632. Early in the history of the colony, he had created a disturbance in which lives had been lost; and in 1638, one or two of his adherents were executed on the charge of piracy and murder. He availed himself of the establishment of the commonwealth, and of the consequent confusion, to seize the supreme power, and to establish a board of ten commissioners, to whom the government of the colony was intrusted. One of the first legislative acts of the new party, was to exclude "popery, prelacy, or licentiousness of opinion," "from the freedom of conscience granted to all other beliefs." The act met with a rebuke from Cromwell, who bade the commissioners "not to busy themselves about religion, but settle the civil government." For a time discord prevailed, but in 1660, the assembly claimed full legislative power, and the liberties of the colony, which by this time contained ten thousand inhabitants, were established on a firm basis.[2]

We have already seen that at the time of the original formation of the Virginian plantation, another colony was projected in the territory, which was afterwards New England. In 1607, it was determined to send out a colony, under the charter of the North Virginia Company. George Popham was appointed president, and Ralegh Gilbert admiral, and with one hundred settlers, they sailed from Plymouth on the 31st of May 1607. On the 8th of August they landed at the mouth of the Kennebek, where they built Fort St George. They made friends with the natives through the agency of two Indians, whom they had brought with them, and forty-five men were left as a colony.

[1] Bancroft, vol. i., pp. 253, 254.   [2] Bancroft, vol. i., pp. 254-265.

Unfortunately for the new settlement the winter was exceptionally cold. Popham died; Gilbert was obliged to return home, owing to the death of his father, and the colony was broken up, having only served to establish a belief in the unendurable severity of the climate.[1]

One of the most energetic in organising this colony had been Sir Fernando Gorges. His interest in the colonisation of America had originally been aroused by the possession of three Indians brought back by Weymouth from America in 1605. The report which he had received from them of their country, "its goodly rivers, stately islands, and safe harbours," had impressed him with the value of settlements on the coast of North America, and in 1606, he had sent out one Captain Challoungs with two of these Indians. Challoungs was captured by the Spanish fleet before he reached America, and the expedition came to nothing. Notwithstanding this failure, and that in the following year, he determined to renew the attempt, "not despairing," as he quaintly says, "of means, when God should be pleased to make it appear, it would yield both profit and content to those that aimed thereat, these being truly, (for the most part), the motives that all men labour, howsoever otherwise adorned with fair colours and goodly shadows." Under the pretext of fishing and trade, he sent out several voyages to inspect the country, but saw no prospect of a settlement.[2] In vain Smith represented the capacities of New England as a fishing station. The ill-success with which Virginia had hitherto met, was discouraging, and the New England patent remained unused. Various fishing voyages were made, but their chief effect was to discredit the English with the natives, by the "beastly demeanours" of the fishermen.[3]

[1] Sir Ferdinando Gorges' "Description of New England," [Massachusetts' "Historical Collection," 3d series, vol. vi.,] pp. 54, 56. Travayle into Virginia, pp. 161–179.

[2] Gorges, pp. 51, 56–63.

[3] Gorges, p. 70. It was in one of these voyages that Hunt kidnapped a number of Indians, one of whom afterwards escaped, and acted as an interpreter for the

The colonisation of New England, incredible as it might seem to Gorges, was to proceed from other motives than "aiming at profit and content." That which the wisest and bravest Englishmen of the Elizabethan age had failed to do, which the most enterprising merchants and gentry of England had only done after a succession of failures, was destined to be accomplished even more fully, by a small and obscure band of exiled enthusiasts. "I will make them conform, or I will harry them out of the land," said King James at the Hampton Court Conference. "I protest my heart melteth for joy, that Almighty God, of His singular mercy, has given us such a king as since Christ's time has not been," was the pious comment with which Bancroft received the declaration of the royal policy.[1] King and primate alike little knew of how great a work God's counsels had made them the unconscious instruments. In 1608, a troop of men, women, and children, were gathered together on a lonely beach between Grimsby and Hull. They had been "harried out of the land," they were "going into a country they know not but by hearsay, where they must learn a new language, and get their livings they knew not how." Holland was in that age the one spot of dry land on which the tossed and troubled ark of freedom had found rest. Thither Ames had fled when Oxford had driven him forth, and there the disciples of Barrowe and Greenwood had found the home which England under Elizabeth had refused them.[2] The goods and the greater part of the men were on board, the women and children were just ready to embark, when "the master espied a great company, both horse and foot, with bills and guns and other weapons, for the country was raised to take them." The Dutchman seeing that, swore his country's oath ('sacrament') and having the wind fair, weighed his anchor, hoisted sail and away." At first it seemed as if those who had

---

Plymouth pilgrims. Discovery and Plantation of New England. Massachusetts' Historical Collection, 2d series, vol. ix., p. 4, and New England's Memorial, p. 54 ; ed. 1855. [1] Stoughton's "Spiritual Heroes," pp. 68, 69.
[2] Belknap's "American Biography," p. 274, n.

been left behind had fared better. A fearful storm arose. For seven days "they neither saw sun, moon, nor stars, and were driven to the coast of Norway; the mariners themselves often despairing of life, and once with shrieks and cries gave over all, as if the ship had been foundered in the sea and they sinking without recovery." Truly the pilgrims might have said, "quid times! Cæsarem vehis." The outcasts who, after fourteen days in the deep, landed at Amsterdam, were to be the founders of an empire which, perhaps, shall influence the world even more mightily than did Cæsar's. The wives and children whom they had left behind them, homeless, and penniless, after being "hurried from one place to another, and from one justice to another," and "thus turmoiled a good while," were at last let go, their persecutors being glad to be rid of them, and joined their husbands and fathers in Holland.

Their historian tells with almost scriptural simplicity and pathos, how "in the low countries, they saw many goodly and fortified cities, strongly walled and guarded with troops and armed men;" how "they heard a strange language and beheld the different manners and customs of the people, with their strange fashions and attires all so far differing from that of their plain country villages, wherein they were born and bred and had so long lived, as it seemed they were come into a new world." After sojourning a year at Amsterdam, they removed to Leyden, "a fair and beautiful city and of a sweet situation" and there "fell to such trades and employments as they best could, valuing peace and spiritual comfort above all riches whatsoever; and at length they came to raise a competent and comfortable living, and with hard and continual labour." There they "continued for many years in a comfortable condition, enjoying much sweet and delightful society and spiritual comfort together." The little colony formed a refuge for Nonconformists from various parts of England, till they became a great congregation. Their honesty and industry gained them employment, and so peaceful was their life, that the magistrates held them up as an example to the turbulent Walloons. Yet their position was a hard, and in many respects a painful one. They saw their children growing up to a life of almost ceaseless toil, or becoming sailors and soldiers, and acquiring the rudeness and often the vices of their associates. Above all, "they had a great hope and inward zeal of laying some good foundation, or at least, to make some way thereunto, for the propagating and advancing the gospel of the kingdom of Christ in remote parts of the world." Sixty years before, Coligny had conceived the idea of establishing that home for religious liberty in the New World which was denied to it in the Old.[1] To America the thoughts of the Leyden puritans now turned. Guiana and Virginia were both proposed. Guiana was overruled as being unhealthy and exposed to the Spaniards, while in Virginia, it was feared they would be in danger of the same persecution which had driven them from England. Their lines were to be cast in a spot seemingly far less pleasant than Virginia or Guiana, but had the wisest political foresight guided them, they could not have chosen more discreetly. "If men desire to have a people degenerate speedily, and to corrupt their minds and bodies too, and besides, to take in thieves and spoilers from abroad, let them seeke a rich soile that brings in much with little labour; but if they desire that piety and godliness should prosper accompanied with sobriety, justice and love, let them choose a country such as this (New England) is; even like France or England which may yield sufficiency with hard labour and industry; the truth is, there is more reason to fear wealth than poverty in that soile."[4]

At length it was determined to settle by themselves under the general government of Virginia, and two deputies were sent to England to treat with the Virginia Company. The company gladly accepted this offer, and were willing to grant them a patent, with as ample privileges as they had or could grant. The king, however, refused to tolerate them by his public authority, though he gave a general promise that he would

[1] Bancroft, vol. i., p. 61.   [2] The Planter's Plea. Force, vol. ii., p. 18.

connive at them, and not molest them, if they carried themselves peaceably. At first this "made a damp on the business." But the principal men in the congregation were disposed to attach little importance to the royal sanction, arguing, with a knowledge of Stuart principles, which showed that enthusiasm had not diminished their worldly wisdom, that "if there should be a purpose or desire to wrong them, though they had a seal as broad as the house floor, it would not serve the turn, for there would be means enough found to recall or reverse it." Their attempt was delayed by internal dissensions then prevailing in the Virginia Company. At length, in 1620, they got a patent in the name of John Wincob, "a religious gentleman, then belonging to the Countess of Lincoln, who intended to go with them." In the meantime the company for New England had obtained a renewal of their patent in precisely the same terms as the Virginia patent. The pilgrims were, for a time, inclined to settle under this, but nothing came of the design, and they adhered to the patent they already had. The terms of it were that the shares should be of £10 value each; that every planter of the age of sixteen should be considered as having one share in the adventure. That all property and land should be common for seven years, at the end of which time this should be divided.[1] On the 5th of September, after crossing over from Leyden, they sailed from Southampton. For a time it seemed as if their second departure from England was to be as disastrous as their first. Owing to the smaller of their two ships being overmasted they had, after sailing more than three hundred miles, to put back and leave it with its passengers, and to sail with the Mayflower alone. Yet the outcasts carried away a grateful recollection of the country from which they had been driven forth, and the name of their settlement commemorated kindness received on the last spot of English soil on which they rested.[2]

[1] The whole of this account of the early wanderings of the Pilgrim Fathers is taken from Bradford's "Letter Book," published in Davis' edition of "New England's Memorial." [2] Belknap's "American Biography," vol. ii., p. 323.

In November 1620 they reached Cape Cod. They then directed their shipmaster to make for Hudson's river. But the same good fortune which had before saved them from settling in Virginia still attended them. The territory about Hudson's river was much richer and more fertile than Cape Cod, but the latter district had been recently depopulated by a pestilence, and was therefore peculiarly fitted to be the settlement of a weak and unwarlike people. Their shipmaster being bribed by the Dutch, who were hostile to the plantation, refused to take them further south, and they were constrained, almost in the dead of winter, to land in "a hideous and desolate wilderness, full of wild beasts and wild men." On the 11th of November 1620 the fathers of New England met to constitute themselves a body politic. The heads of the forty-six families who composed the little republic signed a solemn combination, binding themselves to submit to "such just and equal laws as shall be thought most meet and convenient for the general good of the colony." They then appointed William Carver their governor. Their next proceeding was to find a habitation. On the 16th they sent out sixteen men, well armed, to explore. They met with no Indians, but found some of their wigwams, and, what was of the utmost importance to them, some seed-corn for the new year. On the 6th of December they sent out a second expedition in the shallop to explore the bay. On the same day that they sailed they perceived, near the shore, some ten or twelve natives, the first that they had seen. The next morning, about dawn, they heard "a great and strange cry," which was speedily followed by a flight of arrows. Most of their arms were in the shallop, but fortunately they had four muskets, and with them they kept them at bay, and "soon stayed their violence." None of the savages seem to have been killed, but at length one of the English "taking full aim at" a savage, "made the bark or splinters of the tree fly about his ears; after which he gave an extraordinary shriek, and away they went all of them." After returning solemn thanksgiving for their deliverance, they again set sail. On returning, they landed at Plymouth, and there spent their Sabbath. On the Monday they sounded the harbour, and found it suitable for shipping, and finding also corn-fields and running water, they chose the spot for their settlement. On the 16th of December, the whole body of pilgrims landed at Plymouth, and on the 25th the first house was begun. The hardships of the voyage, the sufferings from cold and lack of food which the emigrants had undergone soon began to tell upon them, and in three months they were reduced to about fifty. Sometimes there were not more than six or seven well. But the spirit of Christian fortitude and brotherhood which they had brought with them into the wilderness did not fail under these trials. The few who had strength ministered night and day to the sick, " not shunning to do very mean services to help the weak and impotent." Had the savages taken advantage of their weakness, the pilgrim colony could not have lived through a single summer. But various circumstances hindered the Indians from an attack. I have already mentioned that they had suffered severely from a pestilence. So widespread had been the destruction, that the sites of their villages were strewed with bones and skulls, and the forest seemed " a new-found Golgotha."[1] Moreover, the savages had about three years before captured the crew of a French ship at Cape Cod, and put nearly the whole of them to death. One of the survivors, who was kept in captivity, having learnt their language, warned them that their crime would not go unpunished. Shortly after, the plague fell upon them, an event that made the survivors henceforth scrupulous in their dealings with the white men. In March they met an Indian, the first with whom they had spoken, who hailed them with "Welcome, Englishmen." A few days afterwards, they received a visit from Massasoit, the sachem of Pokanoket, with whom they made a league. Two years later, this friendship was confirmed by a fortunate circumstance. Massasoit fell ill, and his life was despaired of. The colonists, hearing of

[1] New England's Canaan. By Thomas Morton. Force, vol. ii., pp. 18, 19.

this, sent Winslow to see him. By the use of some simple medicines, he restored Massasoit, and the sachem was ever after a firm friend to the colonists.[1]

With the appearance of summer, the health of the settlers improved, but in April they were deprived of their governor, Carver. He was succeeded by Bradford, a brave and pious descendant of a family of English yeomen.[2] The same autumn, several other chiefs entered into an alliance with the colony, and gave in their allegiance to the English king. So prosperous was the past summer, that when thirty-five more emigrants appeared on the 9th of November, the arrival excited no fear of lack of stores. The colonists could write home to their friends in England,— "By the goodness of God we are so far from want, that we often wish you the partakers of our plenty."[3] They had, however, overrated their strength, for before the next harvest they again suffered for lack of provisions. Shortly after the departure of the ship which brought the emigrants, an ambassador arrived from Canonicus, the sachem of Narraganset, bearing a bundle of arrows in the skin of a rattlesnake. Bradford answered the challenge in kind by sending back the skin stuffed with powder and ball, accompanying it with the message that if the Indians preferred war to peace, they were welcome to attack them; they would not find them unprepared. The colonists, after this, thought it prudent to palisade their village, to place sentries, and to divide their little force into four squadrons to guard the different quarters. In the next summer they built a fort "both strong and comely," and it was characteristic of these soldiers of the

---

[1] The narrative of this visit, written by Winslow, is published in New England's Memorial, pp. 367–375. It is worthy of notice that Winslow was accompanied by "one Master John Hampden, a gentleman of London." It was probably the presence of this John Hampden in the colony, that gave rise to the idea that the celebrated John Hampden intended at one time to emigrate to New England. The improbability of such an intention is shown by Bancroft, vol. i., pp. 411, 412.

[2] Belknap's "American Biography," vol. iii., p. 1.

[3] Moint's "Relation," in Massachusetts' "Historical Collection," 2d series, vol. ix., p. 60.

"holy war," that the same building served them for their place of defence and of worship.

In the summer of 1623 it was found necessary to abandon the system of common labour, and to apportion the land into holdings, the soil itself being as before common property, but the labour and produce divided. They had now spent two winters and three summers in the colony, and had still a hard battle to wage against poverty. They had as yet no cattle,[1] and by the time "their corn was planted all their victual was spent, and they were only to rest on God's providence." Shell-fish was the principal staple of their food.[2]

Before proceeding further, it may be well to review the position of the corporation under which the Plymouth colonists occupied their lands. In 1620, the New England company obtained a fresh patent. Under this the Plymouth colonists had obtained a patent in the name of one John Pierce. Pierce had made two unsuccessful attempts to visit New England, but had been frustrated, once by a leak in his vessel, and once by storms. Finally, he had given up the idea, and assigned his patent to the company for £500.[3] The company treated the Plymouth colonists with liberality in the matter of grants, giving them such patents as were necessary for the Indian trade.[4] But in 1627, difficulties arose. The colonists felt the restrictions on the trade irksome, and the company were dissatisfied with the small profits.[5] Accordingly, Allerton, the deputy-governor, was sent over to make an arrangement by which the colony might be independent of the company. Seven or eight of the leading men among the colonists entered into an agreement by which the

---

[1] The first neat cattle was expected to New England in 1624. Josselyn's "Chronological Observations of America." Massachusetts' "Historical Collection," 3d series, vol. iii., p. 375.

[2] This account of the settlement of Plymouth is taken from Morton's "New England's Memorial."

[3] New England's Memorial, pp. 61-63. Belknap's "American Biography," vol. iii., pp. 28, 29.

[4] Bancroft, vol. i., p. 320.

[5] Belknap's "American Biography," vol. iii., pp. 32-34.

company agreed to sell all their shares, stocks, merchandise, lands, and chattels, for a sum of £1800, to be paid by instalments, those who made the agreement being responsible on behalf of the colonists. The money had to be raised at extravagant interest, but the stimulus of independence more than compensated for the immediate expense. The land and stock were divided into shares; every person was to have a single share, and in addition, heads of families were allowed to purchase one share for every member of the family. In July the same eight "directors," if we may so call them, who had arranged these regulations, determined "to run a great venture," and to pay off the debt due to the company, and all other debts at once, and to take the trade of the colony for six years in payment under certain conditions.[1] Thus, in less than seven years from its first settlement, did Plymouth become an independent society, with full tenure of the land which it occupied. More than twenty years later, a young Oxford scholar amused the courtiers of St James by representing New England as a land of simpletons, the paradise of adventurers and sharpers.[2] The history of Plymouth was a sufficient answer to the lying prophet, but the history of Plymouth was only on a small scale

[1] Prince's "New England Chronology."
[2] Cartwright in "The Ordinary," acted in 1651. Three Swindlers—Sharpe, Slicer, and Hearsay—are represented laying their plans—

"*Sharpe.* There is no longer tarrying here; let's
Swear fidelity to one another, and so resolve for
New England.
Hearsay. 'Tis but getting a little pigeon hole
Reformed ruff.
Slicer. Forcing our beards into the orthodox set.
Sharpe. Nosing a little treason 'gainst the king,
Bark something at the bishops, and we shall
Be easily received.
Hearsay. No fitter place.
They are good silly people; souls that will
Be cheated without trouble; one eye is
Put out with zeal, t'other with ignorance,
And they think they're eagles.
Sharpe. We are made
Just fit for that Meridian; no good works
Allowed there; faith, faith is that they call for,
And we will bring it 'em.
Hearsay. For what Old England can't
Afford New England will; you shall hear of us
By the next ship that comes for proselytes."
—ACT V., SCENE 5.

the history of the nation. In the meantime, other settlers had followed in the path which Plymouth had opened. In 1623, Robert Gorges obtained a patent and a commission from the New England company, constituting him governor-general of New England. He established a plantation in Massachusetts Bay, but his governorship of New England came to nothing.[1] In 1622, one Wiston, who had been at one time an adventurer in the Plymouth company, sent over a colony of sixty "lusty men," who settled near Plymouth. They proved "an unruly company and no good government over them, and by disorder fell into many wants." They ridiculed the Plymouth plantation as a weak settlement, hampered by women and children. But in one year they were reduced to so wretched a condition, that some were glad to sell themselves as slaves to the Indians, while others brought the settlers into disrepute with the savages by stealing their corn, and by other abuses. After a year, having changed their settlement, and having been rescued from famine and massacre by the men of Plymouth whom they had despised, they broke up their colony. Some were incorporated into Plymouth, others returned to England.[2]

For several years Gorges and Mason had made several attempts to establish a plantation; but the territorial grants, though imposing on paper, led to little practical result. Scattered settlements were established along the banks of the Piscataqua, but Mason's death in 1635 prevented any attempt on a grand scale, and New Hampshire struggled into being the most independent of the American colonies.[3]

It seemed as though the task of settling New England was specially set apart for Puritans. Already, in 1625, a small body had separated from the colony at Plymouth, and established themselves at Naumkeak, in Massachusetts Bay.[4] In 1628 a number of merchants and gentry in London, Lincolnshire, and

---

[1] New England's Memorial, pp. 67-70.
[2] Bancroft, vol. i., p. 319. New England's Memorial, pp. 53-57.
[3] Bancroft, vol. i., pp. 328-330. [4] New England Chronology.

the west country, friends to the movement for further church reform, had resolved to enlarge the small settlement at Naumkeak into a Puritan plantation. For this purpose they obtained a patent from the Council of Plymouth, and on the 4th of March 1629 they obtained the charter of Massachusetts. The government was placed in the hands of a governor, a deputy-governor, and eighteen assistants, to be elected by the freemen or members of the corporation.[1] In 1628 Endicott was sent over with a small party. On his arrival he joined himself to the colony at Naumkeak, the whole not amounting to more than sixty, and founded the first town on Massachusetts Bay, afterwards to be known as Salem.[2] The next year in June three ships came over bringing colonists for Salem, "many godly Christians," and two nonconformist ministers, who were duly appointed pastor and teacher. The ships brought out not only colonists and ministers, but means for their support, cattle, goats, and horses in great abundance.[3] 1629 was the most important year in the annals of New England since the first colonists had sailed from Plymouth. At a general court held on the 28th of July, it was proposed to "transfer the government of the plantation to those that should inhabit there." On the 26th of August John Winthrop, Thomas Dudley, and ten others, entered into a solemn covenant, binding themselves, if the court would transfer the government and the patent to them, to form a colony in New England. The subject was brought forward two days after, and it was then resolved that the government and patent should be settled in New England. On the 20th of October Winthrop was elected governor of the new colony, and on Easter Sunday, in 1630, the colonists set sail in six ships, and on the 12th of June they landed in New England.[4] Others followed in seven

---

[1] Bancroft, vol. i., p. 342.
[2] Bancroft, vol. i., p. 341. Hubbard's "History of New England." Massachusetts' "Historical Collection," 2d series, vol. v., p. 109.
[3] Bancroft, vol. i., pp. 346, 347. Hubbard, pp. 112, 113. New England's Memorial, pp. 97, 98.
[4] Bancroft, vol. i., pp. 351-354. Winthrop's "History of New England," vol. i., pp. 1-29.

ships, in all about seven hundred.¹ On the 17th of June, Winthrop explored the country in search of a site for the colony. Charlestown was ultimately selected, but the colonists scattered, and Dorchester, Malden, and other towns date from this settlement.² At first the colony, like all its predecessors, underwent hardships. By December two hundred had died, and a hundred more returned to England. Provisions ran short, and the colonists were saved from famine only by the timely arrival of a provision ship from Bristol.³ At first it seemed as if the report of their ill success had daunted their brethren at home, and in 1631 only ninety emigrants came out.⁴ But the spirit of enterprise only flagged for a moment, and in 1632 and 1633 about six hundred men settlers came over.⁵ In Winthrop the colony had a governor well worthy to head the list of New England's statesmen. He was one of those high-minded and far-seeing Puritans, who so effectually redeemed their party from the oft-repeated charge of poverty or narrowness of views. His principles made him severe, while his temper inclined to lenity, and no man ever more truly carried out Fuller's principle that "one may be a lamb in private wrongs, but on hearing general affronts to goodness, they are asses which are not lions."⁶

We have already seen how the intolerance of England had established the New England colonies. The time was at hand when those colonies should in their turn alienate from them their own children, and be the unwilling parents of a fresh state. In 1631, there arrived at Boston a young minister, Roger Williams, "godly and jealous, having precious gifts."⁷ Williams had been educated at Charter House and at Pembroke College, Cambridge, and under the patronage of Lord Coke, he had

---

¹ New England's Memorial, p. 108. Hubbard, pp. 132, 133.
² Bancroft, vol. i., p. 358.
³ Winthrop, vol. i., p. 49. Bancroft, vol. i., p. 360.
⁴ Bancroft, vol. i., p. 361. ⁵ Winthrop, vol. i., pp. 93, 94, 107, 121, 129.
⁶ For instances of this, see Belknap's "American Biography," vol. iii., pp. 162, 163.
⁷ Phrase quoted by Bancroft, vol. i., p. 361.

studied jurisprudence. His theological doctrines seem to have been those generally received among the Puritans, but in questions of church discipline, he went far beyond most of his sect. He was a rigid separatist, and carried the doctrine of toleration, or, as perhaps it might be more properly called, state indifference, to its fullest length. Accordingly it was impossible to employ him as a minister at Boston. He went to Salem, which was then without a preacher, and was appointed to the vacant office. But a message from Winthrop and the assistants compelled the church of Salem to retract its choice, and the young enthusiast withdrew to Plymouth. In 1634, he incurred the displeasure of some of his congregation by putting forward the doctrine that no tenure of land could be valid which had not the sanction of the natives. His doctrine was censured by the court at Boston, but on his satisfying the court of his "loyalty," the matter passed over. But before long he put forward doctrines, in the opinion of the government, yet more dangerous. He advocated complete separation from the Church of England, and denounced compulsory worship and a compulsory church establishment. Carrying the doctrine of individual liberty to its fullest extent, he asserted that the magistrate was only the agent of the people, and had no right to protect the people against itself; that his power extends only as far as such cases as disturb the public peace. The occasion gave special importance to the assertion of such doctrines. The English government had lately shown aggressive tendencies, and it seemed as if the authority of the colonial magistrates needed to be strengthened, rather than made looser.[1] On the 8th of August 1635, Williams was summoned before the general court; his opinions were denounced as "erroneous and very dangerous," and notice was given to the church at Salem, that unless it could explain the matter to the satisfaction of the court, Williams must be dismissed. In October, Williams was again brought before the court, and after a "disputation" with Mr Hooker, which failed to reduce him from any

[1] Bancroft, vol. i., pp. 369-371, 407.

of his errors, he was sentenced to depart out of the jurisdiction of Massachusetts in six weeks. The church of Salem acquiesced in the condemnation of their pastor. Their own experience might have taught the fathers of New England, that the best way to strengthen heresy is to oppose it. The natural result followed: The people were "much taken with the apprehension of Williams' godliness," and a large congregation, including "many devout women," gathered round him. Since they had failed to check the evil, the Massachusetts government resolved to exterminate it and to ship Williams for England. The crew of a pinnace was sent to arrest him, but, fortunately for the future of New England, he had escaped.[1] With five companions in a canoe, he had set out for the territory of Narraganset, and there founded the village of Providence. The little settlement of outcasts became the nucleus of a flourishing colony, and Rhode Island grew into existence the first pure democracy founded by Englishmen on American soil.[2] A few years later, the government of Massachusetts bore the highest testimony to his character. They were glad to avail themselves of his services to bring about a league with the Mohicans. In a canoe, without a companion, the forgiving apostle of the Indians ventured among a savage people on behalf of the state from which he had been banished.[3] Seven years later, Williams was sent to England by the colony that he had founded, to obtain for it a charter. The affairs of the colonies had at that time been placed by the parliament under the control of Lord Warwick as governor-general, assisted by a council of five peers and twelve commoners. Among these was Vane. He had known Williams in former days, and could sympathise with the liberal-minded enthusiast. His services as an Indian missionary were represented to parliament, and in consideration of them, they granted a free and absolute charter constituting Rhode Island an independent state.[4]

[1] Winthrop, vol. i., pp. 193, 194, 204, 209, 210.
[3] Bancroft, vol. i., p. 398.
[2] Bancroft, vol. i., pp. 379, 380.
[4] Bancroft, vol. i., p. 425.

I have dwelt thus at length on the career of Williams, because it is one of the most striking instances of the exclusive and narrow spirit of the New England Puritans. No doubt, a young colony is justified in using measures to secure the unity of the commonwealth, which would be intolerable in an established state. An established state need impose no tests of either political or religious orthodoxy on its citizens. It can offer them protection to life and property, a career, numerous advantages which they cannot obtain elsewhere, or if it cannot, it has only itself to blame. But a newly-founded colony has no such guarantee for the good conduct of its citizens. Such considerations may justify the rulers of an infant state in exercising a degree of inspection over the acts of its subjects, which would be otherwise unwarranted. But they cannot justify, though they may extenuate, the expulsion of a man like Williams. His life was blameless; he was, as his future history shows, gifted with great political sagacity, and guided by the most exalted principle of justice. But because he could not conform to a rigid code of Church discipline, New England would find no place for him. Yet New England was not the only state in which Roger Williams would have been a martyr. He was one of those catholic spirits who are of no age, and whom their own age therefore has ever rejected. The effect of such men's lives is not to be measured by the outward fruit of their actions. They keep alight the torch of freedom; they awaken a sense of its existence in the hearts of those whose lips condemn them.

In 1631, a number of influential men among the Puritan party in England, including Lord Brook and Lord Say and Seal, obtained a grant for the territory of Narraganset. No attempt, however, was made to settle under this patent till 1634. In that year, a number of the inhabitants of Massachusetts, finding themselves straitened for room, made application for liberty to emigrate. The project met with much opposition, on the ground that the defection would weaken Massachusetts, and that the new colony would be exposed to danger. In the next year, the desire for emigration became general, and on the 15th of October, sixty men, women, and children, with their horses and cattle, commenced their journey to Connecticut river. The journey was a difficult and weary one, and it was winter before they reached their new settlement. Their goods had been embarked in small vessels, many of which were cast away. Their provisions failed, and by the beginning of December, "famine and death looked the inhabitants sternly in the face." Some of them attempted to return to Massachusetts, and would have perished by the way but for the assistance given them by the Indians. In spite of this, the next summer saw more than one hundred settlers, many of them " persons of figure, entire strangers to fatigue and danger," on their way from Massachusetts to Connecticut. Under the governorship of John Winthrop, son of the governor of Massachusetts, the colony made rapid progress. Houses were built, roads were made, a good fort was erected, and by the end of the year, the whole colony numbered eight hundred persons.[1]

In 1635, the New England Company came to an end. Like the Virginia Company, it had done its work, and could only be a restriction on the growth of the colonies. Such portions of the unoccupied land as were supposed to be most eligible for plantation were divided among eight of the former patentees. Among them was the indefatigable Gorges. His career is interesting, not for its own sake, but as a link connecting the Elizabethan explorers with the actual colonists of New England. In his old age, he resolved to become a colonial legislator. He divided his territory into bailiwicks, and subdivided it into hundreds, and resubdivided it into parishes and tithings. He appointed a deputy-governor, a chancellor, a treasurer, a marshal, a judge-marshal, an admiral, a master of the ordnance, a secretary of state, and a council of eight deputies. He made laws for the transfer of lands. He established a judiciary and a constabulary force.[2] The practical result was hardly worthy of this

[1] Turnbull's "History of Connecticut," pp. 27, 58–68.
[2] Gorges, pp. 83–86. Gorges does not seem to have devoted himself to the

imposing array of officials. In 1642, the state numbered three hundred citizens, and in 1650 it was incorporated together with New Hampshire into Massachusetts.[1]

At Newhaven a state had grown up under very different influences. A territory was purchased from the Indians; the freemen met in a large barn, and, in a very formal and solemn manner, proceeded to lay the foundation of their civil and religious polity; a covenant was drawn up pledging the inhabitants to be guided by the rule of Scripture. Seven commissioners, "pillars," were chosen to form a constitution. Church membership was made a qualification for citizenship, and thus more completely than in any of the New England colonies was the idea of a Christian state for a time fulfilled.[2]

The growth of New England soon excited the jealousy of the home government. In 1622 the king's privy council having been advised of the "consequences that might follow so unbridled spirits," resolved that the oaths of supremacy and allegiance should be imposed on all emigrants. For several years, however, it was thought unnecessary to enforce the oaths. But, in 1631, "the daily reports brought over word of their continued misdemeanours," and, in 1633, an order was issued that no emigrants should sail without special inquiry.[3] But little practical result ensued. Greater danger was to be apprehended from internal division. A considerable party in New England feeling their own government, not unnaturally, irksome, were short-sighted enough to wish to set up the authority of the mother-country as a check upon it. Had they been successful they would assuredly have realised the fable of the horse and the stag. But the majority of the country were firm, and the long parliament set an example that another English parliament, at a

colony he had founded, for in 1645 we find that the inhabitants elected Vines deputy-governor, not having heard from Gorges for a long time. *Early Records of Maine* in Massachusetts' "Historical Collection," 1st series, vol. i., p. 102.

[1] Bancroft, vol. i., pp. 429–431.
[2] New England's Memorial, pp. 132, 133. Hubbard, pp. 317–323. Turnbull, vol. i., pp. 104–106. [3] Gorges, p. 82. Hubbard, p. 153.

later day, might well have imitated. Winslow, their agent, declared that "if the parliament of England should impose laws upon us having no burgesses in the House of Commons, nor capable of a summons by reason of the vast distance, we should lose the liberties and freedom of English indeed." The answer of parliament set their fears at rest. "We leave you," they said, "all the freedom and latitude that may be duly claimed by you."[1] With the establishment of the commonwealth all present danger was at an end. Cromwell consistently befriended New England, and the parliament offered them a charter, but Massachusetts, either from timidity or far-sighted policy, did not stake their freedom on the precarious existence of a republic. The restoration did not affect their liberties. In 1662 Charles II. granted a charter to Connecticut giving them full and independent legislative powers. The next year a full charter was granted to Rhode Island, giving them equal powers, and establishing full liberty of conscience.[2]

In 1664 New Netherlands passed by conquest into the power of the English, and the acquisition was confirmed by the treaty of Breda. The territory was soon divided into New Jersey and New York. New Jersey was granted to Lord Carteret and Lord Berkeley, New York to the Duke of York. The newly-acquired territory was fertile, and abounded in timber and minerals.[3] The population, in number about twenty thousand, was composed of motley elements. Every persecution which had disgraced the Old World had contributed its share. There were not only Calvinists from Holland and France, but Lutherans from Germany, and Hussites from Bohemia."[4] Such was the community which now became a part of British America. The difference of race was never a strong enough solvent to interfere with the unity of the empire, but in the War of Inde-

---

[1] Bancroft, vol. i., pp. 437–443.   [2] Bancroft, vol. ii., pp. 54, 55, 62, 63.
[3] An Account of the European Settlements in America (commonly attributed to Burke), vol. ii., pp. 185–190.
[4] Bancroft, vol. ii., pp. 300, 301.

pendence we can trace a want of cordiality and consideration on the part of New England towards New York, which may have been in some measure due to this cause.[1]

In 1674 James II. conceived the idea of consolidating the whole of New England and the newly-acquired territory into one state under a royal governor. Andros was sent out as the first satrap. The selection for New England was a happy one. Andros was a man of no ability, whose idea of ruling the colonies was to play the king "in scarlet and lace,"[2] whose tyranny irritated without destroying or permanently injuring. He prohibited town meetings, extorted unlawful fees and imposed illegal taxes.[3] The men of Ipswich resisted his arbitrary taxation, and were arrested without regard to the Habeas Corpus Act. On their trial they were told that they must not suppose that the liberties of Englishmen followed them to the ends of the earth. They were fined, disqualified from office, and compelled to provide sureties for good behaviour.[4] Lynde of Charlestown was told that an Indian deed for his land was "worth no more than the scratch of a bear's claw."[5]

In 1687, Andros dissolved the government of Rhode Island. Massachusetts refused to surrender its charter, and the men of Connecticut hid theirs in a hollow tree.[6] But the tyranny of Andros in New England was but the last effort of despotism that was tottering to its ruin. When the news of the revolution arrived at Boston on the 4th of April 1689, there was "a general buzzing among the people, great with expectation of their old charter, or they know not what."[7] The people rose "with the most unanimous resolution that ever inspired a people." Andros endeavoured to escape, not in his governor's robes, but in

---

[1] Bancroft, vol. vi., pp. 366 ; vol. viii., p. 276.   [2] Bancroft, vol. ii., p. 425.
[3] The Revolution in New England Justified, published in 1691. Force, vol. iv., pp. 2, 3, 12, 13. An Account of the Late Revolution in New England, published in 1689. Force, vol. iv., p. 7.
[4] The Revolution Justified, pp. 15-17. An Account, &c., p. 8.
[5] Bancroft, vol. i., p. 428.
[6] Bancroft, vol. i., pp. 429, 430.
[7] Expression used by Andros, quoted by Bancroft, vol. ii., p. 446.

woman's clothes, but his shoes betrayed the disguise. The people achieved a bloodless victory. The movement spread through New England. Everywhere Andros's officers were expelled or imprisoned, and the colonies renewed their democratic government.[1]

By 1640, upwards of twenty thousand people had emigrated to New England, and by 1675, fifty-five thousand.[2] The trials proper to a new country had been overcome. The climate was found to be healthy, and the inhabitants were both long-lived and prolific.[3] The soil never attained to the fertility of Virginia, but it afforded sufficient corn to export to the West Indies, and to trade with the natives for beaver. The inhabitants grew their own flax, and made their own linen. Cotton they imported from the West Indies, and manufactured themselves.[4] Fish were so plentiful, that they were used as manure.[5] The relations with the savages were friendly. The only exception to this was in Connecticut. At the first settlement of the colony, the Pequods had harassed and plundered the English, and in 1634 they had connived at the murder of eight Englishmen, perpetrated by some of their confederates. Soon after, the Pequods, being pressed by the Narragansets, sent a messenger to treat of peace with the English. The English demanded the surrender of the murderers, which the Pequods refused, averring that the English had given provocation, and that only two of the criminals were living. A treaty was at length made, but in the next year some Narraganset Indians who had murdered an English trader took refuge with the Pequods. Accordingly, in 1636, Endicott was sent with ninety volunteers to exact satisfaction. The Indians fled into the woods, and the only result of the expedition was to " exasperate, without subduing, a haughty and warlike enemy." Sasacus, the chief of the Pequods, was a man of vigour and ability. He saw that the

---

[1] Bancroft, vol. ii., pp. 446–449. An Account, &c., pp. 4, 5.
[2] A Perfect Description of Virginia, p. 12. Bancroft, vol. ii., p. 92.
[3] New England's First Fruits, p. 246. "A sup of New England air is worth a draught of Old England's ale." New England's Plantation.
[4] New England's First Fruits, p. 247.
[5] A Perfect Description of Virginia, p. 12.

only hope of driving out the white intruders lay in a union with the Narragansets. Had they been willing to enter into these schemes, and to forego their revenge against the Pequods, nothing could have saved the young colony of Connecticut. The Narragansetts, however, allied themselves with the strangers rather than with their hereditary enemies. During the whole of 1636, the Pequods harassed the settlers, burning their hay, and killing their cattle, and reducing the colony to a state of severe distress. In May 1637, the colonists determined on an offensive war. They raised one hundred and eighty men, while Massachusetts and Plymouth contributed two hundred and forty. They were aided by seventy of the Mohican Indians, a powerful and warlike tribe. Mason was sent in advance with a force of about eighty English, and the Mohican allies. Subsequently he was joined by two hundred Narragansets. With this force he resolved to attack Sasacus in his own fort. Such a proceeding was probably unheard of in Indian warfare. The fort was attacked and set on fire, and between five hundred and six hundred Pequods perished. "Parents and children, the old man and the babe, perished in promiscuous ruin." The Pequods made a desperate resistance, but their bows and arrows were useless against fire-arms. The Mohicans and Narragansets took advantage of their weakened state to satisfy their ancient grudge, and by the end of the summer only two hundred Pequods survived. They were so reduced as to make terms with the English to obtain protection against their foes. A treaty was made by which the surviving remnant of the Pequods was broken up and incorporated with the Mohicans and the Narragansets, and soon there was not one "that was, or at least dare call himself, a Pequod."[1] From that time, New England

---

[1] New England's First Fruits. Massachusetts' "Historical Collection," 1st series, vol. i., p. 246. The above account of the Pequod war is taken from Turnbull, vol. i., pp. 69-93. The first New England war did want a "vates sacer." A versified account of Winthrop's "Embassy to England," was written by Roger Wolcott, his successor in the government, and is published in the Massachusetts' "Historical Collection," 1st series, vol. iv., pp. 204-295. Winthrop gives a description of the war to King Charles. The Pequod chiefs hold a council in

suffered from no Indian war for nearly forty years, though in 1643 apprehensions were entertained of an attack from the Narragansets, and it was thought prudent to unite the four colonies of Massachusetts, Plymouth, Connecticut, and Newhaven into a defensive confederation.[1]

The constitutions of the New England colonies were, as I have mentioned, different. Rhode Island was a pure democracy, every man having a voice in the government. Plymouth was also a democracy, with a governor elected by universal suffrage, and a council. In time the increase of the colony rendered it impossible that every inhabitant should have a direct voice in the government, and assemblies to which each town sent a representative were substituted for the town meetings.[2] In Massachusetts a council was elected by the freemen of the province, and the council chose the governor and deputy-governor from among their own number.[3] Connecticut had a governor and a council of six magistrates elected by the whole body of freemen, and a general assembly of deputies from the towns.[4] In Massachusetts none but church members were admitted as freemen.[5] The provincial legislature generally was marked by the same character. The first duty of government was to protect religion and morality. Laws were passed against fornication, drunkenness, idleness, pro-

---

Homeric style, and Sasacus warns them of the proselytising designs of the English—

"You must not have so many handsome wives
That don't consist with mortified lives."

In relating the catastrophe of Sasacus' death, he tells us how he fled to the Mohicans, who

"To cure the passions of his breast,
Cut off his head, and all his cares released."

The Puritan fathers do not seem to have carried out with them the muse of Milton and Waller.

[1] Turnbull, vol. i., p. 226.   [2] Bancroft, vol. i., p. 322.
[3] Early Laws of Massachusetts. Massachusetts' "Historical Collection," 3d series, vol. viii., pp. 200, 201.
[4] Turnbull, vol. i., pp. 100-102.
[5] Description of Salem. By the Rev. William Bentley. Massachusetts' "Historical Collection," 1st series, vol. vi., p. 60. Belknap's "History of New Hampshire," p. 70. An Abstract of the Laws of New England, as they are now Established. 1641. Force, vol. iii., p. 5.

fane swearing, and Sabbath-breaking. Blasphemy, idolatry, witchcraft, and propagation of heresy were all capital crimes. Yet, where religious prejudices were not touched upon, the code was lenient. Theft was never a capital crime. Even rape at first was not, though it afterwards became so. In other ways the protective character of the political system showed itself. No dwelling-house was to be more than half a mile from a church. To preserve the original division into townships, no land was allowed to be sold to a man of another town without the consent of the fellow-townsmen of the seller.[1] Rigid sumptuary laws were enforced. The drinking of toasts was forbidden. Restrictions were placed on female dress. Men were obliged to wear their hair short. No person with an income of less than £200 a-year was allowed gold or silver lace, or silk hoods or scarfs. Any person violating this law was to be assessed accordingly.[2]

That such legislation was practicable, that it did not bring all government into contempt, is in itself the highest testimony to the character of the people. Nothing could have made such a system possible but that strong religious character which colours not only the laws of New England, but its social life, and even its wars. In 1631, a deputy-governor of Massachusetts wrote home, "If any come hither to plant for worldly ends that can live well at home, hee comits an errour of which he will soon repent him. But if for spiritual, and noe particular obstacle hinder his removal, he maye find here what may well content him."[3] "It concerneth New England," said Higginson, "to remember that they are originally a plantation religious, not a plantation of trade. The profession of the purity of doctrine, worship, and discipline is written upon her forehead. Let merchants, and such as are increasing cent. per cent., remember this, that worldly gain was not the end and design of the people of New England, but religion.

[1] An Abstract of the Laws of New England, as they are now Established. 1641. Force, vol. iii.
[2] Belknap's "History of New Hampshire," vol. i., pp. 66, 67.
[3] Governor Thomas Dudley's Letter to the Countess of Lincoln. March 1631. Force, vol. ii., p. 12.

And if any make religion as twelve and the world as thirteen, such an one hath not the spirit of a true New England man."[1] The early history of New England presents the unique spectacle of a sect growing into a nation. There was the narrowness and exclusiveness of a religious sect mingled and contrasted with the sense of an independent national existence. If we would see English Puritanism in its best form, we must study it in the early fathers of New England. The idea that a Puritan was a tasteless misanthrope, is of course absurd. The greatest epic and the greatest allegory in the English language are a sufficient answer to that charge. But it cannot be denied, that the Puritan in England too often acquired the morose fanaticism which his enemies represented as natural to him. To live in danger of being "harried out of the land," and having their ears grubbed out by the hangman's knife, is not calculated to make men gentle or loving to the world around them. In New England all this was different. There the Puritan was no longer a bondman in Egypt, he had reached the Promised Land. The dark past was separated from him by a vast ocean, the bright future was what he had to live for. In England we have almost lost sight of the domestic and civil life of the Puritan, we know him only as a preacher or a soldier; if we would contemplate him as a citizen, we must turn to America. Much, no doubt, of our disgust at the phraseology of the Puritans proceeds from our own want of earnestness, but much is really offensive to a more cultivated taste. Scriptural phrases, when united with denunciations of false hair and stage plays, or used as war-cries, naturally grate somewhat on our ears. But in New England the life and the language seemed to match. There was nothing unreal about the Puritan's use of biblical language. The Hebrew Scriptures were to him not a formal record which it was heresy to disbelieve and irreverence to act upon; not a narrative of another world from that in which we live, to be got rid of by phrases about Judaism and a later dispensation. The heroes of Jewish history were to the New

---

[1] Belknap's "History of New Hampshire," vol. i., p. 61.

England Puritan real men of flesh and blood, fighting the same battle, beset with the same troubles as himself. Was he a wanderer in a strange land? So had Abraham been. Was he likely to perish from famine? He remembered Jacob, and contrasted the flocks and herds of the patriarch with his own poverty. Were the Pequods a mighty people? So were the Amalekites.[1]

With the earnestness of their Puritan forefathers, the New Englanders inherited a full share of their intolerance. We have seen how they treated Roger Williams. In 1637, Mrs Hutchinson, "a gentlewoman of a nimble wit, voluble tongue, eminent knowledge in the Scriptures, of great charity, and notable helpfulness,[2] was accused of introducing antinomian doctrines. After a long contest, and a display of fanaticism in which it is painful to find Winthrop taking a prominent part, she was expelled.[3] Some years later, one Samuel Gorton, "a proud and pestilent seducer, deeply leavened with blasphemous and familistic doctrines,[4] became a prominent character in the religious controversies of New England. His theological opinions and personal character are veiled in considerable obscurity, different writers giving different accounts. After causing considerable disturbance, he was imprisoned for six months, and afterwards banished.[5] Of Ann Hutchinson and Gorton, we can at this distance of time know little. A juster inference as to the intolerance of the early New Englanders is to be drawn from their treatment of the Quakers. The language used of the Quaker tenets would be ludicrous if the bigotry and uncharitableness of good men could ever be so. Their doctrines are "corrupt and abominable; dreams and conceits tending to gross blasphemy and atheism."[6]

---

[1] New England's Memorial, pp. 5, 67. New England's First Fruits, p. 246.

[2] Hubbard, p. 283. Winthrop says, "A woman of a ready wit and bold spirit," vol. i., p. 239.

[3] Hubbard, pp. 283–285. New England's Memorial, pp. 133, 134. Winthrop, pp. 239–241, 304–311.

[4] New England's Memorial, p. 135.

[5] New England's Memorial, pp. 135–138. Hubbard, pp. 401–408.

[6] New England's Memorial, p. 185.

To become a Quaker was to sink to the lowest depth of heresy.[1] Nor did this hostility confine itself to words. In 1658 Quakerism was made a capital offence. In 1659 the members of a Quaker family were publicly sold. In 1660 two Quakers were hanged in Boston. In 1662 "it was moderation to obtain that these unhappy people should be whipped only in three towns."[2] The idea of toleration was utterly foreign to the mind of the New England Puritan. The very name of it was loathed by him:

> "Let men of God in courts and churches watch
> O'er such as do a toleration hatch,"

were the lines found in Dudley's pocket after his death.[3] Ward, a shrewd and vigorous writer, did not scruple to say, "He that willingly assents to toleration of divers religions, or of one religion in segregant shades, if he examines his heart by daylight, his conscience will tell him he is either an atheist, or an heretick, or an hypocrite, or at best a captive to some lust; polypiety is the greatest impiety in the world." "Persecution of true religion, and toleration of false, are the Jannes and Jambres to the kingdom of Christ, whereof the last is far the worst." "It is said that men ought to have liberty of conscience, and that it is persecution to deprive them of it; I can rather stand amazed than reply to this. It is an astonishment to think that the brains of men should be parboyled in such impious ignorance."[4] In the first colonists of New England there is much to extenuate intolerance. The victims of Laud and Strafford might well believe that the safety of a commonwealth depended on the purity of its faith, and might be excused for not having learnt that the means they adopted to preserve that faith were the worst possible for the purpose. New England outgrew the fanaticism of her

---

[1] "One Hickes began to be unsettled about the ordinances of the Church. . . . The issue was this poor unsettled man fell yet further and further, and at last became a Quaker." Account of the Church of Christ at Plymouth. Massachusetts' "Historical Collection," 1st series, vol. iv., p. 121.

[2] Description of Salem. By the Rev. W. Bentley. Massachusetts' "Historical Collection," 1st series, vol. vi., pp. 259-262.

[3] New England's Memorial, p. 167.

[4] The Simple Cobbler of Agawam. Force, vol. iii., pp. 7-11.

youth, but we shall see hereafter how the stern religion of the early pilgrims degenerated into childish superstition, and at how fearful a cost the demon of bigotry was exorcised.

One influence alone saved New England—that which alone can save a civilised nation from becoming heartless sensualists, or priest-ridden bigots. From the first it had been the care of New England that none of her citizens should grow up without education unless by his own fault. In 1636 the general court of Massachusetts voted a supply for the foundation of a college, and in 1638 Harvard, "a godly gentleman and a lover of learning," bequeathed his estate, £850 and half his library to the college. Other benefactions followed. The college was built at Cambridge, and was soon followed by a grammar school.[1]

Such was early New England, a state founded on principles which the world had ever rejected and despised. Those principles were not enforced by institutions established once for all by an overruling will. New England was no Sparta, forced, often unwillingly, into a particular mould by the mechanism of laws and discipline. Her government was an expression of the free will of her people. Nor was the Puritanism of New England a burst of temporary enthusiasm engendered by persecution and destined to fall when that persecution ceased. Time modified it, but did not change its inmost nature. The citizens of Boston during the revolution, orderly, submissive to their leaders, never impetuous, scrupulous even to slowness, were in spirit as well as in blood the descendants of the Pilgrim Fathers.

I have dwelt at considerable length on the early growth and characteristics of Virginia and New England as being the best representatives of the two types of national life, presenting some features of similarity, but more of contrast. In Virginia we have a colony founded by the most influential and far-seeing statesmen of the age, watched over with care, blessed with a fertile soil and a genial climate. In New England we see a small band of religious enthusiasts, tolerated from their very insignificance,

[1] New England's First Fruits, pp. 242, 243.

legislated for by no king or courtiers, landing on a bleak and barren shore. The people of Virginia had wealth, leisure, everything commonly supposed to be favourable to intellectual culture; the New Englanders were a set of rude husbandmen, toiling from day to day for their bread. Yet a governor of Virginia could boast, more than fifty years after the colony had been founded, that it did not contain a school or a printing press, while New England had a college in sixteen years. The Virginian colonists carried out with them the spirit of feudalism, modified but not destroyed by the exigencies of colonial life. The passion for landed possession characterised them from the first, a passion sure to produce, when aided by the noxious influence of slavery, a system of caste and contempt for industry. The colonists of New England were from the first led by the spirit of democracy, resting not on laws, but on the surer basis of social institutions and feelings. Almost at the same time that a Virginian governor was demanding that his salary should be doubled because he was a nobleman, a leading statesman of New England was declining a military command because his wife was sick and had no servant, and his cattle and fields demanded his care.[1] Both colonies were strongholds of popular liberty; but in the one it was the liberty of lawlessness, in the other it was freedom from every law which interfered with the highest law of all. In the early history of Virginia we have an insurrection, but at the same time continual and often successful encroachments on the part of government; in New England we have no violent outburst of the popular will, but a uniform and successful resistance to any exercise of arbitrary authority.

As early as 1620, a patent had been obtained for Carolina by Sir Robert Heath, and an attempt made to colonise it from Virginia. The project came to nothing, and the patent was rendered void. More than thirty years later, a small band of emigrants from New England had endeavoured to establish themselves near Cape

[1] Letter from James Cudworth to Josiah Winslow. Massachusetts' "Historical Collection," vol. vi., pp. 81, 82.

Fear, but had been repulsed by the hostility of the Indians. In 1663, a colony from Virginia was more successful. Berkeley granted them a separate government. Drummond, their leader, was created governor, and Virginia became the parent of North Carolina. A colony from Barbadoes increased the little State, and for a time flourished, though its very site is now disputed. In the same year, a number of proprietaries, including Lords Albemarle and Shaftesbury, Berkeley and Carteret, obtained a grant of Carolina. The greatest philosopher of the age was called on to form a constitution for the projected colony. It might have seemed as if the scheme of a model state was never likely to have so fair a trial. There was no fear of anything visionary or Utopian in a constitution framed by Locke. He was not likely to be misled by any impracticable optimism. A state adapted to the wants of man as a producing and a consuming animal would be the natural outcome of his philosophy. Experience of the past, and distrust of human capacity for self-government, were the basis of the constitution. The land was to be divided into five equal parts. Of this, one-fifth was to be the inalienable property of the proprietaries, and another the inalienable and indivisible estate of the two orders of nobility. The rest was to be held by the people. There were to be four estates,—the proprietaries, the landgraves, the caciques, and the commons. The proprietaries represented the sovereign. They were a permanent corporation of eight, the dignity to be hereditary; in default of heirs, the survivors to elect a successor. One of their number was to act for them in the colony. The landgraves and the caciques formed the nobility, and sat as an Upper House. The Lower House consisted of representatives; freeholders of fifty acres alone had votes, and a property qualification of three hundred acres was necessary for a representative. In New England, a little commonwealth, with no territorial rights, founded by a band of religious exiles, became the foundation of an empire. Carolina began its career under different auspices. The territory was enormous, and the constitution proportionately imposing. Nothing was wanting but colo-

F

nists to till the land, and to be governed by the laws. The result was not encouraging to the philosophy of common sense. The institutions of Carolina remained a dead letter, and her citizens formed a constitution for themselves, suggested not by the dictates of philosophy, but by a knowledge of their own wants. In 1665, the colonists of Albemarle formed a government, and drew up laws which remained in force for fifty years. In 1777, the state numbered eight thousand inhabitants. In 1778, an insurrection broke out, provoked apparently by the interference of the proprietaries, and resulted in a compromise which practically left the government in the hands of the people. Sothel then misgoverned the colony for five years, but his rapacity was as offensive to the proprietaries as to the colonists, and when the people rose against him and deposed him, the proprietaries did not interfere.[1]

In South Carolina, the attempt to establish the model constitution was equally unsuccessful. In 1670, the first colony was sent out, and, disregarding their instructions, established a government consisting of a council and a house of representatives.[2] In 1672, they founded Charlestown, and soon outstripped their brethren of North Carolina. In 1685, the persecution of the Huguenots drove a large portion of the most industrious and intelligent artisans of France to America. In South Carolina, they found full liberty of conscience, and a climate that reminded them of the most favoured spots in their native land. Struggles between the people and the proprietaries soon began. Religious differences aggravated political hostility. In 1690, Colleton, the proprietary governor, was ejected from his office, and banished. For years, "dissensions, tumults, riots, tore the colony to pieces."[3] In 1715, an Indian war was added to the troubles of the colony. The natives planned a general massacre, and slew four hundred

---

[1] Bancroft, vol. ii., pp. 128-166. An Account of the European Settlements, vol. ii., pp. 236-238.

[2] A Narrative of the Proceedings of the People of South Carolina in the year 1719. Published, London, 1726. Force, vol. ii., p. 6.

[3] An Account of the European Settlements, vol. ii., p. 237.

inhabitants. The colony, in its weakness, had to send for assistance to Virginia. The Indians were completely defeated, but at the conclusion of the war, South Carolina had contracted a debt of £8000. Their application to parliament for relief was refused on the ground that they were a proprietary colony. As the colonists had never gained anything from their connection with the proprietaries, they naturally resolved to terminate it. They desired Johnson, their governor, to take possession of the government in the name of the king. Johnson refused, upon which they threw off their allegiance to the proprietaries, established a government, and elected a governor. They then sent a delegate to England to state their grievances. The proprietaries surrendered their charter, Cartaret alone retaining his share, and North and South Carolina were constituted royal provinces, under governors appointed by the crown.[1]

Hitherto the divisions of the colony had interfered with its material prosperity, but when they were removed South Carolina rapidly became a flourishing community. By 1757 land had risen to four times its previous value. Indigo, rice, tar and deerskins formed the staple exports. The abundance of navigable rivers made the conveyance of goods easy and inexpensive. The climate was healthy though variable. Poverty, except as the result of vice, was unknown. The great bane of the colony was the prevalence of slavery. Three thousand negroes were imported annually, and in 1734 they outnumbered the white inhabitants as five to one.[2]

In North Carolina a different state of society prevailed. There nothing existed of that industry and commercial activity which the Huguenots had done so much to introduce into South Carolina. The planters grew up a race of backwoods' hunters,

[1] A Narrative of the Proceedings, &c. Bancroft, vol. ii., pp. 166-187; vol. iii., pp. 13-15, 326-331.
[2] Description of the Province of South Carolina in the Gentleman's Magazine for 1737. Account of the European Settlements, vol. ii., pp. 241-254. Extract from the Journal of Mr Commissary Van Beck, giving an account of the voyage of the Salzburgers to Georgia. London, 1734. Force, vol. iv., p. 9.

wilder even than those of Virginia. It was "a country where there's scarce any form of government." "Every one did what was right in his own eyes, paying tribute neither to God nor to Cæsar."[1]

In Pennsylvania a community came into existence like that of New England, separated from the world by rigid lines of demarcation, and claiming equally to rest on a divine and spiritual basis. It might, at first, seem as if the difference between the Puritan and the Quaker were only merely of degree, as if the Quaker had carried out, to their logical conclusion, those doctrines which were the basis of the Puritan community. Both set authority at defiance; both regarded forms as strongholds of superstition; both believed in direct spiritual influences and in a rigid separation between true believers and the world. In reality the resemblance was superficial, the difference fundamental. The Puritan threw aside ordinances and outward forms, not from a general principle of hostility to them, but because they were, in his eyes, the instruments of spiritual tyranny. His very intolerance, his attempts to establish a system of authority, often stricter than that which he had thrown off, bore witness to this. When the remembrance of the tyranny, which to the Puritan was associated with external forms, had had time to subside, there was nothing to prevent him from acknowledging that they might have a value, that they had once had a value, not as substitutes for spiritual truths, but as symbols of, and witnesses to it. The Quaker had severed the connection with the historical past more completely. If he was right the rest of mankind, past and present, were wrong. Outward forms were not the vestibules through which the soul is led up to the Holy of Holies, but prison-houses in which it is for ever debarred from the enjoyment of light. Thus the Quaker was cut off from the world. He was pledged either to conquer it or to keep up a rigid and impracticable separation from it. The early Friends accepted neither alternative, and their descendants have held

[1] Expressions quoted by Bancroft, vol. iii., p. 21.

their ground, as citizens of the world, only by sliding gradually further and further from the position that their fathers took up. The early Quakers abjured all forms; their descendants are separated from the world only by a barrier of forms. The early Quakers avowed themselves to be not of the world; in no sect have material interests predominated more strongly than among modern Quakers. Yet the patience, the integrity, the active philanthropy of the early American Quakers, above all, the character of that extraordinary man, with whom their name is indissolubly linked, are not less pleasing subjects of contemplation than the more robust and enduring virtues of the New England Fathers.

The disciples of Fox, in search of a refuge from a world with which they were at war, naturally turned to America. We have seen how they fared in Virginia and New England. In 1676 circumstances opened to them a means of effecting a settlement. William Penn was the son of a naval commander who had served with distinction against the Dutch in 1664. At the age of sixteen his hostility to forms led to his expulsion from Oxford. A scholar and a traveller, of good family and high position, gifted with abilities and influence that must have secured him a brilliant career, graced with all the accomplishments of an educated gentleman, he forsook the world, and consented, for the sake of religion, to be driven from his father's house, to be the ridicule of his fashionable friends, and to be cast into prison.[1] In 1676 he became a trustee for the estate of one Byllinge, who had purchased half the territory of New Jersey from Lord Berkeley. Penn and his fellow-trustees agreed on a division of the province with the other proprietor, Sir George Carteret. Carteret retained East New Jersey; West New Jersey fell to the share of the trustees. They then divided the land into a hundred lots,

[1] Clarkson's Memoirs of William Penn, vol. i., pp. 6-30. "Mr Pen, Sir William's son, is come back from France, and come to visit my wife: a most modish person, grown, she says, a fine gentleman." "Mr William Pen is a Quaker again, or some very melancholy thing." Pepy's Diary, vol. ii., p. 162; vol. iii. p. 332.

ten of which they made over to one Fenwick, who had a claim on Byllinge's American possessions, and the rest they advertised for sale, while at the same time they drew up a settlement for their new colony. The legislature was to be in the hands of an assembly of representatives chosen by the people. Every man was to have a vote. The executive was to consist of a governor and twelve assistants. There was to be a trial by jury. No imprisonment for debt was allowed, and full liberty of conscience was secured. An advertisement was also published setting forth the condition and prospects of the colony. The friends availed themselves of the refuge opened to them, and West New Jersey became a Quaker colony.[1] Andros, the governor of New York, claimed jurisdiction over the soil, but the question was referred to the decision of England. The Duke of York also claimed the right of exacting customs from the vessels that sailed up the river which lay in his territory of Delaware. The colonists claimed full right of legislation and taxation. Their arguments are interesting as anticipating much that was said when the general question of colonial taxation was in dispute. "If we could not assure people of an easy, free, and safe government, liberty of conscience, and an inviolable possession of their civil rights and freedoms, a mere wilderness would be no encouragement. It were madness to leave a free country to plant a wilderness, and give another person an absolute title to tax us at will." "By what right are we thus used? The king of England cannot take his subjects' goods without their consent." "To exact such unterminated tax from English planters, and to continue it, after so many repeated complaints, will be the greatest evidence of a design to introduce, if the crown should ever devolve upon the duke, an unlimited government in England." The question was referred to an English judge, and the Duke of York acquiesced in a decision in favour of the colonists.[2]

In 1680 the increasing persecution of the Quakers made Penn desirous to furnish a further refuge for them in America, where

[1] Clarkson, vol. i., pp. 167-175. [2] Bancroft, vol. ii., pp. 357-360.

he might convert and civilise the Indians, and raise up a theopolity, "a virtuous empire in the New Land which should diffuse its example far and wide, and to the remotest ages."[1] £16,000 were due to Penn on account of money lent by his father to government. In lieu of this, he petitioned for a grant of land to the north of Maryland. The grant was opposed both in the Privy Council and by the Lords of Trade and Plantations, and also by the Duke of York, as proprietary of Delaware, and Lord Baltimore of Maryland. These objections, however, were overruled, and on the 4th of March 1681 the charter of Pennsylvania was granted. It constituted Penn absolute proprietary, with the power of making laws, with the advice, assent, and approbation of the freemen of the territory, and of dividing, selling, or alienating any part of the territory.[2] In the same year a society of traders in Pennsylvania was formed, and three ships sent out with colonists. Before their departure, Penn published a rough draft of a constitution to be thereaf ~ considered by the bulk of the colonists. The first article in the code of laws was a broad declaration of the principle of liberty of conscience. The government was entrusted to a governor, a council, of whom one-third were to retire every year, and an assembly of representatives elected annually. The principle of the constitution was, in his own words, "to leave himself and his successors no power of doing mischief, that the will of one man may not hinder the good of a whole country."[3] In the next year the Duke of York made over to Penn his rights over the district of Delaware, or, as it was then called, the Territories.[4] In the same year Penn himself sailed for America. On the 10th of January 1683 the first assembly met. They passed an Act of Union annexing the territories to the province, and an Act of Settlement. The frame of government before referred to was then passed, and some other laws added. The tenor of several of these laws shows that, enthusiast though he might be, Penn was, in the principles of

[1] Clarkson, vol. i., pp. 273-278. [2] Clarkson, vol. i., pp. 273-278.
[3] Clarkson, vol. i., p. 289. [4] Clarkson, vol. i., pp. 278-289, 299-309.

political philosophy, far in advance of his age. All children were to be taught some useful trade. All legal processes were to be as short as possible. Punishments were to be reformatory, and all prisons were to be considered as workshops where the offenders might be industriously, soberly, and morally employed.[1] On the 20th of January, the governor asked the assembly whether they would prefer a new charter. They requested a new one, with certain alterations, which was granted.

Of all the philosophers who have conceived ideal schemes of government, Penn is almost the only one who has put his Utopia into practice with success. That he should have done so at all is high praise. But that he should have framed a government to satisfy the wants of his people rather than to embody his own preconceived ideas,—that, having strong and distinct political opinions, he should have been willing to entrust the people with self-government at the risk of their defying those opinions,—that he should have seen that no laws or institutions, however perfect in themselves, could be so good as those which expressed the free-will of the people,—proves that Penn was not merely a speculative philosopher, but a practical statesman of the highest order.[2]

But the peculiar glory of Penn's early proceedings was his conduct towards the Indians. With the first colonists, Penn sent out his relation, Colonel William Markham, with several commissioners, to confer with the Indians and arrange a treaty. He himself sent a letter in his own hand, declaring his kind intentions towards them, and his "desire to win and gain their love and friendship by a kind, just, and peaceable life," and promising them speedy satisfaction if any of the colonists should wrong them.[3] After his arrival, he himself held a conference with them at Shakamaxon.[4] The peaceful mystic and enthusiast might

---

[1] Clarkson, vol. i., pp. 332-335. Proud's "History of Pennsylvania, vol. i., p. 235. Colden's "History of the Five Nations," vol. ii., pp. 18-200.

[2] Penn's own doctrine was, "Governments, like clocks, go from the motion men give them, and as governments are made and moved by man, so by them they are ruined too." Colden, vol. i., p. 185.

[3] Clarkson, vol. i., pp. 290-292.   [4] Clarkson, vol. i., p. 329.

seem to have little in common with the wild savage, but Penn's doctrines taught him that there was a sense of right in the savage as well as in the white man, to which he would not appeal in vain. His humanity to the Indians bore fruit. They ministered to the wants of the early colonists, and treated them uniformly with love and affection.[1] In after days, the memory of the father of Pennsylvania lingered among the Indians, and the highest praise that could be awarded a white man was, that he was like "Onas."[2]

Colonisation was no longer the irksome and even dangerous task that it had been when the wilds of Virginia and New England were first subdued by Englishmen. The Swedes and Dutch had already prepared the way, and the hardships of the early Pennsylvanians were little more than those with which the inhabitants of a new country are necessarily familiar. In 1683, the legislature of Pennsylvania became involved in a dispute with Lord Baltimore about boundaries, and in the next year a forcible entry was made on several plantations from Maryland. Penn, however, asserted his claims firmly, and for the time the matter dropped. In 1685 the dispute was renewed, and was finally settled by the Lords of Plantations. In 1691, a dispute arose between the territories and the legislature of Pennsylvania. Penn regretted the division, but his moderate and liberal temper restrained him from any attempt to force a distasteful union on the territories. He constituted them a separate government under Markham, and thus became the founder of Delaware.[3]

Penn's friendship for the fallen dynasty was naturally no recommendation at the new court, and in 1692 he was deprived of his government of Pennsylvania, and a commission given to Fletcher. Unjust as this was, the colonists were the gainers by it, for they learnt the lesson of resistance. The whole of Fletcher's government was spent in fruitless altercations with the assembly.

[1] Proud, vol. i., p. 224.
[2] Proud, vol. i., pp. 214, 215. Colden, vol. ii., p. 18.
[3] Proud, vol. i., pp. 355-357.

In 1694, through the instrumentality of Rochester and other noblemen, Penn was reinstated in his government, and in 1699 he returned to the colony.[1] In 1701, the reported intention of Parliament to abrogate the colonial charters necessitated Penn's return to England.[2] Before he left the colony, he granted a third charter. True to the principles which Penn had ever upheld, it granted full liberty of conscience to all who admitted the existence of God, and it opened office to all Christians, of whatsoever denomination. In its general provisions, it was substantially the same as the preceding charter.[3]

In its late history, Pennsylvania did little either to preserve its individuality or to leaven the rest of America with its own character.[4] The only permanent influence of Quakerism was a moderation degenerating at times into timidity, and widely alien from the stern democratic character of New England, or the lawless independence of Virginia. Yet the repeated contests between the assembly and the proprietary government kept alive a spirit of resistance, and helped to prepare Pennsylvania for playing her part in the national struggle for freedom.

For fifty years after the foundation of Pennsylvania, no fresh settlement was established in America. The colonisation of Georgia in 1732 will be ever associated with one of the purest and noblest characters in American history, James Oglethorpe. The associate of Johnson, educated at Oxford, aristocratic by birth, profession, and sentiment, he devoted his life to the service of the poor and friendless. He was the Howard of his age. His pity had been especially moved by the sufferings of debtors in

[1] Proud, vol. i., pp. 377-400. [2] Proud, vol. i., p. 436.
[3] Proud, vol. i., pp. 443-450. As a proof of Penn's advanced views it should be mentioned that he abolished the iniquitous law which punishes the children of a suicide by making his property forfeit, and which to this day compels every jury, which tries a case of suicide, to be guilty of perjury.
[4] Their Quaker principles seem to have sat lightly on the later Pennsylvanians. The assembly, on one occasion, refused to grant a supply for the purchase of powder. They, however, voted an aid of £3000 to be applied to the purchase of bread, flour, wheat, or other *grain*. Franklin subsequently proposed to his own party, when a cannon was wanted, that they should move for the purchase of a *fire-engine*. Autobiography of Franklin in his Works, vol. i., p. 154.

prisons. In 1728, he acted as a commissioner for inquiring into the state of jails, and by his exertions, "he restored to light and freedom multitudes who, by long confinement for debt, were strangers and helpless in the land of their birth." Colonisation, it seemed to him, might afford a permanent alleviation of this misery. He looked to

> "Where, beyond the spacious ocean, lies
> A wide waste land beneath the southern skies;
> Where kindly suns for ages rolled in vain,
> Nor e'er the vintage saw nor ripening grain,
> Where all things into wild luxuriance ran,
> And burdened nature asked the aid of man."[1]

There Oglethorpe thought he might found a home for English paupers and the distressed Protestants of Europe.[2] In 1732, a charter was granted, constituting the whole territory between the rivers Savannah and Alatamaha into the Province of Georgia, to be held by a coporation under a quit-rent. The charter set forth—1. The need of emigration to relieve poverty; 2. The necessity of establishing a protection for the frontier of South Carolina. It then constituted a body of thirteen trustees for establishing the colony of Georgia in America, and created it a corporation. The corporation was to appoint the governor and all officers for twenty-one years. After that time, the right was to revert to the crown. The declared intention of the trustees was, "to relieve such unfortunate persons as cannot subsist here, and establish them in an orderly manner, so as to form a well-regulated town." To carry out the intentions of the promoters of the scheme, and to make the colony a community of resident and working proprietors, no person was allowed to hold more than five hundred acres of land, and no alienation was allowed. The importation of slaves was forbidden as putting free labour on an unfair footing, and giving the rich an undue advantage. The vicinity of the Spaniards also would have made a servile insurrection peculiarly dangerous. As it was to be a military

---

[1] "Georgia," a Poem. By Samuel Wesley.
[2] Bancroft, vol. iii., pp. 418, 419.

colony, and a protection to the frontier of Carolina, it was provided that every inhabitant should be trained to the use of arms. The culture of mulberries for the production of silk was rendered compulsory. Another less judicious, because almost impracticable, law was passed, forbidding the importation of rum. Liberty of conscience was granted to all, Papists alone excepted. Rich men invested their capital, and Parliament voted a grant of £10,000.[1]

On the 17th of November 1632, Oglethorpe, with one hundred and thirty persons, sailed from Gravesend, and on the 20th of January, they landed at Beaufort town. Oglethorpe went up the river to select a spot for a settlement, and entered into an alliance with Tomochichi, the chief of a tribe of Indians. On the 1st of February, the colonists arrived at the spot selected by Oglethorpe. The infant colony was supported by the kindness of its neighbours in South Carolina, who helped them with food and labour. On the 18th of May, Oglethorpe held a conference with the chief men of the eight Creek cantons. The Indians brought a present of buckskins and professed themselves friends to the white men, and ready to protect them against the Cherokees if necessary. On the 21st, a treaty was signed, and the Indians went away with presents, including ammunition, and, it is painful to add, eight kegs of rum.[2]

In the next year, on the 24th of March, the colony was reinforced by the emigration of a band of Salzburgers. They were received kindly, both by the Indians and the English. "The blessing of God," they said, "seems to have gone along with this happy undertaking; for here we see industry honoured, and justice strictly executed, and luxury and idleness banished from this happy place, where plenty and brotherly love seem to make their abode;" and in the Savannah they found a river to remind

---

[1] A True and Historical Narrative of the Colony of Georgia. Force, vol. i., pp. 2-19.

[2] A Brief Account of the Establishment of the Colony of Georgia. Force, vol. i., pp. 8-12.

them of their native Rhine. Oglethorpe gave them their choice of a plantation, and they pitched on a spot about twenty-one miles from Savannah, and thirty miles from the sea. Their industry, and the rapidity with which their settlement grew up, astonished the English.[1]

In April 1734, Oglethorpe returned to England, taking with him Tomochichi and others of the Creek chiefs.[2] That the results of the colony were not altogether satisfactory, may be inferred from the fact that the trustees gave notice, "that as they found that many of the poor who had been useless in England were inclined to be useless likewise in Georgia, they determined that 'these embarkations should consist chiefly of persons from the Highlands of Scotland, and persecuted German Protestants.'"[3] In 1735, a small body of Moravians emigrated to Savannah, and a colony of Highlanders established themselves at New Inverness in Darien. Oglethorpe returned in 1736 with three hundred emigrants.[4] In the winter of the same year, Oglethorpe again visited England. He was able to report that the colony was doing well, and in the autumn of 1737, he returned with a commission as brigadier-general and a regiment. His men worked laboriously, and a fort was soon erected.[5] In spite of the above-mentioned dissatisfaction, the liberality of parliament was continued to an extent which was hardly recompensed by the results. In seven years they granted £94,000, and during that time the number of emigrants had only reached two thousand two hundred, of whom nearly seven hundred were foreign Protestants. There were one hundred and nine freeholders in Savannah, and twenty-seven thousand one hundred acres of land had been divided in private grants.[6] As might be

[1] Extract from Van Beck's Journal, pp. 8-11.
[2] Bancroft, vol. iii., pp. 425, 426.
[3] An Account showing the Progress of the Colony of Georgia. Published by Order of the Trustees. 1742.
[4] Bancroft, vol. iii., p. 427.
[5] Bancroft, vol. iii., p. 433. A state of the province of Georgia attested upon oath in the Court of Savannah. 1740. Force, vol. i., p. 17.
[6] Account published by Trustees, p. 15.

expected from the character of the colonists, Georgia did not escape internal dissensions. Several of the colonists drew up and published a memorial attacking Oglethorpe.[1] Its character may be judged of by the fact that the points which it selected for attack, were Oglethorpe's humanity to the natives, whom it calls "a parcel of fugitive Indians—useless vagrants," and his refusal to relax the restrictions on the importation of rum and negroes. John Wesley, who visited the colony in 1736, is in the same document accused of being a papist.

In 1736, difficulties as to boundaries had arisen with the Spaniards, and the colonists suspected that their Indian allies were being tampered with. In 1742, the young colony was to feel the danger of its proximity to the Spanish frontier. Party spirit had engaged England in one of the most unjust of all unjust wars. A Spanish force was collected at Cuba for the invasion of Georgia. Oglethorpe was ready to lay down his life for the state which his devotion had founded. "We are resolved not to suffer defeat; we will rather die like Leonidas and his Spartans, if we can but protect Carolina and the rest of the Americans from desolation," was his message to Savannah. On the 4th of July, the Spanish force landed, and marched on Frederica, but the frontier selected for the fort had been a strong one, and the courage of the Highlanders repelled the invaders with loss. On the 18th, after an unsuccessful attack on Fort-William, which was defended with great bravery, the Spanish force re-embarked and sailed south, and on the 24th of July, Oglethorpe published an order for a general thanksgiving.[2] The father and saviour of the colony soon returned to England. For ten years he had devoted himself to the cause of Georgia. "Instead of allowing himself the satisfaction which a plentiful fortune, powerful friends, and great merit entitle him to in

---

[1] Given in Force, vol. i. The introduction to the Account, published by the Trustees, stigmatises it, apparently with perfect justice, as "a mean, low sneer, a malicious, ill-natured invective, published by a few persons of no estate, and as little character."

[2] Bancroft, vol. iii., pp. 443-446.

England, he has inured himself to the greatest hardships that any the meanest inhabitant of this new colony will be exposed to; his diet has been mouldy bread, or boiled rice, instead of bread, salt beef, pork, &c. His drink has been water, his bed the damp earth, without any other covering than the canopy of heaven to shelter him, and all this to set an example to this new colony, how they might bear with such hardships in their new settlements."[1] He never revisited Georgia, but during the rest of a long and honourable life, he was ever the firm friend of the colonies.[2]

For a time the new colony was unprosperous. Dissensions arose, and the inhabitants emigrated till the colony was finally reduced to about eight hundred inhabitants. The conversion of it into a royal province improved its condition and obliterated the peculiarities of its institutions. The restrictions on the alienation and accumulation of land disappeared. The indolence of the settlers and the facility of employing slave labour, triumphed over the conscientious scruples of the Germans and the Highlanders, and in all respects Georgia became assimilated to the other southern colonies.[3]

I have traced, briefly and imperfectly, the growth and development of these thirteen colonies, which up to the middle of the eighteenth century formed the Anglo-American empire. In that empire there was apparently little of the material for national unity. Its inhabitants were not of one race or one speech, still less were their institutions or worship the same. One thread alone bound them together—the common spirit of independence and self-government. We can easily understand the democratic character of New England, but it is harder at first to see what influence extended that spirit to the southern colonies. Something is due, no doubt, to the self-reliance and freedom from

---

[1] Preface to the Account, published by Order of the Trustees, p. 4.
[2] In 1768 he distributed pamphlets, in behalf of America, among the leading public men in England. Bancroft, vol. vi., p. 148.
[3] Account of the European Settlements, vol. ii., pp. 261-272.

restraint engendered by colonial life. But that alone is not a sufficient explanation. In truth the colonies did not become democratic; they took out democratic principles with them. The outward manifestation of those principles was checked in England by the remaining forms of feudalism, but they were not the less real. By the middle of the seventeenth century, English loyalty had become a sentiment rather than a principle of action. The complete isolation of the colonies from the mother country removed most of the checks which that sentiment still imposed on popular liberty. How, it may be asked, can this be said, while the outcry of loyalty with which a colony greeted an English prince is yet ringing in our ears? But it is not certain that an English prince would not have been received as enthusiastically in America in 1760, nor is it certain that Australia would not defend her rights against the mother country if necessary, as readily as America did a hundred years ago. But if we are at a loss to trace the causes of the growing spirit of democracy in America, we cannot fail to perceive its manifestations. Nothing illustrates more strikingly the really democratic character of the American colonies than their system of representation. The member of the provincial assembly often went from his constituents with a clear and definite set of instructions;[1] he was a delegate rather than a representative. Such a system might be unfavourable to the production of great statesmen. It gave America that without which great statesmen are useless, an independent and self-reliant people.

---

[1] The history of the War of Independence furnishes us with many such instances. Several copies of instructions are to be found in Wirt's "Life of Patrick Henry," and in Hutchinson's "History of Massachusetts."

CHAPTER III.

GENERAL VIEW OF THE COLONIES FROM 1688 TO 1760.

I HAVE hitherto said nothing, save in the way of reference, of that remarkable people who occupied the soil of America before it was known to Europeans. The nationality of the North American Indians is one of the most vexed questions of ethnology. In the limited space of such an essay as this it will be enough to notice a few of the more salient peculiarities which apparently connect them with some of the races of the Old World. In several of their customs, the observation of separation and purification by the women, the practice of placing their altars on twelve stones, their fasts and feasts, they bear a remarkable resemblance to the Jews.[1] In other respects the reader of Herodotus cannot fail to be struck with the likeness of some of their customs to those of the ancient Scythians. They scalped their foes and cherished the scalps as trophies, and, like the Scythians, the prairie Indians used the scalps as decorations for their bridles, customs so peculiar that one can hardly suppose the coincidence fortuitous.[2] Like the Scythians they used the vapour bath.[3] The challenge of Canonicus to the New Eng-

---

[1] Clarkson, vol. i., pp. 397, 398. Catlin's "Letters and Notes on the North American Indians," vol. ii., pp. 232-234.

[2] Herodotus, book iv., chap. 64-75.

[3] Travayle into Virginia, p. 108. Catlin, vol. i., pp. 97, 98, 186. Beverley, p. 172. Roger Williams' Key to the Language of the Indians of New England. Massachusetts' "Historical Collection," 1st series, vol. iii., p. 237. It is also worthy of notice that the Finns, who, if we suppose the Indians to be Mongols, may be connected with both them and the Scythians, also use the vapour bath.

landers is a repetition of the Scythian message to Darius. The advocates of each theory find arguments in the personal appearance of the Indians. Penn avers "that a man would think himself in Duke's Place or Berry Street in London, when he seeth them,"[1] while some of the early navigators were struck by their Mongolian appearance."[2]

To many of these good qualities all the early writers bear witness. Their chastity was universally acknowledged, even by their revilers.[3] In no instance had any white women cause to dread dishonour at their hands.[4] Both to the English and among themselves they were hospitable and generous, giving with the thoughtless liberality of children, and expecting presents with equally thoughtless acquisitiveness.[5] In scarcely a single instance can they be justly charged with commencing hostilities. In Virginia they did not molest the colonists till provoked by Granville's ill-judged severity, and in New England they had been prejudiced against the English by the misconduct of the fishermen who frequented the coast. In Pennsylvania they reciprocated the kindness of the colonists by uniform friendship and fidelity.[6] Prisoners, when taken young by them, often bore away so grateful a recollection of their captivity that when restored they endeavoured to escape to their former life.[7] Of the arts of life the Indians understood enough to satisfy their simple requirements, and they were restrained from useful industry rather by the pride of savage independence than by inability. They comprehended the teaching of their religious instructors rapidly, and often showed considerable aptitude for speculative thought. They raised difficulties in morals and theology which have puzzled wise men in the Old World.[8] An Indian could

---

[1] Clarkson, vol. i., p. 397. [2] Purchas, p. 818. [3] Roger Williams, p. 230.
[4] Colden, vol. i., p. 9.
[5] "In liberality they excel, nothing is too good for their friend." Penn in Clarkson, vol. i., p. 389. Colden, vol. i., pp. 12, 13. Roger Williams, p. 208.
[6] Proud, vol. ii., p. 325. [7] New England's First Fruits, pp. 254, 264.
[8] "The Clear Sunshine of the Gospel breaking forth upon the Indians in New England." By Mr Thomas Shepherd. Massachusetts' "Historical Collection," 3d series, vol. iv., p. 63.

even defend his drunkenness by an appeal to final causes.[1] Of their social life, and the relative position occupied by the sexes, is difficult to form clear ideas. Polygamy was allowed and divorce was common,[2] yet conjugal infidelity seems to have been almost unknown.[3] Woman was regarded as a drudge, whose function was to save man from the degradation of labour,[4] yet we hear of "Sachem squaws."[5] Such conflicting accounts may perhaps be explained by some distinct difference of character founded on difference of race, like that which divided the Gauls and Germans in the time of Cæsar. Their religion is scarcely a less puzzling question than their social state.[6] All writers agree that they were theists,[7] but of the details of their belief we know little that is authentic. They seem to have regarded the God of the white man as difference from their own God, but of local or tribal worship we find no trace. Idolatry, though not unknown, was rare, but fetichism seems to have been common.[8] Their political system appears to have been based entirely on race,

[1] An Indian, apologising for his drunkenness, said, The great Spirit who made all things, made everything for some use, and whatever use He designed anything for that use, it should always be put to. Now when He made rum, He said,—Let this be for the Indian to get drunk with, and it must be so.—Franklin's Autobiography, vol. i., p. 164.

[2] Travayle into Virginia, p. 51.   [3] Roger Williams, p. 230.

[4] "Man was made for war and hunting, and holding councils; squaws and hedgehogs were made to scratch the ground." Report of a Committee, &c., pp. 19, 20.

[5] Travayle into Virginia, p. 55.

[6] Colden, p. 17. It is hardly likely that they would be communicative on the subject, or that, if so, their statements would be trustworthy. Beverley gives a long account of their religious system, pp. 156, 157. But when we find that he had taken the precaution of giving his informant "plenty of strong cider to make him good company and open-hearted," we may attach less importance to the expositions of t' e Indian theologian. The statement of a New England divine ("New England's Plantation") that the Indians worship two gods, Tantum and Squantum, may probably take ranks with the Mophi and Crophi of Herodotus.

[7] Travayle into Virginia, p. 82. "All the Indians have two things, religion and a bow and arrows." Roger Williams, p. 226; Clarkson, vol. i., p. 391, and many other authorities.

[8] See Catlin's Account of the Sanctity attaching to the Medicine Bag, vol. i., pp. 35–37. An English pig, introduced by the early colonists of Virginia, terrified them, as they thought he was the god of the pigs. Purchas, p. 829.

and so to have been an immediate development of the patriarchal mode of life. The authority of the king was usually lax,[1] varying, no doubt, with his personal qualities.[2] Their mode of succession was, at least among the Virginian tribes, peculiar. The sovereign power, though held chiefly, if not exclusively, by males, descended in the direct female line, and was transmitted, firstly, from brother to brother, and then from brother to sister's son, so that the direct line did not succeed till all the collateral claimants were exhausted, a provision probably established chiefly with a view to securing an adult leader.[3] Of political union between different tribes they seem to have had little or no idea. To this there is one striking exception, in that remarkable confederacy, called the Five Nations. The political condition of the Five Nations appears to have been far more advanced than that of any other tribe of the continent. The permanence of their union, and the practice of keeping up their numbers by adoption,[4] all point to a higher development than we find elsewhere. In the French war the alliance of the Five Nations continued to be a matter of great importance. Yet their history is itself an illustration of a fact which is one of the most striking

[1] Thus we find that Powhatan was obliged to tell the English privately of offences committed by his subjects for fear of offending them. Travayle into Virginia, p. 51.

[2] Thus, as we have seen, (p. 27), Opitchapan was virtually superseded in consequence of his infirmities by his brother Opechancanough. At the same time we should notice that Menatonon (p. 14) is described as impotent in his limbs, showing that mere physical qualities were not the great essential.

[3] Beverley, p. 150. Travayle into Virginia, pp. 69, 70. The mode of succession may be best illustrated by a sketch thus. (Those signified by capital letters are chiefs. Those marked * are females).

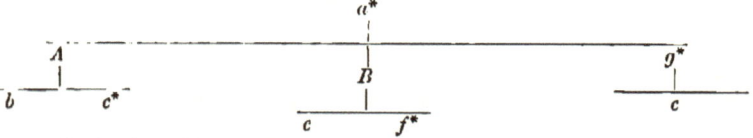

Thus at *A*'s death, *B*, his younger brother, succeeds to the exclusion of *b* and *c*; and at *B*'s death, *c*, his sister's son, succeeds to the exclusion of *e* and *f*. But this mode of succession does not seem to have extended to the Northern tribes, and was perhaps confined to Virginia.

[4] Colden, vol. i., p. 5.

proofs of the incapacity of the Indians for civilisation. No tribe appears to have continued great for any space of time. The Five Nations themselves were only stimulated into vigour by the aggressiveness of the Adirondacs, then the most powerful tribe on the continent, but who absolutely disappeared before the strength of the new-born confederacy.[1]

The general history of the American Indians is by no means a pleasing subject of contemplation for an Englishman. From the day that white colonists set their foot on the soil of North America, the natives of that soil were doomed. The acquisition of fire-arms made them reckless in their destruction of game, and rendered their petty wars more frequent and more bloody.[2] The substitution of our cottons and calicoes for their own furs and deerskins was a fertile cause of sickness and consumption.[3] "Firewater" was a still more potent engine of evil.[4] We could give them nothing to compensate for these evils. "What," says Colden, "have we done to make them better? We have indeed reason to be ashamed that these infidels, by our conversation and neighbourhood, are become worse than they were before they knew us. Instead of virtues, we have only taught them vices that they were entirely free from before that time."[5] The labours of Eliot, and Gookin, and Williams are among the most praiseworthy efforts in missionary history; yet they bore no permanent fruit.[6] The opinion which the savages formed, and with too

---

[1] Colden, vol. i., p. 239.

[2] Observations on the Indians of North America, in a Letter from General Lincoln. 1795. Massachusetts' "Historical Collection," 1st series, vol. v., pp. 7, 8.

[3] Report of a Committee, &c., p. 26. General Lincoln's Letter, p. 7.

[4] Catlin, vol. ii., p. 251, and elsewhere. Franklin's Autobiography, vol. i., p. 163.

[5] Colden's Dedication, p. 6. So Penn says, "They are the worst for the Christians who have propagated their vices, and yielded their tradition for ill, and not for good things." Clarkson, vol. i., p. 396. Beverley says, in the same spirit, "They have reason to regret the arrival of the Europeans, by whose means they seem to have lost their plenty as well as their innocence." Beverley, p. 185.

[6] The religious instruction imparted does not seem to have been always received in a very Christian spirit. Colden tells of an Indian convert, whose comment, after hearing the account of the crucifixion, was, that if he had been there he would have had Pontius Pilate's scalp. Colden, vol. i., p. 207.

much apparent justice, of the results of Christianity, was expressed by one of them in Georgia:—" Christian much drunk! Christian beat men! Christian tell lies! Devil Christian! Me no Christian!"[1] The French were guilty of atrocities towards the Indians far surpassing anything ever perpetrated by the English,[2] yet their attempts to civilise and Christianise them were somewhat more successful. No wilderness was so inhospitable, no tribe so savage, that the Jesuit missionary did not brave their perils.[3] Their creed was naturally more acceptable to the childish temper of the savage than the stern Calvinism of New England. The more versatile and plastic character of the Celt lent itself better to the exigencies of savage life. Many of the French on the Canadian frontier lived among the Indians, married with them, and thus formed a bond of national union.[4] Yet they produced nothing worthy of the name of civilisation. In truth, the Indian had not the rudiments of civilisation in his character. He had no sense of the obligation of law, he had no capacity for settled industry. To endeavour to civilise him was but to destroy his native virtues, and to give him no others in their stead. "The Great Spirit," he said himself, "gave the white man a plough, and the red man a bow and arrow, and sent them into the world by different paths, each to get his living in his own way."[5] An American writer has drawn a happy picture of the mongrel that was produced by the attempt to impose the training of a white man on the native temper of the savage, and of his degraded condition. "His new friends profess love to him, and a desire for his improvement in human and divine knowledge, and for his eternal salvation, but at the same time endeavour to make him sensible of his inferiority to themselves. He is put to school, but his fellow-students look upon him as a being of inferior species. He is neither a white man nor an Indian; as

---

[1] Southey's "Life of Wesley," vol. i., p. 80.
[2] Colden, vol. i., pp. 79, 120–122, 193–196.
[3] Colden, vol. i., p. 60.   [4] Colden, vol. i., p. 260.
[5] Report of a Committee, &c., pp. 19, 20.

he has no character with us, he has none with them."[1] The best of them would shun such a condition, and prefer to die with Sasacus and Philip as the champions of national freedom. What legislation could do for their protection the colonial legislation did. It forbade enslaving them, it restricted the sale of spirits, it debarred them from alienating their lands. It regarded their lives as equally sacred, in the eye of the law, with those of its white subjects.[2] But no legislation could save the barbarian when brought face to face with the civilised man. Yet the fate of the Indian, though inevitable, is not the less sad. One can acquiesce in the extinction of the scarce human Bushmen, or the aborigines of Australia; but the destruction, and, even worse, the utter demoralisation of a brave, generous, and high-spirited race, must ever be one of the saddest chapters in the history of America.

I have already given one specimen of the ferocious energy with which the fathers of New England set to work to root out the heathen from their Canaan. For nearly forty years no other nation exposed itself to the fate of the luckless Pequods. In 1670, Alexander, the sachem of Pokanoket and the son of Massasoit, the faithful ally of the English, was suspected of hostile schemes. Death, however, anticipated his designs, and his brother Philip succeeded. Philip, like his father Massasoit, was resolutely opposed to Christianity. In 1671, he made a treaty with the English and surrendered his arms. Four years later, finding his territory becoming more and more restricted, he resolved to strike a last blow for the liberty of his people. Happily the English were warned in time, and the attack had to be made before the preparations for it were fully ripe. During the whole summer of 1675, Philip's men ravaged the colony, plundering, murdering, and desolating everywhere. Happily for the colonists many of the Indians stood neutral, and some were

[1] Report of a Committee, &c., p. 30.
[2] Winthrop, vol. i., p. 323. Hening, vol. i., pp. 248, 252, 253; vol. ii., p. 138; vol. iv., p. 286.

moved by rewards to take up arms against Philip.[1] Yet the English dared not pursue their enemy into the forests. "It is ill," they said, "fighting with a wild beast in his own den," and they confined themselves to defensive measures. But in the winter, when the forests were clear, a force of one thousand men under the command of Josiah Winslow, marched against the enemy. The treachery of an Indian fugitive guided them to the camp of Philip. The fort was taken with comparatively small loss of life, and the scene of horror which we have witnessed in the Pequod war was now re-enacted. Nearly one thousand Indians, many of them women and children, perished either by the weapons of the English or in the flames of their own wigwams. Philip and the survivors renewed the war during the ensuing summer, and inflicted severe loss on their enemies. But their cause was utterly hopeless. Their women had perished, and their fields remained untilled. Many of the neutrals began to take the side of the English, and even Philip's own people were brought over by the hope of pardon. Betrayed and surrounded, the Arminius of North America was hunted down and shot like a wild beast in the forests where his fathers had reigned.[2] Like his German prototype he had lived long enough to see his wife and son the prisoners of his foes. Neither the consistent kindness received from Massasoit, nor the respect due to a brave enemy, saved the young sachem from being sold as a slave to the Bermudas.[3] Philip's war was the last unaided attempt of the red men in New England to expel their invaders. It was marked by actions worthy of the dying effort of a heroic people. The English surrendered one of their prisoners to the Mohicans, who tortured him horribly and asked him tauntingly whether he liked the war then. "The insensible and hard-hearted monster did answer that he liked it very well, and found

---

[1] The reward was a coat for every enemy slain, two for every prisoner. The reward offered for Philip was forty coats if taken alive, twenty if killed.

[2] The above account is taken from Hubbard's "Present State of New England," being a narrative of the troubles with the Indians. London, 1677.

[3] Bancroft, vol. ii., p. 108.

it as sweet as Englshmen did their sugar." Another prisoner in a spirit of Roman patriotism, consented to die rather than take back proposals for a peace.[1] If the revenge taken was severe, so was the suffering. Six hundred men, a twentieth of the whole able-bodied force of the colony had fallen. Whole towns were destroyed, and six hundred houses were burnt to the ground.[2]

The Indians were not the only inferior race with whom the white man in America was brought in contact. In 1619, a Dutch ship landed twenty negroes at Jamestown.[3] These are the first negro slaves on American soil of whom there is any record. For a considerable time the slave trade was in the hands of the Dutch, and, as I have before mentioned, in 1653 the number of whites in Virginia exceeded that of negroes as twenty to one. But the poison had been introduced, though its operation might be slow. We have seen that the union of the races was from the first looked on with disgust. Yet it is not till the eighteenth century that we meet with much in the legislation of Virginia to remind us of the existence of an inferior caste. In 1705 we find an ominous law protecting negro slaves against ill-treatment, and in 1711 we find that their testimony was not to be received on the same footing as that of white men. The evil did not confine itself to the degradation of the negroes. There grew up "a feculum of beings called overseers, a most abject, unprincipled race."[4] I do not find any explicit record of the existence of such a class in early times in the other colonies, but we can hardly doubt that in South Carolina the preponderance of the negro population must have produced the same evils in even an intensified form.

[1] Hubbard, who tells of these actions, adds a strange comment. "Instances of this nature should be incentives unto us to bless the Father of lights, who hath called us out from the dark places of the earth, full of the habitations of cruelty." It would be hard, one would think, to find "darker places of cruelty," than existed in the hearts of men who could tell of such actions with no other feeling than self-righteous exultation.
[2] Bancroft, vol. ii., p. 109.   [3] Beverley, p. 37.
[4] A private letter, quoted in Wirt's "Life of Patrick Henry," p. 32.

We find no mention of negroes in New England till eighteen years after their first appearance in Virginia. In 1763, out of a total of about two hundred and fifty-one thousand souls, a little over five thousand were negroes; and in the next thirteen years, while the whole population was increased by one hundred and twelve thousand, the number of negroes was about stationary.[1] Here a caste feeling prevailed, though not as strongly as in Virginia. A negro striking a white man was liable to be sold out of the province. Mixed marriages were punishable, and the officiating clergyman was liable to a fine of £50, though the marriage, when once celebrated, could not be annulled. No negro might be in the streets after nine o'clock. Slavery, no doubt, was opposed to the principles, and even more to the social character, of New England, but it was not to these wholly or even chiefly that the difference between the Northern and Southern colonies is due. The difference of climate, and even more of soil, is the real explanation. Not that, as is sometimes alleged, the climate of the Southern States is such as to render white labour in any way impossible. The Salzburgers and Oglethorpe's highlanders worked diligently, while the broken tradesmen who had been sent to Georgia out of charity clamoured for negroes. The difference is, not that white labour is impossible in the South, but that black labour is impossible in the North. The climate was ill-suited to the African, and the barren soil required a more scientific system of tillage than he could carry out. The labour of a gang of human machines working under the whip of an overseer could not stand in competition against the active New England yeoman. In the Southern colonies, the richer soil and the simpler agriculture placed the free labour and the slave far more nearly on the same footing.

I must not altogether pass over without notice those strange and tragical events which, towards the close of the seventeenth century, threw so dark a cloud over the hitherto tranquil career

---

[1] Answers, by the Rev. Dr Bellinap, to questions proposed by Judge Flecker. Massachusetts' "Historical Collection," vol. iv., pp. 191-198.

of New England. The penal code of Massachusetts, based as it was on that of the Jews, included witchcraft among its capital crimes. The early New England Puritan no doubt thought himself a firm believer in possession and in the power of witches. But he had no time for such follies. He had to fight Satan by nobler means than by hanging old women. It was not till he had leisure to mix up Indian demonology with crude theological notions and the conceits of his own brain, and till the stern unreasoning bigotry of Dudley had given way to the hypocritical self-justifying bigotry of Cotton Mather, that the penalties imposed on witchcraft became a real evil. In 1656, a Mrs Hilbers, widow of a leading citizen of Boston, and sister to the deputy-governor, had been hanged, as an old pastor said, "for having more wit than her neighbours." In 1685, a miserable Irishwoman was hanged as a witch at Salem. One of those supposed to have been bewitched worked on Cotton Mather's credulity and vanity till he thought he saw an opportunity of serving of God, and distinguishing himself by a general crusade against witchcraft. About the same time, there were dissensions in the church at Salem. Beside the town, a separate community, Salem village, had grown up. Disputes had arisen between the two churches. Burroughs, the favourite minister of Salem village, had been expelled, and his successor, Parris, had involved himself in incessant disputes with his parishioners. In 1691 he allied himself with Mather, and they commenced their campaign. They obtained a complete triumph. The inhabitants were seized by one of those epidemics, of which there are other instances in history, but of which the laws are as yet unknown. The life of every man, woman, and child in Salem was at the mercy of a vindictive priest and a vain pedant. No age, no rank was safe. A life of blameless virtue was no protection. A child of four years old was accused; a gentlewoman of eighty, of good family and exemplary character, was hanged. An aged man suffered himself to be pressed to death rather than let himself be convicted, and his goods forfeited. Burroughs, the predecessor and rival of Parris, was among those executed. No show of justice was observed in the trials. So weak did the prosecutors feel their own case, that, when some of the accused fled to the other colonies, they did not dare to demand them. At length, the good sense of the people came to the rescue. The terrible infection was checked, but not before twenty innocent persons had perished on the gallows. Under the wise and gentle management of a new pastor, the dark cloud left by the witch tragedy passed away. Some of the "possessed" children repented with open confession, and expiated their misdeeds by acts of kindness to the relations of those whom they had helped to murder. Mather and Parris, on whose heads the main guilt rests, died unrepentant.[1]

For more than a hundred years, the colonists knew nothing of war save the ferocious, but ill-organised and short-lived attacks of the savages. But it was soon evident that America must become the battle-field of England and France. The French held Louisiana and Canada. Could they but establish a line of communication along the valleys of Ohio and the Mississippi, they would have a complete belt along the whole English frontier. For years that had been the policy of France, and her relations with the natives had all been directed to that end. In 1753 matters drew to a crisis. The French began to encroach on the unoccupied valley of the Ohio territory, claimed by England as part of Virginia. In April Duquesne, with a force of twelve hundred men, marched into the valley, disregarding the feeble protest of the natives. In the autumn of that year Dinwiddie, the governor of Virginia, sent by the direction of the home government, "a person of distinction" to demand an explanation from the French commander. The ambassador selected was George Washington, a young Virginian gentleman, twenty-one

---

[1] I have taken this account from Bancroft, vol. iii., pp. 75-78, 84-98. A letter from Thomas Brattle, F.R.S., giving a full and candid account of the delusion called witchcraft, which prevailed in New England, 1692, and from an article on Salem witchcraft, lately published in the *Edinburgh Review*.

years old, brought up as a land surveyor. The French commander boldly avowed his purpose of holding the valley of the Ohio. On Washington's return, it was decided to adopt prompt measures. The Ohio company erected a fort, and Washington was sent with a hundred and fifty men to hold the territory. Aided by the Indians, he attacked the French at Great Meadows on the 27th of May, and defeated them. But he was unsupported, and could do nothing towards holding the valley against the constantly increasing French forces. On the 4th of July he capitulated, and retreated with all his effects, leaving the French in possession of the valley.[1]

French aggression was to lead the American colonies to take the first step towards national unity. On the 19th of June a congress of representatives from every colony north of the Potomac met at Albany. Among these representatives was Benjamin Franklin. Self-made and self-taught, the journeyman printer had risen to be one of the leading statesmen of his country. His name was not yet associated with those great discoveries which have now made it immortal, but he had already shown himself one of the most active and public-spirited citizens of Philadelphia. He had organised a public library and a fire company, and had induced the citizens to establish an academy. The city owed it to him that its streets were paved and swept.[2] Nothing was so vast as to be beyond his comprehension; nothing so minute as to escape his attention. In everything he undertook, great or small, he showed that most rare combination of qualities, an unresting desire for improvement, with the capacity for seeing what improvement was possible, and the readiness to acquiesce in going no further. There have been natural philosophers who have bequeathed even greater gifts to the world; there have been statesmen who have left their mark more indelibly stamped on the character and institutions of their country; there have been philanthropists who have rendered greater public services. But

[1] Bancroft, vol. iv., pp. 106-121.
[2] Franklin's Autobiography, published in his Works, vol. i., pp. 99, 133, 158.

in all history we can scarcely find a character who combined in himself so many and such varied means of usefulness to his fellow-men, and who employed them so ungrudgingly and so wisely.

He now laid before the congress a scheme for uniting the colonies in a confederacy. The immediate grounds set forth for this measure were the necessity for resistance to the French, the failure of that resistance in the present year, owing to the absence of co-operation, and the confidence which such a state of disunion tended to inspire in the enemy. The plan of union proposed "that humble application be made for an Act of Parliament of Great Britain, by virtue of which one general government may be formed in America, including all the said colonies, within and under which government each colony may retain its present constitution, except in the particulars wherein a change may be directed by the said act." The plan then provided "that the said general government be administered by a president-general, to be appointed and supported by the crown; and a grand council to be chosen by the representatives of the people of the several colonies met in their several assemblies." The council was to be elected every three years. The number of representatives allotted to each colony should be proportionate to its contribution to the general treasury. The president-general was to have a veto on all laws. The council was to have power to raise soldiers and build forts for the protection of any of the colonies, or equip ships for the defence of the empire generally, but might not impress men in any colony without the consent of the colonial legislature. It was also to have power to make laws and levy taxes, with due regard to the convenience of the people, "rather discouraging luxury, than loading industry with unnecessary burdens." All laws were to be transmitted to England for approbation. Military and naval officers were to be nominated by the president, and approved by the council; civil officers to be nominated by the council, and approved by the president. The separate states were still to keep up their own military establishments, and if they should be put to any expense in self-defence, the general government was to defray it, so far as it was reasonable.[1] The congress approved of the scheme, and the project of union seemed at first likely to create general enthusiasm. But the centrifugal tendency was still too strong for the centripetal, and the confederation of the American colonies was postponed.[2]

The home government now took up the cause of the colonies. Provisions were made for the settlement of the Ohio valley, and the direction of American affairs was entrusted to the brave and ferocious Cumberland. Braddock, a man of no military genius, violent, brutal, and overbearing, was appointed commander-in-chief. Orders were given that the provisional officers should hold no rank while serving with the regular troops.[3] At the same time, Dieskau sailed with troops from Canada. Everything spoke plainly of war. On the 9th of July 1755, Braddock, with twelve hundred picked men, forded the Mononhangela, and entered the valley of the Ohio. Franklin had reminded him of the dangers of backwoods warfare, and the fear of ambuscades, but he had scorned the warning as coming from a provincial and a civilian.[4] At one o'clock, just after the whole force had crossed the Mononhangela, they heard a quick and heavy fire in their front. The two front detachments of five hundred men fell back, and the whole force was in confusion. The officers, conspicuous on horseback, were picked off by riflemen. Braddock had five horses killed under him, and was at length mortally wounded. The officers behaved with unparalleled courage, and strove to rally their troops, but to no purpose. The men, deaf to the exhortations of their officers, fired away all their ammunition, and then fled, leaving their artillery, provisions, and baggage. Washington, who had resigned his commission in disgust at the stigma cast on the American officers, was present, and, with his despised provincials, "behaved the whole time with the greatest

---

[1] Franklin's Works, vol. iii., pp. 22-55.
[2] Bancroft, vol. iv., pp. 125, 126.
[3] Bancroft, vol. iv., pp. 167-170.
[4] Franklin's Autobiography. Works, vol. i., p. 190.

courage and resolution."[1] The total loss in killed and wounded was seven hundred and thirteen, while that of the enemy did not amount to one hundred."[2] Braddock died in the space of two days, and was buried secretly to save his corpse from the fury of the Indians.[3]

In Canada, the colonists had done better for themselves than the regular troops had done for them. A force of New England militia had defeated the enemy near Fort-Edward. The loss on each side had been about equal, but among the French who fell was their leader, the brave Dieskau.[4]

Meantime, in another part of the continent, a scene had been enacted, more full of human suffering than many battle-fields. In 1714, the treaty of Utrecht had given to Great Britain the French colony of Acadia. The inhabitants of that province were loyal and attached subjects of France, and they stipulated that, under the British government, they should not be called upon to bear arms against their native country. On the whole continent, there was not a more peaceful and tranquil community than that of Acadia. They were "a society of brethren, every individual of which was equally ready to give and receive what he thought the common right of mankind." Vice was unknown. None lived single, and when a young couple married, the community furnished them with a house and ground, and supplied them with the necessaries of life for a year. Agriculture was their staple occupation, and the produce of their own fields and flocks supplied nearly all their wants. The English government granted them the benefit of complete neglect. "No magistrate was ever appointed to rule over them. No rents or taxes of any kind were ever exacted from them. Their new sovereign seemed to have forgotten them, and they were equally strangers to him."[5]

---

[1] Original Account of Braddock's Defeat. By Orme, (his aide-de-camp.) Published in the Massachusetts' "Historical Collection," 2d series, vol. viii., pp. 153–155. Franklin's Works, vol. i., p. 191.   [2] Bancroft, vol. iv., p. 191.
[3] Hutchinson's "History of Massachusetts," ed. 1828, p. 32.
[4] Bancroft, vol. iv., pp. 207–212.
[5] Some account of the late inhabitants of Acadia, translated from the French of the Abbé Raynal, and published in the Annual Register, vol. xix.

Surely the storm of European war might pass by and leave these Acadians to the enjoyment of their tranquil life. But when did such considerations weigh as a feather in the balance in the schemes of the rulers of mankind? The peaceful happiness of the people is no part of the statesman's care; that is only the province of visionary enthusiasts like Penn and Oglethorpe.

The peace of Acadia was threatened in 1755 by the establishment of a British force among them. War between their countrymen and their rulers was close at hand. Yet they only desired to stand neutral. The English government was not satisfied. "They possess the best and largest tract of land in this province; if they refuse the oaths, it would be much better that they were away," was the report of Lawrence, the Lieutenant-Governor of Nova Scotia. It was not hard to find pretexts for carrying out the desired policy. The Acadians had refused the oath of allegiance, though almost immediately afterwards, they had repented and offered to take it. They were declared "Popish recusants," and their deportation was ordered.[1] The whole population of Acadia, probably the happiest and most prosperous settlement in America, was driven out at the point of the bayonet. Families were broken up, husbands sent to one colony, their wives to another far distant. One thousand of them landed at Boston in the dead of winter, utterly unprovided for. The government had made no arrangements for their reception, and but for the humanity of the citizens, many of them must have perished of cold and hunger. The kindness shown to men of an alien race and a detested religion, shows that the New Englanders had added tolerance and charity to the virtues of their Puritan fathers.[2]

In 1751, war was declared between England and France, and in 1758, the conquest of the Ohio valley was again attempted The first attack on Fort Duquesne failed, like Braddock's, through the foolhardiness of the English commander, Grant, and as in Braddock's defeat, the courage of the provincials helped to save

[1] Bancroft, vol. iv., pp. 194-206. [2] Hutchinson, pp. 39, 40.

the force from destruction. In November, two thousand five hundred men marched against Fort Duquesne, under the command of Forbes, with Washington at the head of the provincials. Braddock's defeat was avenged, but by a bloodless victory.[1] The French garrison set fire to the fort and fled. The spot was named Pittsburg by the victors, in honour of the great dictator who had revived the glory of the English arms. If equal success attended them in Canada, the future expansion of the Anglo-American empire would be bounded only by the Pacific.

In the campaigns of 1757 and 1758, the ability of the French General Montcalm was assisted by the incapacity and supineness of the English commanders. But Wolfe's arrival introduced a fresh spirit, and the campaign of 1759, was crowned by the surrender of Quebec. With that event the war in America was virtually at a close. A question now remained to be settled of vital importance to the colonies. Should England retain Canada, or cede it in consideration of receiving Guadaloupe? The voice of the colonists was unanimously in favour of Canada. To have Canada under the same government as themselves would relieve them from the expense of guarding a vast frontier, and would diminish the danger of Indian warfare. On the other hand, there were those in England who argued that the extent of territory would tend to make the colonists independent, both commercially and politically, of the mother country. Against these views, Franklin published a pamphlet, urging the superior value of Canada to England.[2] The increase in the number of subjects need be, he pointed out, no source of alarm. The extension of territory would be in itself a security against the colonists undertaking manufactures. Increase of population might drive them to it, but extension of territory would serve to confine them to agriculture. The idea that the colonies would be induced to aim at independence he utterly ridiculed. Could it be supposed that these separate colonies with different forms of government, different

[1] Bancroft, vol. viii., pp. 308-311.
[2] Published in Franklin's Works, vol. iv., p. 153.

laws, different interests, and some of them different religious persuasions, and different manners, would ever be bound together in one empire. Would these colonists who would not unite for self-defence against the French and Indians, unite against their own nation, which protects and encourages them, and with which they have so many ties of blood, interest, and affection? The idea that Canada in the possession of the French acted as a check on the colonies, he denounced as a barbarous scheme for employing the French and Indians to restrain the colonists, and he pointed out that independence of each other, and separate interest, was the guarantee which England had for the security of her American possessions. At the same time he took occasion indirectly to remind the government of the duty they owed to the colonies. "While the government is mild and just, while important civil and religious rights are secure, subjects will be dutiful and obedient. The waves do not rise but while the winds blow." Franklin's policy, or rather the design of Pitt, for amassing and consolidating a great English empire prevailed, and Canada became British territory.

CHAPTER IV.

THE CONTEST FOR INDEPENDENCE.

WE have seen the colonies at the end of a severe and exhausting, but not destructive war. Their services were acknowledged by the mother country, and considerable, though probably inadequate, compensation was voted to them. But though the war had taxed them heavily, in other respects the yoke of English supremacy sat lightly on the neck of the colonists. The severity of the navigation laws was in practice mitigated by the lenity with which they were carried out. The excise officers systematically connived at the evasions of the law.[1] Of the million and a half pounds of tea consumed annually in the colonies, not more than a tenth came from England.[2] The commercial monopoly of Great Britain was regarded, according to the economical principles of that age, as a politic and necessary measure.[3] The severe restrictions on colonial industry were indeed felt, but so many and so varied were the fields for labour, that though these restrictions might impede the progress of the colonies, they never could produce actual want. The rapid growth of their commercial prosperity closed the eyes of the Americans to the severity of the trade regulations. "After the war, and in the last years of it,

---

[1] Annual Register, vol. iii., pp. 219, 220. Bancroft, vol. iv., p. 158, and vol. v., p. 87. Franklin says, (vol. iv., p. 325), "The needy wretches who, with poor salaries, were trusted to watch the post day and night, found it easier and more profitable not only to wink but to sleep in their beds; the merchant's pay being more generous than the king's."

[2] Bancroft, vol. iv., p. 158, *note*.

[3] Franklin's Works, vol. iv., p. 181; vol. v., p. 7.

the trade of America had increased far beyond the speculations of the most sanguine imaginations. It swelled out on every side. It filled all the proper channels to the brim."[1] In other respects, America might well be content with her political relations to the mother country. "She had, except the commercial restraint, every characteristic mark of a free people in all her internal concerns. She had the image of the British constitution. She had the substance. She was taxed by her own representatives. She chose most of her own magistrates. She paid them all. She had, in effect, the sole disposal of her own internal government."[2] Consequently, "she had not only a respect, but an affection for Great Britain, for its laws, its customs, and manners. Natives of Britain were always treated with particular regard; to be an old England man was of itself a character of some respect."[3] The principal grievance was the character of the governors, many of whom were, like the Roman pro-consuls, needy adventurers, who came out to retrieve their fortunes, and to acquire resources for future extravagance at the expense of the colonies.[4] Projects of raising a revenue and maintaining a civil list had occasionally been heard of, but they had taken no definite form, and the colonists might well feel that the sufferings they had undergone, and the loyalty they had shown in the late war, would exempt them from any such burdens. Not that the materials for resistance were wanting whenever the need of them should come. All the traditions of their origin pointed to freedom as their birthright, to resistance against tyranny as their duty. Nor had the old Puritan spirit died for lack of nourishment or exercise. Massachusetts had had struggles with her governors, Pennsylvania with her proprietors, Virginia with her clergy. The democratic training of the New England townships had not

---

[1] Burke's Works, vol. ii., p. 391.   [2] Burke's Works, vol. ii., p. 385.
[3] Franklin's Examination before Parliament, in his Works, vol. iv., p. 169.
[4] Franklin's "American Discontents," vol. iv., p. 248. Rules for Reducing a Great Empire into a Small One, vol. iv., pp. 389, 390. Franklin states (vol. iv., p. 469) that in 1764 Bernard was convicted of corruption and collusion with smugglers, and still allowed to retain his office.

perished. Public libraries had diffused knowledge among the people.[1] The late war had taught them the strength of a colonial militia. But though the nation was gradually and secretly developing its fitness for freedom, the idea of independence had never consciously presented itself. A few far-seeing statesmen and enthusiastic patriots may have discerned on the horizon the "little cloud like a man's hand," which contained within it the storm of civil war, but separation from the mother country would have seemed to the mass of Americans a wild dream.[2] In 1764, Otis, the leading statesman of Massachusetts, said publicly, "The true interests of Great Britain and her plantations are mutual, and what God has in providence united, let no man dare attempt to pull asunder."[3]

Nor was there anything in the internal state of England to make the Americans apprehend danger. England, at the accession of George III., was, beyond all doubt, the freest of the nations of Europe. The principles of liberal government had, for nearly a hundred years, made steady progress.[4] There had been a steady

---

[1] Franklin's Works, vol. i., p. 97.

[2] Lord Chatham stated to Franklin, in a conversation in 1774, that it was commonly believed in England that America was aiming at independence. Franklin's answer was, "that having more than once travelled almost from one end of the continent to the other, and kept a great variety of company, eating, drinking, and conversing with them freely, he had never heard, in any conversation, from any person, drunk or sober, the least expression of a wish for such a separation." Franklin's Works, vol. v., pp. 6, 7. Dr Price, in his "Additional Observations on the Nature and Value of Civil Liberty, and the War with America," published in 1777, quotes [pp. 80-82] private letters from New York, written as late as 1775, disavowing any idea of independence in very strong terms. Horace Walpole, wise after the event, says in his "Memoirs of George II.," vol. i., p. 397, that suspicions had been entertained as early as 1754 that America was aiming at independence. I can find no evidence for such a supposition, much against it. See Franklin's Works, vol. iv., pp. 432, 477, 485, 496, 498, 503. Annual Register, vol. xix., p. 96. Bancroft, vol. v., pp. 148, 201, 202, 205, 217, 271; vol. vi., p. 73. The Critical Moment on which the Salvation or Destruction of the British Empire Depend, by Janus, published, 1776, p. 81, and Thoughts on the Letter of Edmund Burke, Esquire, to the Sheriffs of Bristol on the Affairs of America, by the Earl of Abingdon, pp. 56, 57. Compare with such statements the repeated disavowals of independence, both by provincial assemblies and continental congresses.

[3] Hutchinson, p. 102.

[4] For an account of this movement, see Buckle's "History of Civilisation in England," vol. i., chap. 7.

diminution of the royal prerogative. The king no longer attended cabinet councils or debates in the House of Lords. The two first Hanoverian princes were restrained by indolence and ignorance from interfering in the affairs of the nation. Whenever their influence was exercised it was only in foreign, not domestic, politics, and though parliament acquiesced in that influence the nation protested against it. The prime minister no longer held office by the will of the sovereign. The king was forced by the Pelhams to dismiss Granville; he was forced by the nation to accept Pitt. The once strong party of prerogative was, as a political force, extinct, and when the Whigs, after ruling England for forty-five years, were at length overthrown, it was by weakness within, not by attacks from without. The publication of the debates of parliament at once indicated the interest which the nation felt in the proceedings of its rulers, and strengthened its power of criticising them. Political newspapers had sprung up, and eminent statesmen did not think it unworthy of them to fight their battles in the popular arena, and to appeal to the voice of the multitude.[1] By various means knowledge had been widely diffused. Circulating libraries and book clubs were organised. Lectures were delivered, and treatises written on scientific subjects in a popular and untechnical style.[2]

It would exceed the limits of my subject were I to attempt to trace in full the causes which had combined to produce this movement. In the first place various circumstances had effectually debarred the king from the use of arbitrary power. A disputed succession not only acted as security for good behaviour, but alienated from the throne the only party who would have been likely to support it in any encroachments on popular liberties. The king's own claim to the throne rested on the people's right of self-government. The king's own party, the Whig aristocracy, was like himself pledged to the cause of liberty. Additional security was provided by the national debt, which gave so large a portion of the community a direct interest in the security of parliament.[3]

[1] Hallam, vol. iii., p. 298. [2] Buckle, vol. i. pp. 393, 394.
[3] Cooke's "History of Party," vol. ii., p. 409.

Mainly, however, the growth of liberal principles was due to this, that a new political force had come into being. The power of the aristocracy had been relatively lessened; that of the landed gentry was at best stationary, while that of the mercantile and professional classes, the most progressive and enlightened part of the nation, had greatly increased. A time was at hand which was to test the value of that movement. It was yet to be seen whether national liberty did not require a wider basis; whether the Whig party were capable of resisting the encroachments of arbitrary power, or whether they might not themselves become the willing instruments of arbitrary power. It yet remained to be seen how far the progress which England had made during the eighteenth century could be checked by a reactionary king and subservient ministers, how far it was a permanent law and principle of her growth.

In the accession of George III. there seemed nothing to awaken the fears of British subjects, much to raise their hopes. The new king spoke the language of his people; he avowed himself a Briton. England, not Hanover, was to be the object of his affection and interest. The last hope of the Stuart dynasty had perished, and all fear of a disputed succession was at an end. Time was to show how far these changes in the position of the king were subjects of congratulation. The new system soon bore fruit. In less than a year Pitt, the minister of the people, had resigned. The words that then passed between him and Granville foreshadowed the spirit of the coming reign. The people, said Pitt, had called him to the ministry, and to them he was responsible. "When," said Granville, "a minister talks of being responsible to the people, he talks the language of the House of Commons, and forgets that at this board he is only responsible to the king."[1] In another year a ministry was in office fully prepared to carry out Granville's principles. The self-styled patriots who, eighteen years before, had driven out Walpole, and overthrown his party, must have rued their success when

[1] Cooke, vol. ii., p. 404.

they contrasted the present ministry with that sturdy autocrat. They had promised themselves a pure parliament and a patriotic cabinet. Instead of that, they had a parliament more corrupt and subservient than ever, led by ministers with no more principle than Walpole, and without a tithe of his ability. The three principal figures in the cabinet were Bute, Granville, and Townshend. Bute was a brainless courtier, the mouthpiece of the king; Granville was, according to the political notions of the time, honest, but he was a pedant, a slave to precedent and system, ready to worship the Stamp Act as his "idol,"[1] and to talk in parliament of the "sacredness"[2] of the navigation laws. Townshend was by far the ablest of them; he was a brilliant debater, and ready at mastering the details of any subject which his official duties imposed upon him, but without any sense of the responsibilities of statesmanship. He looked on the House of Commons as a debating society in which to fire off brilliant paradoxes. Incapable of fixed and far-seeing ambition, his only aim was to win the applause of a moment. He was ready to impose a tax, at the risk of ruining an empire, rather than suffer a political opponent to taunt him with cowardice. Such were the men to whom, under the "over-ruling influence"[3] of the king, himself, if possible, more arbitrary, ignorant, and obstinate than any of them, the destinies of England and her colonies were intrusted.

As we have seen, projects had been more than once entertained for an American revenue. When Keith, the governor of Pennsylvania, made the proposal to Walpole, he met with the answer, "I have Old England set against me, and do you think I will have New England likewise."[4] In 1754, Halifax had proposed a "certain and permanent revenue" to be adjusted by commissioners, one from each province.[5] Several of the pro-

---

[1] Burke's speech on American Taxation, April 19, 1774, in Burke's Works, vol. ii., p. 391.
[2] Walpole, quoted by Bancroft, vol. v., p. 294.
[3] Expression used by Pitt in Parliament. Bancroft, vol. v., p. 384.
[4] Annual Register, vol. viii., p. 25.   [5] Bancroft, vol. iv., p. 166.

vincial governors came forward with suggestions, but at such a time it would have been unsafe to weaken the loyalty of the colonies, and the projects came to nothing. The next year, however, the subject was again mooted. Halifax insisted on the propriety of raising a revenue. Huske, an American patronised by Townshend, urged a reform in the colonial administration, and a system of taxation by parliament. The colonial governors almost unanimously joined in the cry. So serious did it seem, that in November, Massachusetts gave its agent instructions "to oppose everything that should have the remotest tendency to raise a revenue in the plantations."[1] None of these proposals produced any immediate result, but they had the effect of familiarising parliament with an idea of an American revenue, and with the necessity of checking colonial independence. Had parliament been gifted with political foresight, it might also have seen in the spirit which these encroachments elicited, the germ of future resistance. When it was suggested in 1760 by some English officers at New York, that a revenue should be raised by a system of quit-rents virtually amounting to a land tax, Livingstone, an American landholder, cried out, grasping his sword, "While I can wield this weapon, England shall never get it, but with my heart's blood."[2] In the next year a dispute arose at Boston about molasses' duties. The custom-house officers demanded the assistance of the executive in their search for contraband goods, and the colonists refused it. This was the opening scene of American resistance. The case was tried before Hutchinson and the council. Gridley, the crown lawyer, appealed to a statute of William III. Otis, "the great incendiary," replied, "I am determined," he said, "to sacrifice estate, ease, health, applause, and even life, to the sacred calls of my country in opposition to a kind of power, the exercise of which cost one king of England his head, and another his throne." He denounced the writs of assistance as a violation of personal liberty and security; he appealed to the charter of Massachusetts, and

[1] Bancroft, vol. iv., pp. 178–181.   [2] Bancroft, vol. iv., p. 371.

he denied the power of parliament to issue such writs, since they were opposed to the first principles of law.[1] Otis lost his case, but the spirit which he had awakened did not perish. The next year furnished him with another opportunity of asserting the rights of the colonies. The inhabitants of Salem and Marblehead petitioned that a ship might be sent to protect their fisheries against the French. A sloop was sent, and the assembly was ordered to make provision for the expense. They protested, and Otis drew up a remonstrance claiming for the colony "their most darling privilege, the right of originating all taxes," and averring that to withhold it was "to annhilate one branch of the legislature."[2]

But the attacks on American liberty were not confined to the question of taxation. Hitherto the colonial judges had held their appointments during good behaviour, and had been dependent on the local assemblies for their salaries. In 1761 a blow was struck at the independence of the judiciary, by the appointment of Pratt to the post of chief-justice of New York, during the king's pleasure. To meet this, the assembly of New York resolved to withhold the judge's salary till the form of the order was changed. This gave an opening for further encroachment. "Shall," said Colden, " the chief justice of so considerable a province as this be left to beg his bread of the people?" The Board of Trade therefore recommended that the judge's salary should be paid out of the royal quit-rents, pointing out, at the same time, that this would give the judge a direct interest in protecting the crown domains against encroachments. The recommendation was adopted, and the judges were no longer responsible to the colonial governments.[3]

This was but the first step towards remodelling the whole colonial system. The conclusion of peace removed the last obstacle which had interfered with such a policy. In 1763, Townshend, holding the post of First Lord of Trade with the

---

[1] Bancroft, vol. iv., pp. 414, 415. Hutchinson, pp. 89-94.
[2] Hutchinson, p. 97. [3] Bancroft, vol. iv., pp. 427-429, 440.

administration of the colonies, brought forward his policy. His first measure was a declaration, that for the future direct taxation was to supersede requisitions. With the revenue thus raised, a civil list was to be maintained, so that every person in public employment should be immediately dependent on the home government. The charters were to be superseded, and a new territorial arrangement introduced. The navigation laws were to be strictly enforced, and as a necessary condition for the success of these measures, a standing army was to be maintained. The general assembly at New York protested, but the protest fell to the ground. The system of making the judges answerable only to the crown was established, and twenty regiments were voted as a standing army for America. On the 9th of March, Townshend brought forward his scheme of American taxation. The first measure was to lower the excise duties on the French and Spanish trade,—duties which, I have said before, had been hitherto systematically evaded,—and to enforce them rigidly. To enable this policy to be carried out, Granville brought in a bill, empowering the commanders of ships in the regular navy to examine, and on suspicion, to apprehend smuggling vessels, and encouraging their activity in this service by the hope of rewards.[1] Before Townshend could proceed further with his policy, events had driven him from the cabinet. His successor, Shelburne, refused to have anything to do with the taxation of America,[2] and it was left to Granville to complete the measures which Townshend had begun. If the colonial system was to be remodelled, it was to be regretted that the task was not in Granville's hands from the beginning. Unlike Townshend, he had political principles, and those principles, narrow though they were, would have withheld him from imposing arbitrary government on America. But that part of the task which devolved on him was the very one for which he was the least fit. Moderately liberal in general politics, in commercial matters he was a slave to the spirit of protection, and his pride and obstinacy made him

---

[1] Bancroft, vol. v., pp. 86–92.   [2] Bancroft, vol. v., p. 136.

incapable of withdrawing from a policy to which he had once pledged himself. In justice to him, it must be said that he did not propose his measures without due inquiry. Unhappily, the class of men who then held government offices in the colonies, was such that it was useless to look to them for authentic information. He learnt that a Stamp Act might be reckoned on to produce an annual revenue of £60,000.[1] Accordingly, on the 23d of September, the secretary of the treasury was instructed " to write to the commissioners of the stamp duties, to prepare a draft of a bill to be presented to parliament for extending the stamp duties to the colonies."[2] The ministry, however, considered that there were other measures of more pressing importance than the Stamp Act.

The first step was to provide for the execution of the Navigation Act. Every power that could be put in action, governors and officers, civil, military, and naval, were to help at this task. In the words of Franklin, "the brave honest officers of the *navy* were to be converted into pimping tide-waiters and colony officers of the *customs*. Those who, in time of war, had fought gallantly in defence of the commerce of their country, were in peace to be taught to prey on it."[3] The next measure was to reconstitute the boundaries of British America. The newly acquired territories were divided into three provinces, Quebec, and East and West Florida, and the boundaries of the old provinces, whose uncertainty had been the cause of much confusion, were definitely settled.[4] The whole territory to the west of Lake Nepising and beyond the Alleghanies was forbidden soil to the colonists. "The country to the west of our frontiers quite to the Mississippi was intended to be a desert for the Indians to hunt in."[5] If anything were needed to show the incapacity of the

[1] Bancroft, vol. v., p. 137. Huske, who had in 1755 advocated a Stamp Act, extravagantly promised a result of £500,000. Bancroft, vol. v., p. 170.
[2] Bancroft, vol. v., p. 151.
[3] Rules for Reducing a Great Empire into a Small One. Franklin's Works, vol. iv., p. 395.
[4] Annual Register, vol. vi., pp. 19-21.   [5] Bancroft, vol. v., p. 164.

ministry and the parliament for imperial legislation, it was this cowardly and feeble attempt to check the growth of the colonies.

The reconstitution of the judiciary and of the civil offices stood over for the present. Halifax in vain pressed the point,[1] but it was no essential part of Granville's scheme. His sole object was to raise a revenue and to enforce the commercial supremacy of Great Britain. At that point he was inflexible, but he saw the folly of unnecessarily inflaming the colonies, and upon representation being made to him from various quarters he consented to postpone the Stamp Act for a year. At the same time, as a measure of conciliation, he granted the freedom of the whale fishery to New England.[2] On the 9th of March 1764 he brought forward his budget, and gave notice of his intention to impose a Stamp Act on the colonies, stating that he would be ready to commute such a duty for any other that might seem equally profitable, and was preferred by the colonies. When that fatal proposal of taxing the colonies was first laid before parliament not a voice was raised against it. Beckford alone said, "As we are stout I hope we shall be merciful," and the subject was allowed to rest. Five days later a bill was brought in remodelling the Navigation Acts, and making them still more oppressive to America, and on the 5th of April it received the royal assent. Yet Granville still endeavoured to persuade others, and doubtless did persuade himself that his policy was moderate and conciliatory. He represented to the colonial agents that the Stamp Act was the most efficient and easiest of collection that could be imposed. But although he was willing to adopt an alternative, he had no idea of giving up the policy of taxation.[1] To a

---

[1] Bancroft, vol. v., p. 177.   [2] Bancroft, vol. v., p. 185.

[3] Burke expressly declares, in his speech of April 19, 1774, that Granville never proposed to the colonial agents that the assemblies should tax themselves instead of having a Stamp Act levied by the British Government, and that Granville never availed himself of such a defence. The only ground for the statement is a pamphlet by Israel Mauduit, published in the Massachusetts' "Historical Collection," 1st series, vol. ix., pp. 268-271, which contains a letter from the Massachusetts' assembly to their agent in London, referring to such an offer as having been made by Granville, which is, however, no proof that the offer was really made. Burke's

member of the House of Commons he said, "If the stamp duty is disliked I am willing to change it for any other equally productive. If you object to the Americans being taxed by parliament, save yourself the trouble of discussion, for I am determined on the measure."[1]

The Stamp Act was a completion of the new system on which America was to be governed. At this point we may pause to consider the general nature of that system, and the feelings with which it was regarded in this country and by the Americans. The objects of the ministerial policy were, as we have already seen—firstly, to enforce a strict commercial monopoly; secondly, to impose on the colonists a civil and military system, over which the colonial legislatures should have no control; thirdly, to raise a revenue, partly for the purpose of maintaining this system, partly to relieve a portion of the country from taxation. The scheme was, in fact, to convert the colonies into so many separate satrapies to be governed by and for England. To aggravate the difficulty of the colonists they were forbidden to pay their taxes in paper. It is needless to dwell at length on the injustice of the scheme. To fetter the growing industry and enterprise of colonies for the benefit of the mother country is not only, as we now know, foolish and impolitic, but it is in itself an unjust abuse of national power. Yet there was, at least, this defence for the monopoly system, that it was regarded, according to the erroneous economic theories of that day, as a necessary protection for English labour, and that as such the colonies acquiesced in it. But having already fettered the industry of the colonies, then to levy toll on the fruits of that industry was to impose, in the words of Burke, "perfect and uncompensated slavery."[2] The time selected for the attempt heightened its injustice. The colonies had just gone through an exhausting war

---

statement on such a subject made when he must have known that if false it was open to contradiction, is almost conclusive.

[1] Bancroft, vol. v., pp. 187-191.
[2] Burke's Speech, April 19, 1774, vol. ii., p. 396.

entailed upon them by their connection with England. They were receiving compensation for that war from the very parliament which proposed to take away with its left hand what it gave with its right. Even Bernard, the servile tool of arbitrary government, stated, in a letter written from Boston at the time of the Stamp Act, that the government of Massachusetts, "which was as much beforehand as any," was at that time raising an annual revenue of £37,500 to liquidate its debt, and could not hope to be free till four years later.[1] The question which one naturally asks is, "How could England be so unjust as to pass such measures, so foolish as to believe that they could be enforced?" For all classes alike were implicated. The king favoured the measures, the ministry originated them, the parliament passed them unanimously, the people acquiesced in them. The only answer that can be given is that the king and his ministers were ignorant and arbitrary, parliament was ignorant and subservient, the people were ignorant and selfish. I have already dwelt on the character of the king and his ministers, and I have also shown how some of the checks which had restrained the undue exercise of the prerogative in the two past reigns were now removed. But the arbitrary policy of George III. and the cabinet could have done little harm had parliament maintained its proper ground as the supporter of liberal principles. The decay of those principles was due to a variety of causes. The force of that movement which had arrayed the parliament against the Stuarts was spent, and no fresh impetus supplied its place. In that struggle the commons had been per force the champion of the nation. Just as the barons, who obtained Magna Charta, could not take the narrow standing ground of class interest, but were obliged, while fighting their own battle, to fight that of the commons, so the commons, in opposing Charles I., could not rest on the narrow standing-ground of parliamentary privilege. But here the question was not the supremacy of the king over the people, but the supremacy of the English government, of which

[1] Burke's Works, vol. ii., p. 396.

they themselves formed a part, over men separated from them by three thousand miles of sea. Moreover, as I have already pointed out, circumstances had for years identified the royal prerogative with the rights of the people, and the old spirit of resistance had dwindled and decayed for lack of exercise. Walpole's government, too, had done much to demoralise parliament. Not only had he employed wholesale corruption, but he had ruled the House of Commons as a despot, and it was now paying the penalty of that languor and inefficiency which always succeeds despotism. Lastly, the Stamp Act was openly held out by the ministers as giving relief to English landholders by diminishing the land tax. "I well remember," said Burke, "that Mr Townshend dazzled the country gentlemen by playing before their eyes the image of a revenue to be raised in America.[1] Such were some of the causes which account for the English nation ever entertaining such designs. But that they could have believed them to be beneficial, or even practicable, is a proof not merely of selfish indifference to the welfare of the colonies, but of great, and, in the case of a ministry, most culpable ignorance. It proceeded from ignorance, firstly, of the principles of commerce. To imagine that it was necessary to coerce the trade of America in order to limit it to our ports was an error, but in that age of protection a venial one. But to attempt to tax industry, and at the same time to cut off the sources of industry, was self-contradictory and suicidal. It was endeavouring "to cure an emaciated body by leaving it no juices at all."[2] Secondly, From ignorance of the true principles of colonial government. One error pervaded and vitiated nearly all the popular speculations on the relation of the colonies to England. The colonists were regarded as the subjects of the English nation, not as their fellow citizens.[3] As long as this was merely a

---

[1] Burke's Works, vol. ii., p. 388.   [2] Annual Register, vol. viii., p. 22.
[3] Franklin said, in a letter to Lord Kames, quoted in Life, vol. i., p. 309, "Every man in England seems to consider himself as a piece of a sovereign over America; seems to jostle himself into the throne with the king, and talks of our subjects in the colonies." Pownall, writing in 1769, said, in a letter quoted by

phrase, the colonists might afford to regard it with contempt; but when the idea began to translate itself into action, it was clear that they had no longer any alternative but slavery or independence. Thirdly, A degree of ignorance amounting to fatuity seems to have existed in this country as to the state of America. That a nation who had just incurred a debt of £2,600,000 in a war undertaken on behalf of the mother country should be expected to pay a revenue into the Home Treasury, seems incredible. Again, nothing is more common in the writings of the time than to find the colonies taxed with ingratitude and unreasonableness for expecting protection, and giving nothing in return. Yet the legislature had itself admitted, by granting compensation for the expenses of the war, that the debt was on the side of England, to say nothing of the benefit derived from the monopoly of the colonial trade. That any rational man should have imagined that America was indebted to England, and not England to America, seems now incredible; yet it was then the opinion of a vast majority of the nation.[1] Equally erroneous ideas obtained in England as to the willingness and capacity of the colonists to resist.[2] They forgot that the Americans were the children of men who had fled into a wilderness from the tyranny of the Stuarts; who had faced savage men and wild beasts rather than endure Laud and Strafford; who had encountered the despotism of James II., not with secret intrigues, not by the treachery of the king's children and favourites, but by the open resistance of New England farmers and

---

Bancroft, vol. vi., p. 267, "We have but one word that is our sovereignty, and it is like some word to a madman which, whenever mentioned, throws him into his ravings, and brings on a paroxysm." See also Franklin's Works, vol. iv., pp. 258-293, 538.

[1] Franklin, vol. iv., p. 292, quotes and animadverts on the statement, occurring in a pamphlet, called "An Inquiry into the Nature and Causes of the Disputes between the British Colonies in America, and the Mother Country,"—"It is very certain that England is entitled to a great deal of gratitude from her colonies." For further remarks on the same subject, see p. 494; vol. v., pp. 85-87.

[2] "The sound of the drum, the piercing squall of the fife, the sight of regular troops without the use of arms, or the thunder of guns, were to frighten the Americans into submission." The Critical Moment, p. 44.

merchants. The ministry and parliament of George III. might be excused if they forgot that Englishmen had ever fought for their liberties, that they ever had liberties to fight for; but the nation cannot be excused for the slanders which it heaped on the loyalty and courage of its own kinsmen. For one hundred years the New England colonies had received no aid in the wars with the Indians;[1] yet in spite of this, in spite of the late war, in spite of their repeated protestations of loyalty, the Americans were commonly regarded as a set of disaffected traitors who were manœuvring for independence, and who only remained loyal for lack of courage to secede. Two causes no doubt contributed to keep the mass of the people ignorant as to the true state of American affairs. The parliament resolutely refused to entertain the petitions of the various assemblies; and the provincial governors, from whose statements the popular ideas about America were derived, systematically traduced and misrepresented the colonists. But, though these facts palliate the guilt of the English nation, they only prove more completely the unfitness of England at that time to be the centre of a great imperial system.

By the more thoughtful in both countries, the relation of the colonists to England was variously regarded. There were those who, like Burke, declined to go into the question of right at all, or like Dickinson, the Pennsylvania farmer, "accepted the undefined relations of the parliament to the colonies as a perpetual compromise, which neither party was to disturb by pursuing an abstract theory to its ultimate conclusions."[2] They must have perceived the anomalies of the existing system; they must have seen that the supremacy of the mother country might at any time, must inevitably at some time, clash with the wellbeing of the unrepresented colonies, but they preferred the known evils of a theoretically imperfect union to the unknown dangers of separa-

---

[1] Franklin's Works, vol. iv., p. 190. Hutchinson, in a letter quoted by Bancroft, vol. v., p. 208.
[2] Bancroft, vol. vi., p. 105.

tion. Others there were who, like Chatham and Otis,[1] passionately loved England and upheld her imperial supremacy, yet thought it possible to reconcile that supremacy with the freedom of the dependencies. The ambition of Chatham's soul was to make England a great imperial power, monopolising the commerce of India and America, and recompensing them for that monopoly by its protection. There were others, both here and in America, less sanguine, but, as the event would seem to prove, more far-seeing. Long before any dispute had arisen, Camden prophesied that the folly of England would one day rob her of her colonies.[2] In America, Henry seems to have understood from the beginning of the struggle that the interests of the two countries were incompatible. No doubt it would have been possible, if England had been temperate and just, to maintain the connection longer, yet some time the rupture must have come. The Americans must have seen, sooner or later, that the right of self-taxation which they claimed was only a part of the larger right of self-government. If England could not tax the colonies because they were unrepresented, on what principle could she involve them in a war, or exercise any of the legislative rights which an imperial state must necessarily claim? That taxation should have been the first point on which the colonies resisted was but natural; it was historically the battle-ground of English liberties. "On this point the ablest and most eloquent tongues had been exercised, the greatest spirits had acted and suffered." The strongest defenders of popular rights in England "took infinite pains to inculcate, as a fundamental principle, that in all monarchies the people must in effect themselves mediately or immediately possess the power of granting their own money, or no shadow of liberty could exist."[3] But sooner or later the contest would have extended to the whole question of government. Nor does it seem likely that the difficulty could have

---

[1] Bancroft, vol. v., p. 202; vol. vi., p. 118. Hutchinson, p. 339.
[2] Franklin's Works, vol. i., p. 373, *note*.
[3] Burke's Speech on Conciliation with America, in his Works, vol. iii., p. 50.

been overcome by a system of colonial representation. Burke has pointed out how impracticable such a scheme must have been,[1] nor is it certain that it would have been acceptable to the colonists. In any case England was utterly unfit to become, as Chatham wished her to be, a centre of a great colonial empire. The whole conduct of the American dispute, from first to last, showed how low and petty were the notions prevalent in this country as to colonial government. It was clear that our colonies were regarded by the aristocracy merely as affording so many places of emolument for their own class, and by the bulk of the nation as a means of increasing their commerce and decreasing their taxation. With provincials of an inferior race, such a system would have been dangerous; with men of English blood, and with English traditions, and with English ideas of liberty, it was impossible. That we have lost for ever the opportunity of displaying to the world a great Anglo-Saxon confederation, bound together by the ties of race, speech, and religion, may indeed be cause for regret; that England, under George III., was no longer permitted to hold a supremacy at once oppressive to the governed and demoralising to herself, can only be matter for thankfulness.

We have already seen that Granville was impolitic enough to give notice of the Stamp Act a year before it was to be put in force. The delay gave the colonists time to concert measures of resistance. They had been forewarned of the danger. Already had the proceedings of the colonists foreshadowed the coming conflict. A month before the news of the bill arrived, Boston, under the leadership of Samuel Adams, had claimed the right of self-taxation. When the news actually came, a statement was drawn up by Otis, and forwarded to the agent in London. New York showed a similar spirit. Her assembly sent an address to the king, a manifesto to the Lords, and a petition to the Com-

---

[1] Burke's Works, vol. iii., pp. 137-141. "It is questionable whether representation, even if practicable, would have been acceptable to the colonists." Franklin's Works, vol. iv., pp. 156-283.

mons. Her citizens vowed to wear only homespun, and to drink no wine until the act was repealed. Massachusetts established a committee of correspondence. Rhode Island followed their example.[1] Nor were the southern colonies backward in resistance. Virginia appealed to the King, the Lords, and the Commons.[2] The assembly of North Carolina claimed the right of self-taxation, and appointed a committee to correspond with Massachusetts.[3] Thus, with one unanimous voice, did the colonies proclaim their intention of resisting the threatened injury. They protested, not against the immediate act of oppression only, but against the principle of arbitrary government. The Navigation Acts, already passed, were oppressive; "their bonds were straitened so much, that America was upon the point of having no trade, either contraband or legitimate. They found, under the construction and execution then used, the act no longer tying, but actually strangling them."[4] Yet they did not put this forward as their main grievance. They wisely saw that the issue was not a mere temporary question of taxation, but the permanent principle of colonial liberty;[5] "non agitur de vectigalibus, libertas in dubio est." Yet the Americans still maintained their loyalty, and it was the opinion of Hutchinson that England could get all she wanted by conciliatory measures.[6] In the true spirit of Englishmen, the colonists, as long as they could find a standing ground of precedent, declined to have recourse to first principles. They appealed to their rights as granted by charter, and claimed to be the subjects of the king, and independent of parliament. They recognised that the parliament and not the king was the

---

[1] Bancroft, vol. v., pp. 197–199, 200–217.   [2] Hutchinson. Appendix B.
[3] Bancroft, vol. v., p. 223.   [4] Burke's Works, vol. ii., p. 392.
[5] Franklin, in January 1768, wrote, "If the parliament has a right thus to take from us a penny in the pound, where is the line drawn that bounds that right, and what shall hinder their calling whenever they please for the other 19s. 11d." Franklin's Works, vol. iv., pp. 158, 159. See also the Instructions of the Electors of Boston to their Representatives. Hutchinson, p. 102. In a letter in a New York paper, signed *Freeman*, the writer says, "It is not the tax, it is the unconstitutional manner of imposing it, that is the great subject of uneasiness to the colonies." Bancroft, vol. v., p. 280.
[6] Bancroft, vol. v., pp. 208, 209.

quarter from which an arbitrary exercise of power was to be feared. On the subject of America, the king and the parliament might be at one, yet as long as such a fiction was tenable, they fell back on the sovereign as an imaginary ally to whom they might appeal against the parliament.

In the meantime, Bernard was urging the Home Government to proceed with their task of colonial reconstruction on a plan which he had been for years maturing. There was to be a civil list, an American nobility, and direct taxation if necessary. The charters were to be abolished and a uniform government substituted by act of parliament.[2] With such an adviser, we can scarcely wonder that in England the remonstrances of the colonists called forth only censure. At the opening of the next session on the 10th January, 1765, the king in his speech, called attention to the American question, as one involving "obedience to the laws and respect for the legislative authority of the kingdom." Both houses echoed this sentiment. In spite of the representations of the colonial agents and the protests of London merchants, who had debts in America to the amount of £4,000,000 the ministry was firm. Grenville was resolved "to establish as undoubted the authority of the British legislature in all cases whatsoever." "The colonies," said Townshend, "are not to be emancipated."[3] On the 6th of February, Grenville brought forward his general scheme. With strange self-deception, he strove to reconcile arbitrary measures with his political principles, by the transparent fallacy that the Americans were really represented, though he himself, had just before been considering a scheme for giving them representatives in parliament. The house was full and acquiesced contentedly in the ministerial policy. Still it did not pass altogether unchallenged. Beckford again protested that "taxing America for the sake of raising a revenue would never do." Townshend repeated the charge of ingratitude. "Will these American children," he said, "planted

---

[1] Franklin's Works, vol. iv., p. 408.   [2] Bancroft, vol. v., pp. 229-231.
[3] Bancroft, vol. v., pp. 200, 201.

by our care, nourished up by our indulgence to a degree of strength and opulence, and protected by our arms, grudge to contribute their mite to relieve us from the heavy burden under which we lie." The charge drew forth a burst of eloquent indignation from Barré—"They planted by *your* care! No; your oppressions planted them in America. . . . . They nourished up by *your* indulgence! They grew up by your neglect of them. . . . . They protected by *your* arms! They have nobly taken up arms in your defence; have exerted a valour amidst their constant and laborious industry for the defence of a country whose frontier was drenched in blood, while its interior parts yielded all its little savings to your emolument. And, believe me—remember I this day told you so—the same spirit of freedom which actuated that people will accompany them still. . . . . The people, I believe, are as truly loyal as any subjects the king has; but a people jealous of their liberties, and who will vindicate them if ever they should be violated." In spite of this opposition, the ministerial motion was carried by two hundred and forty-five to forty-nine.[1]

On the 13th, the stamp bill itself was intoduced. Petitions against it were presented from Jamaica, Virginia, South Carolina, Canada, Massachusetts, and Rhode Island.[2] But the house absolutely refused to receive them. In vain did Conway protest against "shutting their ears to the representations of the colonists." In vain did he ask "to receive from the colonies information by which his judgment might be directed, and his conduct regulated." "The light which I desire," he said, "the colonists alone can give."[3] The very act of petitioning was, as he pointed out, an acknowledgment of supremacy, but it was all in vain. Parliament preferred darkness to light, and recklessly voted away the finances of a country of whose condition it knew

---

[1] The account of this debate is taken from Bancroft, vol. v., pp. 236-242. Lord Mahon, in his "History of England," pp. 130, 131, throws doubts on the authenticity of Barré's speech.

[2] Bancroft, vol. v., pp. 244-246.   [3] Bancroft, vol. v., pp. 244, 245.

nothing. On the 27th, the bill passed the commons, and on the 22d March, it received the royal assent by commission. That there would be any difficulty in carrying it out, does not seem to have occurred to the minds of any of the ministers. Grenville said, five years later, that " he did not foresee the opposition to the measure, and would have staked his life for obedience."[1] Even the friends of America in England anticipated no resistance.[2]

The colonies understood their own spirit better. "They may from present weakness submit to the impositions of ministerial power, but they will certainly hate that power as tyrannical; and as soon as they are able, will throw it off."[3]

Little did the English ministry think that a young Virginian yeoman was destined to set that "ball of revolution" rolling,[4] which would not stop till England and the colonies were separate powers. Patrick Henry may share with the patriots of Massachusetts the honour of having opened the contest of independence. Seldom had boyhood promised less for the future man. Utterly averse to books, "he loved idleness for its own sake," and "ran wild in the forest like one of the aborigines of the wood, dividing his life between the dissipation and uproar of the chase and the languor of inaction." His features were coarse, his speech plain, his dress slovenly. At eighteen, a reckless marriage had driven him to labour on a small farm for his livelihood; at twenty-three, he was bankrupt.[5] Yet with all this, he was upright, temperate, and pious,[6] and under the rude exterior there lay the "perfervidum ingenium" of his Scotch ancestors. Two years before the passing of the Stamp Act, he had won his spurs as a champion of popular liberty, and had sounded the boldest note of defiance to arbitrary power that had been yet

[1] Bancroft, vol. v., p. 252.
[2] In a letter published in his Life, vol. i., p. 294, Franklin says, "We might as well hinder the sun-setting—that we could not do. But since it is down, my friend, and it may be long before it rises again, let us make as good a night of it as we can." Compare Wirt's "Life of Patrick Henry," p. 61.
[3] A New York paper, quoted by Bancroft, vol. v., p. 270.
[4] Expression of Jefferson, quoted by Wirt, p. 59.
[5] Wirt, pp. 22-24, 29-31. [6] Bancroft, vol. v., pp. 417-419.

heard in America. The occasion was a trial about the stipend of the clergy. The Virginian clergy had originally received sixteen thousand pounds of tobacco per annum under a law, which was re-enacted in 1748. In 1755, a short crop was anticipated, and it was settled that the stipend of the clergy, as well as the salaries of all the civil officers, should be commuted for money at a fixed rate of sixteen shillings and eight pence per hundred weight, about one-third of the actual value of tobacco. In 1578, a short crop was again expected, and the assembly, as before, passed an act for commuting the stipend of the clergy. The act was, however, opposed by the Bishop of London, and failed to receive the royal assent. The clergy then proceeded to bring actions for the loss they had sustained by the commutation. A verdict was given in their favour, but a fresh issue was raised and a second trial ensued. Henry was retained against the clergy. His speech was not that of an advocate, but a demagogue. Ignoring the legal merits of the case, he took his stand on the broad principle, that the supreme right of legislation lay in the people, and that the royal sanction was unnecessary. The court rang with cries of "treason" from his opponents, while the multitude who crowded around listened in mixed terror and admiration. The jury awarded the clergy nominal damages, but the verdict was the least result. The spirit of resistance was awakened, and the people had learnt that day that they had rights, and that those rights would not want a defender.[1]

Two years later, Henry was elected to represent Louisa county in the assembly of Virginia. The enforcement of the Stamp Act was drawing nigh, and as yet there had been no sign of resistance. More than half the assembly had gone home, when Henry came forward to defend the cause which he had made his own, "the majesty of the people."[2] He proposed five resolutions :—

1. Declaring that the colonists had brought with them the full rights of Englishmen.

[1] Wirt, pp. 38–47. [2] Wirt, p. 53.

2. That these rights were confirmed by the charters.

3. That these rights implied that they could not be taxed without their own consent.

4. That they had hitherto been uniformly acknowledged and never forfeited.

5. That the general assembly alone can impose taxes, and that the subversion of this right would be destructive not only of American but British freedom.

Two more resolutions were drawn up, but not officially proposed. After a severe contest, Henry carried all his measures. Thinking that all was over, he went home the next day, and the government party took the occasion of his absence to reverse the fifth resolution.[1] But all the resolutions went out to the world, as declaring the mind of Virginia, and in the words of Bernard, "rang the alarum bell" to the rest of America.[2]

It did not sound in vain. On the 6th of June, Otis proposed in the assembly of Massachusetts the calling of a congress, to consist of deputies from the various colonies elected by the delegates of the people.[3] The proposal was accepted, and letters were sent to all the assemblies, advising that a congress should meet on the first Tuesday in October.[4] Yet the proposal at first met with a cold reception. Forty years before, Massachusetts had made a similar suggestion, and it had been forbidden by the home government as mutinous.[5] The assembly of Virginia was forbidden by the governor to meet. New Jersey and New Hampshire declined.[6] At length the proposal of Massachusetts met with a response from South Carolina. "Though one of the weakest, it was the first to listen to the call of its northern brethren in their distresses. Massachusetts sounded the trumpet, but to Carolina is it owing that it was attended to. Had it not been for South Carolina, no congress would then have happened."[7]

---

[1] Wirt, pp. 74–76. Hutchinson. Appendix B.
[2] Letter of Bernard to Halifax. Bancroft, vol. v., p. 278.
[3] Hutchinson, p. 118.   [4] Bancroft, vol. v., p. 280.   [5] Hutchinson, p. 119.
[6] Bancroft, vol. v., pp. 292, 293.
Gadsden, quoted by Bancroft, vol. v., p. 294.

On Monday, October 7th, the delegates of nine colonies met in congress.[1] Union was their principle of action. They no longer took their stand on separate charter rights, but on the higher ground of national independence. They passed resolves, expressing loyalty to the king, and attachment to parliament, claiming the right of fixing their own taxes, both on grounds of equity and precedent, and setting forth the right and necessity of petitioning the king and both houses of parliament. They drew up an address to the king, a memorial to the Lords, and a petition to the Commons, conceived in the same tone of loyalty and submission. To the Commons they said, "We glory in being the subjects of the best of kings, and having been born under the best form of government. . . . . We esteem our connection with and dependence on Great Britain as one of our greatest blessings, and apprehend the latter will appear to be sufficiently secure when it is considered that the inhabitants in the colonies have the most unbounded affection for his majesty's person, family, and government, as well as for the mother country, and that their subordination to the parliament is universally acknowledged." At the same time, they asserted unswervingly their right of self-taxation.[2] Two only of the deputies refused to sign, Ruggles of Massachusetts, and Ogden of New Jersey. Ogden was hung in effigy by the people of New Jersey, and Ruggles censured by the assembly of Massachusetts.[3]

The nation responded to the call of congress. When the Massachusetts assembly met in September, they received a message from Bernard warning them that the attempt to prevent the execution of the Stamp Act might lead to civil war, and that before the petition for repealing the act could even be entertained, the act must be formally acquiesced in. Undeterred, they sent back an answer reasserting all the points urged by the congress, and adopted resolves that all courts should do business without stamps. Bernard, seeing their temper, ad-

---

[1] Bancroft, vol. v., p. 334.   [2] Hutchinson. Appendix F–Y.
[3] Hutchinson, p. 134.

journed them till the next month.[1] When they met again, they passed fourteen resolutions asserting that the colonists had, on the ground of justice and precedent, the same rights as Englishmen; that these rights included self-taxation; that representation in England was impossible; that all attempts in parliament to tax them were infringements of their rights and their charter. Finally, they avowed their loyalty to the king and parliament.[2]

The same spirit pervaded the whole continent. When the "mother of mischiefs,"[3] as Franklin called the Stamp Act, was received in New Hampshire, the ships hung their flags half-mast high, and the bells rang muffled.[4] At Boston, copies of the Stamp Act were hawked about the streets, with a black border and a death's head, as an emblem under the title of "England's Folly and America's Ruin."[5] "Great sir, retreat, or you are ruined," was the address of a New England paper to the king.[6] The very children in the streets learned the cry, "Liberty, property, and no stamps."[7] Pictures of Barré and Conway were hung in Fanueil Hall.[8] Bute, Grenville, Huske, and Oliver were hung in effigy.[9] At New York, a figure of Colden was burnt with the wood of his own state coach.[10] The mob of Boston broke open and sacked Hutchinson's house.[11] Yet no violence was offered to life. Though the cannon at Boston was spiked as a measure of precaution, "not a sword was drawn, not a gun fired."[12] The assembly of Boston offered a reward of £300 for the apprehension of any of the ringleaders in the attack on Hutchinson's house, and £100 for the detection of any one concerned in it. A public meeting of freeholders passed a resolution condemning the proceedings of the mob.[13] In the same spirit, the

[1] Hutchinson, p. 131. The Critical Moment, p. 88.
[2] Hutchinson. Appendix E.   [3] Life of Franklin, vol. i., p. 295.
[4] Annual Register, vol. viii., p. 50. Bancroft, vol. v., p. 352.
[5] Bancroft, vol. v., p. 377.   [6] Annual Register, vol. viii., p. 50.
[7] Bancroft, vol. v., p. 352.   [8] Annual Register, vol. viii., p. 51.
[9] Hutchinson, p. 135. Annual Register, vol. viii., p. 51. The Critical Moment, p. 92.
[10] The Critical Moment, p. 92.   [11] Hutchinson, pp. 124, 145.
[12] Annual Register, vol. viii., p. 52.
[13] Hutchinson, p. 125. Franklin's Works, vol. iv., p. 471.

colonists tried to find legal justification for their resistance. They quoted the authority of Coke and Locke.[1] Everything was done to make the colonies independent of English trade. A society of arts, manufactures, and commerce was formed to encourage native industry. No lamb was eaten. People of the highest class wore homespun. "The spirit of industry and frugality took the place of the spirit of idleness and profusion."[2] It was no longer "the pride of the Americans to indulge in the fashions and manufactures of Great Britain," but "to wear their old clothes over again till they could make new ones."[3] Rather than use stamps, they would suffer trade to stagnate altogether. The stamp distributors were all compelled to resign.[4] Various means were adopted to evade the act. Bark was used instead of paper.[5] "The people's wrath was kindled against the stamped paper as if it were fraught with the seeds of a pestilence or a contagious poison."[6] The governors were at last compelled to yield the point, and allow business to proceed without stamps.[7] It was clear that England would have either to retract or to resort to arms, unless the prophecy of Johnson, the pastor of Lyme, was to be fulfilled: "Such councils ended in Israel in such a revolt and wide breach as could never be healed. That this may end in a similar event is not impossible to the providence of God, nor more improbable to Britons, than five years ago this Stamp Act was to Americans."[8]

Meanwhile a ray of hope for America seemed to have revived in England. "The counsellors of Rehoboam's stamp"[9] were no longer in office. The conduct of Grenville's ministry about the Regency Act had so offended the king that he had even desired Pitt to form a government. Had Temple been willing to take office with his brother-in-law it might have been done. It is generally useless to speculate on what might have been, but it is

---

[1] Bancroft, vol. v., pp. 286, 291, 323.   [2] Annual Register, vol. viii., p. 55.
[3] Franklin's Works, vol. iv., p. 198.   [4] Bancroft, vol. v., pp. 310, 314, 316.
[5] Annual Register, vol. viii., p. 54.   [6] Franklin's Life, vol. i., p. 298.
[7] Annual Register, vol. viii., p. 55.   [8] Bancroft, vol. v., p. 321.
[9] Expression of Johnson, quoted by Bancroft, vol. v., p. 321.

difficult not to think, as Pitt evidently thought,[1] that the scene at Hayes, when Temple refused his brother's overture, was one of the great turning-points of history. Had Pitt then come in with the nation at his back, with the disorganised opposition and a House that was ready, as the next session showed, to make any concessions if it could only hide its own weakness under any decent mask, the defection of the colonies might have been indefinitely postponed. But weaker rulers and a sadder fate were in store for the country.

Still the change of ministers was a distinct gain to the colonies. Rockingham, the new prime minister, had avowed that he would rather repeal a hundred Stamp Acts than run the risk of embroiling England with America,[2] and Conway, the secretary of state, had, in the Stamp Act debates, shown himself willing to listen to the appeals of the colonies. In January of the following year petitions were presented from the merchants of London, Bristol, and Glasgow to both houses of parliament, representing the great injury which the Stamp Act would inflict on the commerce of the kingdom, and praying for its repeal.[3] In the same month the ministers made overtures to Pitt. He had not forgotten the treachery of Newcastle, and refused to act with the government, but appeared in the House of Commons as an independent member, as he said himself, "single, unsolicited, and unconnected."[4] He took for his standing point the constitutional Whig doctrine that taxation and representation were inseparable; that commercial restrictions were just, but the direct taxation in the case of America was justified neither by law or equity. "I rejoice," he said, "that America has resisted. If its millions of inhabitants had submitted, taxes would soon have been laid on Ireland; and if ever this nation should have a tyrant for its king, six millions of freemen, so dead to all feelings of liberty as voluntarily to submit to be slaves, would be fit instruments to make slaves of others." He pointed out the meagre results

[1] Bancroft, vol. v., 298.
[2] Bancroft, vol. v., p. 365.
[3] Annual Register, vol. ix., p. 34.
[4] Bancroft, vol. v., p. 383.

which the tax could at best produce, and the danger of enforcing it. He warned them "that in such a cause their success would be hazardous. America, *if* she fell, would fall like the strong man, she would embrace the pillars of the state, and pull down the constitution along with her."[1] In spite of these representations the ministry, before the end of the month, brought in a resolution, to the effect, "that the king in parliament has full power to bind the colonies and the people of America in all cases whatsoever."[2] When the resolutions came before the Lords, Camden, following the example of Pitt, pointed out the injustice and impolicy of their proceedings, and reminded them how Spain, by her obstinacy, lost the low countries. When the Lords divided, Camden, Shelburne, and three others, voted against the resolution, while one hundred and twenty-five supported it. In the Commons the same spirit prevailed. Pitt, Barré, and Beckford in vain pointed out the injustice, the folly, and the hoplessness of the measure, and at the division there were not ten voices to confirm their protest.[3] The ministry, however, though they agreed with the Tory party in maintaining the right to tax, differed from them as to the practical expediency of enforcing it. On the 7th of February it became known that the ministry intended to move the repeal of the Act. That same night Grenville brought forward a motion for enforcing all the American Acts. Pitt, availing himself of the declared policy of the ministry, pointed out to the House the unreasonableness of carrying out measures, the repeal of which was shortly to be the subject of discussion, and for the first time the enemies of America were defeated in a full house.[4] All the evidence that was laid before parliament pointed to the hopelessness of the enforcement. On the 11th, Trecothick was examined at the bar of the House of Commons. "Will the Americans acquiesce," he was asked, "if this act is mitigated?" "No modification will reconcile them to it," he said, "nor will anything satisfy them less than its

[1] Bancroft, vol. v., pp. 383–395.   [2] Bancroft, vol. v., p. 401.
[3] Bancroft, vol. v., pp. 404, 413–417.   [4] Bancroft, vol. v., pp. 422–424.

total repeal."[1] Two days afterwards Franklin was examined. He corroborated Trecothick's statement. When asked, "Do you think the people of America would submit to pay the stamp duty if it was moderated?" "No," he answered, "never, unless compelled by force of arms." He showed that the colonies had sufficient internal resources for their own support, and scouted the idea that they could be starved into submission. At the same time he reminded the house that till the Stamp Act the colonies had been attached to the mother country, and loyal and obedient to parliament, and that they had always acquiesced in commercial restrictions imposed by England, considering an excise duty only a legitimate return for the protection afforded to their trade. He pointed out, too, that America had borne its share in the expenses of the late war.[2]

The time had come when the ministry saw that if they would not commit themselves to the "thorough" policy of Townshend, they must yield. On the 20th of February, Conway moved for leave to bring in a bill for the repeal, and on the 22d July a division took place. The Stamp Act was repealed by a majority of one hundred and eight in a house of four hundred and forty-two.[3] Eight years later, Burke described "with melancholy pleasure" the scene of that night; how "the whole trading interest of the empire, crammed into the lobbies of the House with a trembling and anxious expectation, waited their fate almost to a winter's return of light;" how "from the whole of that grave multitude there arose an involuntary burst of gratitude and transport. They jumped upon Conway like children on a long absent father; they clung about him as captives about their redeemer; all England, all America, joined to his applause."[4] The ministry unhappily marred the boon by bringing in, and passing at the same time, an act declaratory of their right to tax the colonies. In the Lords the repeal act passed, though not without violent

---

[1] Bancroft, vol. v., p. 424.
[2] Franklin's examination, as given in his Works, vol. iv., pp. 161-199.
[3] Bancroft, vol. v., pp. 434-436.   [4] Burke's Works, vol. ii., p. 434.

K

opposition, by a majority of thirty-four. The declaratory act passed both houses, in spite of the attacks of Pitt and Camden.[1] On the 18th of March the acts received the royal assent, and the unity of the empire was respited. The king returned from Westminster amid the cheers of the multitude. Bow Bells rang. The friends of America testified their pleasure by a public dinner. The ships on the river hoisted their colours, and at night the city was illuminated.[2] In America, the joy at the news was not alloyed by any fears for the future. South Carolina voted a statue to Pitt, and Virginia one to the king, and an obelisk to the defenders of American freedom.[3] In Boston the houses were hung with banners by day, and were illuminated by night. Liberty-tree was lit up, and figures of the king, of Pitt, Barré, and Camden were exhibited. Debtors were released by public subscriptions. In the words of the colonists themselves, "they had escaped like a bird from the net of the fowler."[4] The declaratory act and the mutiny act were overlooked in their gratitude, and Bernard himself was compelled to acknowledge "their good humour, temper, and moderation."[5]

This unbroken sunshine was not to last long. In the same month a dispute arose between Bernard and the assembly about the election of the council. The assembly, exercising their right of election, rejected all the government officers. Bernard resisted this, and endeavoured to coerce the assembly; but they reasserted their right, and maintained it successfully.[6] In other matters, Massachusetts showed that the cessation of danger had not extinguished the spirit of liberty. The assembly threw the debates open to the public. Following up the congress of last year, they proposed a conference of delegates, and actually established a committee of correspondence.[7] When petitions were made by sufferers from the Stamp Act disturbances, discussion

[1] Bancroft, vol. v., pp. 444-450.
[2] Bancroft, vol. v., p. 454.
[3] Wirt, p. 86. Bancroft, vol. v., p. 457.
[4] Bancroft, vol. v., p. 458.
[5] Franklin's Works, vol. iv., p. 476.
[6] Bancroft, vol. vi., pp. 10-12.
[7] Hutchinson, p. 166.

arose. In the course of it, Hawley, the member for Northampton, used the ominous words, "The parliament of Great Britain has no right to legislate for us."[1]

The hopes of a more liberal system which the late measures of parliament had encouraged were gradually overcast. On the 25th of August the Rockingham government went out, and it was left to Pitt to form an administration. As before, Temple refused to join him.[2] He had to form a ministry of the most incongruous materials, as Burke described it, "a mosaic of patriots and courtiers, king's friends and republicans, Whigs and Tories, treacherous friends and open enemies."[3] Townshend was Chancellor of the Exchequer, and in him Pitt let in one who was destined to thwart his most cherished designs, to betray his ministry, and to plunge his party into disgrace and confusion. For the present, however, America was in the hands of Shelburne, the only statesman perhaps who was fitted for the post. His moderate and conciliatory tone won the heart of the colonies, and when he requested the assembly of Massachusetts to settle their local differences as far as they could, they gladly acceded, and voted a grant of compensation.[4] But Shelburne's moderation made him odious to the king, and when ill-health drove Chatham into retirement, the colonies were left at the mercy of Townshend. On the 26th of January he took advantage of Chatham's absence to declare his colonial policy. In reply to Granville, who complained that the scheme for colonial revenue had been frustrated, Townshend pledged himself, amid the applause of the house, to bring forward a scheme of American taxation. "I am still," he said, "a firm advocate for the Stamp Act, for its principle, and for the duty itself, only the heats which prevailed made it an improper time to press it. I laugh at the absurd distinction between internal and external taxes. I know no such distinction. It is a distinction without a difference; it is perfect nonsense; if we have a right to impose the one, we

---

[1] Bancroft, vol. vi., p. 38. [2] Bancroft, vol. vi., p. 20.
[3] Burke's Works, vol. ii., p. 420. [4] Bancroft, vol. vi., p. 40.

have the right to impose the other; the distinction is ridiculous in the opinion of everybody except the Americans." And turning to the colonial agents in the gallery,—" I speak this aloud, that all you who are here in the galleries may hear me; and after this I do not expect to have my statue erected in America." And when Granville taunted the ministry with cowardice in not daring to tax America, he instantly rebutted the charge by pledging himself to the measure.[1]

Thus the repeal of the Stamp Act was reversed at a simple stroke by the treachery of an unprincipled politician, and the name and authority of Chatham were used to sanction measures which, less than a year ago, he had risen from his sick-bed to resist. On the head of Townshend, more than of any other man, rests the crime of having driven the colonies into rebellion. Others might plead ignorance, he could not; or if he was misled by ignorance, it was wanton and wilful ignorance—the ignorance, not of stupidity, but of levity and recklessness. Granville was a bigot to his commercial creed; the king was a bigot to his doctrine of prerogative, but Townshend could urge no such defence. Of him Burke said, "Perhaps there never arose in this country, nor in any country, a man of a more pointed and finished wit; and, where his passions were not concerned, of a more refined, exquisite, and penetrating judgment."[2] But he was a slave to that miserable form of ambition, a love of preeminence for its own sake, scarcely to be called ambition, since it lacked all sense of the value and duties of power, and to gratify that passion, he was alike ready to betray a party, or to endanger an empire.

With such an opponent in the cabinet, and with the king for his enemy, Shelburne, though supported by Chatham, could do little. Everything looked more hopeless than ever. Camden had gone over to the supporters of authority. Rockingham

---

[1] My authorities for this are, Bancroft, vol. vi., pp. 46-49; Wirt, p. 96, and Cooke's "History of Party," vol. iii., pp. 91, 92.

[2] Burke's Works, vol. ii., p. 422.

regarded America as a mere party question. Conway stood firm, but was without influence or energy.[1] On the 13th of May, Townshend, on behalf of the government, brought forward his policy for America. The main features of his scheme were,— 1. That New York was to be punished for its disregard of the Billetting Act by being deprived of all legislative power. 2. Port duties were to be levied on Spanish exports, on glass, and other commodities, and especially on tea. 3. The revenue thus obtained was to be placed at the king's disposal, and a civil list established. The plan was received with general approbation. Yet Burke said prophetically, "You will never see a single shilling from America," and Beckford, the constant friend of the colonies, bade the ministry " do, like the best of physicians, heal the disease by doing nothing."[2]

When the news reached America, the spirit of resistance, which had been temporarily laid, re-awakened. "The Rubicon," they said, "is past." " Such counsels will deprive the prince who now sways the British sceptre of millions of free subjects."[3] The disfranchisement of New York in particular warned them on how frail a basis their liberties rested. "The language of the act seems to them to be,—Obey implicitly laws made by the parliament of Great Britain to raise money on you without your consent, or you shall enjoy no rights or privileges at all."[4] Appeals to the law of nature began to be heard.[5] Yet even so they blamed only the ministry and the parliament, and declared themselves, as ever, loyal to England and the king.

Massachusetts, as before, was the first colony to take active measures. In January 1768, they drew up with great care, under the guidance of Samuel Adams, a statement of their case, to be

[1] Townshend said of him at this time, "Conway is below low water mark." Bancroft, vol. vi., p. 64.
[2] Bancroft, vol. vi., p. 75–79.   [3] Bancroft, vol. vi., pp. 97, 98.
[4] Franklin's Works, vol. iv., pp. 447. Hutchinson, p. 171.
[5] Bancroft, vol. vi., p. 102. It is curious to trace the gradual manner in which the Americans shifted their position from the technical and legal ground of charters and constitutional rights to wider ground of equity and natural law. Compare Franklin's Life, vol. i., pp. 307–310.

communicated to the ministry, and laid before the world.[1] They accompanied this with letters to the ministers, and an address to the king. Their next step showed their caution, and, to some extent, the unformed nature of their schemes. It was proposed that circular letters should be sent to the other colonies, apprising them of the steps which Massachusetts had taken. But it was feared that this proposal would be looked upon with suspicion in England, and it was rejected by a large majority. The motion, however, was again brought forward on the 4th of February, and the former vote reversed. A circular letter was drawn up and forwarded to all the colonial assemblies.[2] Meanwhile the burgesses of Virginia had passed resolutions affirming the right of the Americans to be taxed only by their own assemblies. At the same time, they drew up a petition to the king, a memorial to the House of Lords, and a remonstrance to the House of Commons, which were unanimously adopted. Besides this, they not only expressed their sense of the service which Massachusetts had rendered to American liberties, but followed their example by directing their speaker to communicate their proceedings to the speakers of all the assemblies, and to intimate to them the necessity of resistance. New Jersey, Connecticut, and New York all followed the example set by Virginia, and expressed their sympathy with Massachusetts.[3]

But English government was doing more to accelerate colonial independence than any of the assemblies. The 18th of March, the anniversary of the repeal of the Stamp Act, was celebrated at Boston with a temperate festival; as Hutchinson described it, "We had only such a mob as we have long been used to on the 5th of November, and other holidays." Bernard, however, who was a coward as well as a knave, represented it as "a great disposition to the utmost disorder," and made his helpless state a ground for demanding troops.[4] Hillsborough, who had succeeded Shelburne, deceived by Bernard's representations, had given

---

[1] Bancroft, vol. vi., pp. 119-122. [2] Bancroft, vol. vi., pp. 124, 125.
[3] Bancroft, vol. vi., pp. 149, 150. [4] Bancroft, vol. vi., pp. 133-135.

orders to Gage, the commander of troops in America, to quarter a regiment at Boston. The admiralty was at the same time directed to send one frigate, two sloops, and two cutters to remain in Boston harbour, and the castle of William and Mary was to be repaired and occupied.[1] But before these orders arrived, the outrageous conduct of the government officers at Boston had resulted in violence. A ship of fifty guns, the Romney, had been sent from Halifax, at the request of the commissioners of the customs, to lie in the harbour, and its captain had pressed New England seamen in direct defiance of a statute. Shortly after this, the excise officers had seized a sloop, the property of John Hancock, a leading merchant, with circumstances of violence, and had unnecessarily called the Romney to their assistance. A riot ensued, magnified by the partizans of government, into an insurrection.[2] While men's minds were thus inflamed, a letter came from Hillsborough to Bernard with reference to the petition, and other documents, which had been sent over by the assembly in February.[3] The petition had been received by Hillsborough, but was never presented to the king. The letter to Bernard contained instructions to the effect that he should order the assembly to rescind the circular letter; should they refuse to do so, to dissolve them, and to dissolve them repeatedly as long as they should hold out. The governors of the other provinces were instructed to use their influence to prevent the assemblies from entertaining the proposals made in the circular letter.[4] Accordingly, Bernard called on the assembly to rescind. It was a critical question; the existence of the legislature was at stake. The assembly recognised the importance of the occasion, and refused to rescind by ninety-two votes against seventeen. Bernard, in obedience to instructions, dissolved them.[5]

In the mean time, the news of the riots had reached England,

---

[1] Bancroft, vol. vi., p. 153.
[2] Franklin's Works, vol. iv., pp. 481, 482. Bancroft, vol. vi., pp. 154–157.
[3] Bancroft, vol. vi., p. 163. [4] Bancroft, vol. vi., pp. 143–145.
[5] Hutchinson, pp. 195–197.

and it was determined that Massachusetts should be made an example to the other colonies. Town meetings were to be stopped; two more regiments and a frigate were to be sent, and if any person had committed treason under the statute of Henry VIII., he was to be brought over to England for trial.[1] About the same time, a non-importation meeting had been held in Boston; the citizens had pledged themselves to dispense with imported superfluities, and committees of correspondence had been established to further this arrangement throughout the country. The anniversary of the resignation of the tax collectors was celebrated by processions singing patriotic songs.[2] In September, the people of Boston took the most decided measure that had yet been adopted. Bernard had prorogued the assembly, and had refused to summon it. Adams had already striven to familiarise the people with the idea of a democratic government. On the 22d of September, Otis, Adams, and Warren called a town meeting at Fanueil Hall. Four hundred muskets, the property of the town, were deposited there, and these, Otis announced, would be distributed between the citizens when needed. The inhabitants then proposed that a convention of delegates should meet at Fanueil Hall to supply the place of the assembly. Representatives of the town were elected, and were requested to send a circular through the province to give notice of the scheme. A public vote was then passed that the inhabitants should provide themselves with arms and ammunition. Finally, a letter was read, announcing that New York had joined in the non-importation agreement.[3] On the 22d of September, the convention, consisting of the representatives of ninety-six towns and eight districts, met and requested the governor to call an assembly. He refused, and admonished them to disperse, an admonition which they treated with contempt. They then renewed their petition to the king, remonstrating against taxation, against a standing army, and against a civil list, and, after a session of six days, dis-

---

[1] Bancroft, vol. vi., pp. 177, 178. [2] Hutchinson, pp. 201, 202.
[2] Bancroft, vol. vi., pp. 196-199. Hutchinson, pp. 203-205.

solved.¹ The council, in the meantime, led by Bowdoin, a political ally of Adams,² had been equally jealous of the rights of the state. Bernard had ordered the council to take measures, quartering two regiments, expected from Halifax, in the city, pleading Gage's orders. The council refused to entertain the proposal, and took their stand on an act of parliament which required the civil officers to "quarter and billet the officers and soldiers in his Majesty's service in the barracks; and only in case there was not sufficient room in the barracks, to find other quarters for the residue of them." On the 28th of September, the squadron from Halifax arrived, and on the 1st of October, the quartering order was to be executed. The troops marched into the town; Dalrymple, their commander, blustered; Hutchinson cried out at the folly and ingratitude of the citizens; Gage and Bernard grumbled; but the council was firm, and none of the officers dared to transgress the act of parliament.³ "They act with the highest wisdom and spirit; they will extricate themselves with firmness and magnanimity," said a friend of the Americans in London, when he heard of the proceedings at Boston.

Yet, generally, the moderate temper they had shown was taken as a symptom of weakness. Had they resorted to arms and violence they would have been dangerous rebels; as they preferred to trust to law and endurance they were cowardly rebels. All the worst passions of Englishmen were aroused, and nothing but a servile submission would have satisfied them. "America must fear England before she loves her" were Lord North's words in parliament, and he pledged himself never to repeal the objectionable acts till he saw "America prostrated at his feet."⁴ On the 7th of December Beckford and Trecothick moved for a general inquiry into the state of America in preference to special proceedings against Boston. The motion was lost by one hundred and twenty-seven votes against seventy-three, and it was deter-

---

¹ Bancroft, vol. vi., pp. 203-205.
² Hutchinson, p. 293.
³ Bancroft, vol. iv., pp. 201-211.
⁴ Bancroft, vol. vi., pp. 232, 233.

mined that Boston was to be the victim.[1] Yet as little hold had the "incendiaries" given, and so insecure was the ground occupied by the ministry, that no decisive measures were taken. In the Lords, Hillsborough denounced and threatened, and brought forward resolutions, but nothing effective was done. "The ministry," said Choiseul, "covers pusillanimity and fear under the semblance of vigour." Granville scoffed at the resolutions as "angry words."[2] Six months passed, and the English legislature did nothing, either towards coercion or conciliation. The ministers feared equally to use the powers they claimed, or to renounce them. The right of taxing America was like a rusty cannon which they did not dare to fire for fear of the recoil, while they were unwilling to confess their weakness by dismounting it.

On the first of May the ministry came to a decision. They were unanimously resolved to repeal all Townshend's duties, except that on tea. On that the cabinet divided. It produced less than £300 a-year. Should they, for that "paltry sum, lose the affection of two millions of people?" The king, speaking by the mouth of Lord North, gave an affirmative, and the duty remained.[3] The ministry thus threw away its last hope of conciliation. The battle-field was narrowed, but the colonies were not deceived into imagining that the strife was less real. Nor was the ministerial policy of separating the colonies by selecting Boston for their special victim more successful. The assembly of Virginia passed resolutions claiming the sole right of taxation, and denouncing a proposal to try Americans in England. The governor thereupon dissolved them. But, following the precedent of Massachusetts, they met again on their own responsibility, and agreed to a series of non-importation resolves. Delaware and all the southern colonies followed their example.[4] True to the policy in which Massachusetts had led the way they

---

[1] Bancroft, vol. vi., pp. 239, 240.
[2] Bancroft, vol. vi., pp. 245, 246, 254.
[3] Bancroft, vol. vi., pp. 276-278.
[4] Bancroft, vol. vi., pp. 280-282.

"took care of themselves, not by resisting the laws, but by rendering these laws ineffectual in their application."[1]

In Boston itself both parties preserved the same attitude. Bernard, Gage, and Hutchinson were all utterly wanting in resolution, and were glad to defer a struggle, the issue of which they in their hearts distrusted, while the people was obedient to its leaders, who saw that their Fabian policy must in the end be successful.[2] Yet there was no sign of concession. At the election of representatives eighty-one out of the ninety-two who had voted against rescinding the resolutions at the command of Hillsborough were returned.[3] At a town meeting a motion was objected to as implying independence of parliament, upon which Adams said, "Independent we are and independent we will be." The non-importation agreements were rigidly kept. Those who refused to observe them were socially excommunicated.[4] Hutchinson himself, and his sons, who had subscribed to the agreement, and afterwards violated it, were compelled to make restitution. The consignees of tea were compelled to reload it and ship it to England, while the soldiers looked on.[5] When Bernard announced that all the duties, except that on tea, had been repealed, the merchants held a meeting, and declared the concession insufficient. Bernard's departure was celebrated with public rejoicing, bells were rung and cannon fired; flags were hoisted on liberty-tree, and a bonfire lighted on Fort-hill.[6] He carried with him the contempt and hatred of all. He had been true to no party. He had schemed against the people, and slandered them while he professed himself their friend. He had advocated arbitrary rule while he avowed his loyalty to the constitution. His dishonesty and avarice had disgraced the

[1] Franklin's Life, vol. i., p. 322.
[2] "It was an evidence of the influence the mob was under, and that they might have been let loose, or kept up just as their leaders thought fit." Hutchinson, p. 136.
[3] Hutchinson, p. 230. [4] Hutchinson, pp. 265, 268, 269.
[5] History of War of Independence in the Massachusetts' "Collection," 1st series, vol. ii., p. 44. Bancroft, vol. vi., p. 311.
[6] Hutchinson, p. 254. Bancroft, vol. vi., pp. 290–292.

home government. Even as a tool of tyranny the ministry found him worthless, and after his return to England he was hated and shunned by all honest men.¹ Yet his puny animosity had failed to do harm. "He has essentially served us," said a New England clergyman; "had he been wise our liberties might have been lost."²

Occasionally the mob broke out in violence. An informer was tarred and feathered, and an obnoxious printer had his shop sacked.³ But there was nothing like united or organised opposition to authority. It was left for the preservers of law and order to set the example of riot. The mere presence of the soldiers was an annoyance to the quiet inhabitants of Boston.⁴ The noise of drums and fifes broke in rudely upon the sober semi-puritan Sunday.⁵ Cannon were pointed at the door of the room in which the assembly were sitting. One of the officers was detected inciting the negroes to revolt.⁶ One of the regiments quartered was notoriously dissolute and overbearing. A soldier was repeatedly heard to declare that he would never miss an opportunity of firing upon the inhabitants. Yet the citizens confined themselves strictly to legal measures. When a captain gave orders to his men to run any one through the body who touched them he was indicted. At New York the soldiers had provoked the people by cutting down their liberty-pole. Riots ensued, in which the people had the advantage. Shortly after, an informer in Boston was pelted by a mob of boys. He fired among them and killed one. At the funeral the citizens of all ranks followed in solemn procession.⁷ On Friday, the 2d of March, a quarrel arose between the soldiers and some rope-makers, in which the soldiers were beaten. On Monday night the soldiers patrolled the streets,

---

¹ General Oglethorpe drove Bernard out of the Smyrna Coffee-House in London, telling him he was "a dirty, factious scoundrel, who smelt cursed strong of the hangman." A letter in the *Pennsylvania Gazette*, August 30, 1770, quoted by Wirt, p. 99.
² Bancroft, vol. vi., p. 291.   ³ Hutchinson, p. 259.
⁴ Wirt, p. 97.   ⁵ Hutchinson, p. 234.
⁶ Franklin's Works, vol. iv., pp 484–486.
⁷ Bancroft, vol. vi., pp. 314, 331-3 4.

insulting and striking the citizens. Towards midnight a party of them turned out with their arms, rushed about the streets "like madmen in a fury," laying about them with sticks and sheathed cutlasses. At last the disturbance was quieted by the interference of some of the officers and citizens, amongst them a mulatto, Crispus Attucks. Later, however, more soldiers came, and were surrounded and taunted by the mob. At last one of the crowd struck a soldier's musket with his stick. The word "fire" was given; the soldier raised his piece and shot Attucks, who was quietly looking on. The people immediately retreated, but the soldiers continued to fire on them deliberately. Three persons were killed and eight wounded, two mortally. The bells rang in all the churches, the town drums beat. The citizens flocked into the street; everywhere the stains of bloods on the newly-fallen snow met their view. Had the citizens been the "rebels and incendiaries" which their enemies called them, and had been striving to make them, it would have gone hard with every English officer and soldier in Boston. When, however, the troops were confined to the barracks, and Preston, who had given the order to fire, and the soldiers implicated, had been arrested, the mass of the people dispersed, leaving about a hundred on guard.

The next morning delegates were sent from the town-meeting to Hutchinson to demand the immediate withdrawal of the troops. Hutchinson attempted to terrify them by reminding them that to attack the troops would be treason. They renewed their demand and withdrew. By the military instructions for America it was specially provided that in the absence of any officer, above the rank of brigadier, the governor of the province might give orders to the troops. Accordingly, acting on this power, he ordered the 29th regiment, which had especially been implicated in the disturbance, to withdraw to the castle, and retained the 14th, under efficient restraint, in the town. This did not satisfy the townsmen. A committee headed by Samuel Adams, waited on the governor and demanded the withdrawal of the second regiment. Hutchinson yielded, and "troops who had come to overawe the people, and maintain the laws, were sent as law-breakers to a prison rather than a garrison." "There," said Burke, "was an end of the spirited way we took when the question was whether Great Britain should or should not govern America."[1]

As Boston had won its triumph by patience, so it used it with moderation. In order that Preston should have every opportunity of a fair trial, John Adams and Quincy undertook his cause, and when he was acquitted, the people, though they dissented from the verdict, acquiesced in it;[2] "an instance of great temper and equity in a people so exasperated."[3] These were the men of whom Lord North had not scrupled to say in parliament, "the trumpeters of sedition have produced disaffection; the drunken raggamuffins of a vociferous mob are exalted into equal importance with men of judgment, morals, and property," adding, with truth, "the contest in America, which might at first have been easily ended, is now for no less than sovereignty on one side and independence on the other."[4]

On the very day when the victims of British misrule were being buried in Boston, the affairs of America were under the consideration of parliament. It was fully decided to repeal all the duties except that on tea. Of the propriety of a total repeal no thinking man had a doubt. Lord North, in his heart, saw the necessity of it.[5] The parties of Granville and Rockingham were prepared to unite, on the ground that a policy of conciliation once commenced ought to be thoroughly carried out.[6] One man alone was resolved against it, and that man's will ruled the British parliament. The king was determined that there should be no complete concession till America had submitted, and the tea duty remained. Further deliberations on American affairs ensued. Hillsborough was for prompt action; North, humane

---

[1] This account of the massacre is taken from Bancroft, vol. vi., pp. 334-347.
[2] Bancroft, vol. vi., pp. 350, 373, 374. [3] Franklin's Works, vol. iv., p. 486.
[4] Bancroft, vol. vi., p. 322. [5] Bancroft, vol. vi., p. 354.
[6] Annual Register, vol. xii., p. 52.

THE CONTEST FOR INDEPENDENCE. 159

and moderate, though against his better nature the instrument of tyranny, was for waiting, in the belief that the non-importation covenants would fail.[1] There was foresight in the calculation. In nearly all the colonies there had been an evasion of the agreements. Chests had been secretly unpacked and reshipped, filled with rubbish.[2] Rhode Island had imported secretly. Maryland and Virginia had done the same. New England and Pennsylvania had diminished but not cut off their imports. One state alone, New York, had been perfectly true to its engagements.[3] Recriminations ensued, and for a time the motto, "join or die," which had hitherto guided them, seemed to have been forgotten. The people of New York naturally objected to having the burthen of taxation exclusively thrown upon their shoulders, and when it was announced that the tea duty was the only one remaining, New York made overtures to Pennsylvania to resume importation. Pennsylvania, like New York, smuggled nearly all its tea from Holland, and was at first inclined to entertain the proposal, till dissuaded by a letter from Franklin.[4] At length New York resolved to break through the agreement against importation. The packet sailed to England with orders for goods, and the non-importation agreement fell to the ground. Tea alone remained a prohibited commodity.[5]

On the other points the spirit of the Americans was as fixed as ever. Hutchinson tried to remove the assembly from Boston to Cambridge, and pleaded various precedents for so doing. In 1721, he said, Governor Shute had removed the assembly to Cambridge on account of the small pox, but the next year had refused to allow the assembly itself to give a similar order, proving that the removal was at the discretion of the governor. Six years later there had been a dispute upon Governor Burnet attempting to remove the assembly to Salem, but since then, according to Hutchinson, it had always been allowed that the

---

[1] Bancroft, vol. vi., p. 363.   [2] Hutchinson, pp. 330, 331.
[3] Annual Register, vol. xvii., p. 45. Hutchison, p. 261, n. Bancroft, vol. vi., p. 365.
[4] Hutchinson, p. 331.   [5] Bancroft, vol. vi., p. 366.

governor had the right of removing the assembly at his own discretion.¹ Another dispute arose when Hutchinson received orders from Gage to give up Fort William to Dalrymple. It was provided in the charter that the governor should have command of the colonial militia and forts. Consequently to eject the militia, and garrison the fort with regular troops, was a distinct violation of the charter.² The assembly protested in vain, but Hutchinson felt so much alarmed after he had done it that he slept at the castle every night for the next week.³

Massachusetts was not the only colony where arbitrary power had been arrested and defied. The lieutenant of a government ship, the Gaspee, had defied the governor of Rhode Island. His proceedings were sanctioned by the admiral at Boston. Emboldened by this he was guilty of various outrages, insulting and plundering the inhabitants and making illegal seizures. In one of these attempts the Gaspee ran aground. The inhabitants availed themselves of the opportunity to board her and set her on fire.⁴

During the whole of the present year [1772] a kind of intermittent warfare was kept up between the citizens and the governor. An order was sent out to exempt the commissioners of customs from taxation. The assembly resisted, but Hutchinson negatived their measures.⁵ The clergy avowed themselves the friends of freedom by omitting in the annual proclamation of a thanksgiving day, to enumerate among the public mercies, as was usual, the continuance of civil and religious liberty.⁶ At the election the governor's party exerted themselves to prevent Adams from being returned as member for the town, but the attempt only united the party of liberty more closely.¹ But the

---

¹ Hutchinson, pp. 298, 300–307.   ² Hutchinson, p. 319.
³ Bancroft, vol. vi., p. 370.
⁴ History of the War of Independence, in Massachusetts' "Historical Collection," 1st series, vol. ii., p. 72. Annual Register, vol. xvii., p. 45. Bancroft, vol. vi., pp. 417, 418.
⁵ Bancroft, vol. vi., pp. 403–405.   ⁶ Hutchinson, pp. 347, 348.
⁷ Hutchinson, p. 356.

most decisive measure of all was a resolution passed by the assembly, by a majority of eighty-five to nineteen, setting forth that the payment of the governor and the civil officers, by warrants given by the crown, was a violation of the charter. A month later it was announced that provision had been made by the king for the payment of the law officers.[1] This was tantamount to making the judges entirely independent of the people, and, coupled with the assertion of the right to tax, was a complete overthrow of civil liberty. Adams saw how much was at stake. "We are at a crisis," he said; "this is a moment to decide whether our posterity shall inherit liberty or slavery.[2] On the 2d of November, Adams moved at a town meeting for a committee of correspondence to publish the infringements of their rights in the province itself, and in the other colonies.[3] On the 20th of November, the committee laid a statement before the town meeting, enumerating all their grievances. The assumption of absolute power by the British parliament; the exertion of that power to raise a colonial revenue; the appointment of officers, unknown to the charter, to collect the revenue; the unconstitutional authority with which these officers were invested; the establishment of a standing army and a civil list; the oppressive use of royal instructions; the excessive power of the vice-admiralty courts; the restrictions on colonial industry; the threat of trying the Americans in England; the claim of a right to establish a bishop and episcopal courts; the alteration of the colonial boundaries, and the facility which this gave to rapacious governors of extorting money for fresh grants. They then resolved to make an appeal to all the towns in the province. The inhabitants answered to their call. From little inland towns and fishing villages, "infant people in an infant country," who did not "think their answer perfect in spelling, or the words placed," came the cry of liberty. To raise the spirit of

---

[1] Hutchinson, pp. 358–360. Annual Register, vol. xvii., p. 45. Bancroft, vol. vi., p. 420.
[2] Bancroft, vol. vi., p. 426.   [3] Bancroft, vol. vi., p. 429.

resistance yet higher, news came that those who had burnt the Gaspee were to be sent over to England for trial. The people of Rhode Island turned to Adams for assistance, and he told them that the occasion "should awaken the American colonies, and again unite them in one bond; that an attack upon the liberties of one colony was an attack upon the liberties of all, and that, therefore, in this instance, all should be ready to lend assistance."[1]

In Virginia, a still greater contest had arisen, a contest the issue of which was to affect the fate of America and the world in distant ages. The Virginians had resolved to free their state from the curse of slavery. Already the rapid increase of the slaves had become a source of danger. Almost the earliest incident in Jefferson's political career had been to bring in a bill of emancipation. But the legislature considered that the first step to be taken was to suppress the slave trade. Repeated acts had been passed for this purpose, but in every case they had been disallowed. On the 10th of December 1770, the king issued an instruction under his own hand, commanding the governor, upon pain of the highest displeasure, to assent to no law by which the importation of slaves should be in any respect prohibited or obstructed. In 1772, this order was discussed by the assembly, and it is difficult not to believe that, in considering the question, the Virginians were not contemplating the possibility of a war of independence. Finally, it was decided to send an address to the king, setting forth the inhumanity of the trade, and the pernicious influence which it exercised on the settlement of the colony. The petition was ignored, and the officers of the crown were instructed to maintain the slave trade, if any attempt should be made to interfere with it.[2] For nearly a hundred years from that time, negro slavery continued to be the curse of America. It locked the door of material and intellectual progress on a whole race; it made a nation of civilised men into a nation of tyrants. Its evils did not end there. It polluted the chief

[1] Bancroft, vol. vi., pp. 432-434, 439-441.   [2] Bancroft, vol. vi., pp. 413-416.

springs of the community's well-being. It made industry despised; it marred the sanctity of family life. Ere it could be overthrown, a great empire was well-nigh rent asunder. When these things are remembered, it should be remembered, too, that there was a time when the demon of slavery lay bound and helpless, and that an English king stepped in and set it free.

On the 4th of March 1773, the assembly of Virginia met to consider the proposal of Massachusetts for committees of correspondence. Carr, a patriot whom the fates but showed to the world, but whose name was worthy to be linked with those of Henry and Jefferson, moved a series of resolutions for a system of intercolonial committees of correspondence. They were supported by Lee and Jefferson, and unanimously carried. A committee was appointed, and the resolves forwarded to every colony.[1]

About this time, Franklin sent over to America a number of letters written by Hutchinson to various people in England, deliberately advocating measures for subverting the liberties of Massachusetts.[2] They told, better than any acts of parliament, what was the mind of England, and what the colonies had to expect. During the summer, they were widely circulated through all the colonies, and did more for the cause of liberty than even the resolutions of Massachusetts.[3] In Boston itself, against whose rights they were specially directed, they called forth universal indignation. A resolution was passed in the assembly, declaring Hutchinson and Oliver to be public enemies, and petitions were sent both from the council and the assembly requesting their removal.[4]

In September, the news came from England that the East India Company had been authorised to import tea to America, without paying duty in England. The project excited indigna-

---

[1] Bancroft, vol. vi., pp. 454, 455.
[2] There is a full account of these letters in Franklin's Works, vol. iv., pp. 405-456.
[3] Bancroft, vol. vi., p. 463.
[4] Franklin's Works, vol. iv., p. 433. Annual Register vol. xvii., p. 467.

tion throughout the continent. At Philadelphia the agents of the company were compelled to resign. At New York they voluntarily threw up their office, finding that their task would be impracticable. At Boston they were called on by a committee to resign, and on refusing were declared public enemies.[1] On Monday, November 28th, the first tea ship, the Dartmouth, appeared in Boston harbour. The owner of the ship promised not to land it for two days. On Monday, five thousand citizens, forming the largest town-meeting ever known in Boston, came together. They resolved unanimously to keep out the tea. The owners of ships all promised that tea should be sent back unladen. Notice was sent round the country, proclaiming any ship-owner, who should land tea while the act was in force, a public enemy. Volunteers under arms patrolled the streets at night to guard against any attempt to unload the ships. Two more tea ships which arrived were anchored alongside of the Dartmouth, that one guard might serve for all. For a fortnight, nothing was done. On Saturday, the 11th of December, Hutchinson gave orders to level the castle guns, so that no ship could leave the harbour without a permit. After twenty days, it would be legal for the revenue officers to seize the ship and unload her cargo, if she had not already been unloaded. On the 16th of December, a meeting of seven thousand citizens resolved that the tea should not be landed. At six o'clock that night, a band of forty or fifty men, disguised as Indians, took possession of the three ships, and in the sight of the multitude emptied the whole cargo, three hundred and forty chests of tea, into the bay. The council condemned the act, but there was no clue to the perpetrators. The militia and the cadet corps were called on to preserve the peace, but refused. The sheriff's proclamation, denouncing factious meetings, was read publicly, and laughed at.[2]

On the 7th of March 1774, messages were laid before both

---

[1] Bancroft, vol. vi., pp. 471-475.

[2] This account of the tea riot is taken from the Annual Register, vol. xvii., pp. 8, 59. Bancroft, vol. vi., pp. 477-487.

houses of parliament, requiring their action with regard to Boston.[1] Boston was not the only colony that offended. In Carolina the imported tea had been thrown into the river. In New York it was landed under the guns of a man-of-war.[2] But though the other colonies had shared in the guilt, yet the English government saw that it was the spirit of Boston that animated the whole, and hoped, by placing her on a different footing, to alienate the other colonies from her. Accordingly, that day week, Lord North brought in his bill for the immediate punishment of Boston. Its port was to be closed against all commerce till it should make unqualified submission. Other measures of a similar character were brought in. The custom's officers were to be removed to Salem. A bill was brought in "for the better regulation of the government of Massachusetts Bay," proposing to overthrow the constitution of the colony, to do away with the representative element, and place the whole power in the hands of officers appointed by the crown. By another act, recommended by the king, it was provided that any magistrates, revenue officers, or soldiers indicted for murder or any other capital offence, should be removed for trial to Nova Scotia or Great Britain. A fourth act legalised the quartering of troops within the town of Boston. A fifth regulated the government of the province of Quebec, and established the Roman Catholic religion there with a view of enlisting the Canadians against the other colonies.[3] In vain did Burke protest against these measures. In vain did an old member of the house warn it that it was "commencing its ruin from that day." "I am sorry to say," were his concluding words, "that not only has the house fallen into this error, but the people approve of the measure. The people, I am sorry to say it, are misled. But a short time will prove the evil tendency of this bill. If ever there was a nation running headlong into ruin, it is this." In vain did the friends

[1] Annual Register, vol. xvii., p. 59. [2] Annual Register, vol. xvii., p. 51.
[3] Annual Register, vol. xvii., pp. 63, 69, 72, 73. Bancroft, vol. vi., pp. 511, 512, 525-527.

of America plead in her defence the moderate and equitable spirit shown at Preston's trial. Bolland, the agent of Massachusetts, was refused a hearing, contrary to precedent and to the example of the Lords. A petition was presented by the Lord Mayor in the name of several of the natives of America then present in London. It was pointed out that the port act would destroy the means of industry by which twenty thousand people earned their bread, and that for our own commercial interests the measure was suicidal.[1] Justice and self-interest were alike neglected, and the people clamoured for the punishment of Boston as loudly as its rulers.

On the 1st of June 1774, the Port Act came into force. Boston was to be starved out. Should she resist, Gage had orders to employ the troops, and was reminded that they were responsible for any acts they might commit only to England. There was no need of the precaution. Boston remained true to its policy of peaceful resistance. "Nothing," they said, "is more foreign from our hearts than a spirit of rebellion."[2] A solemn league and covenant was drawn up to suspend all commercial intercourse with Great Britain after the last day of August.[3] The house of representatives, now removed to Salem, passed resolutions declaring the expediency of a colonial congress, appointing five representatives for Massachusetts, and voting them £500 for their expenses. This vote the governor refused to sanction. The committee thereupon recommended that the money should be raised by a general subscription. Finally, fearing that a dissolution was impending, they passed a declaratory resolution setting forth the arbitrary designs of government, and recommending the inhabitants to discontinue imports, and to encourage home manufactures till their grievances should be redressed. This resolution came to the ears of the governor, and he sent his secretary to dissolve them. The assembly, however, locked the door of the

---

[1] Annual Register, vol. xvii., pp. 65, 66, 73.
[2] Bancroft, vol. vii., p. 61.
[3] Annual Register, vol. xviii., pp. 10, 11.

house, and the secretary, being refused admission, dissolved them from the stairs.[1]

In its main object, the Port Bill was a failure. The ministry had expected that Boston would be deserted by the other colonies, and would fall an example and a warning to them. "But instead of abandoning, they clung the closer to their devoted sister as the danger increased, and their affection and sympathy seemed to rise in proportion to her misfortunes and sufferings."[2] The citizens of Salem, it was hoped, had been bribed by the transference of the seat of government, and of as much of the commerce of Boston as their harbour admitted. They presented an address to the governor, setting forth their sympathy for Boston, and disclaiming the idea of profiting by the sufferings of their countrymen. "We must be dead to every idea of justice, lost to all feeling of humanity, could we indulge one thought to seize on wealth and raise our fortunes on the ruin of our suffering neighbours."[3] Throughout the colonies sympathy was expressed. New York called for a congress.[4] "Don't pay for an ounce of the damned tea," was the advice of Gadsden, the leading statesman of South Carolina.[5] The assembly of Virginia set apart the 1st of June as a fast-day, an example almost universally followed. For this act of insubordination the governor dissolved them. Forming themselves into a private committee, they resolved on a continental congress.[6] Three months later they met again, confirmed their importation agreement, pledging themselves to export no tobacco after the 10th of August 1775, if the American grievances were not redressed, and recommending the substitution of other articles of agriculture. Maryland, which, like Virginia, depended on its tobacco, passed similar resolutions.[7] Everywhere the same spirit prevailed. The Philadelphians alone were lukewarm, and

---

[1] Annual Register, vol. xviii., pp. 7, 8.
[2] Annual Register, vol. xviii., p. 3.   [3] Annual Register, vol. xviii., p. 9.
[4] Bancroft, vol. vii. p. 42.   [5] Bancroft, vol. vii., p. 62.
[6] Annual Register, vol. xviii., pp. 5, 6. Wirt, pp. 114-118.
[7] Annual Register, vol. xviii., p. 13.

hoped that by a threat of a congress, they might terrify the English government into submission without incurring the loss of their commerce.[1] But they were the only exceptions. Nor was the sympathy so widely shown confined to words. Marblehead placed its harbour, its wharves and warehouses, at the disposal of the merchants of Boston.[2] South Carolina sent two hundred barrels of rice, and promised eight hundred more. Virginia in less than three months gave three thousand seven hundred and twenty-three bushels of wheat, and one thousand five hundred and twenty-five bushels of Indian corn. Quebec shipped one thousand and forty bushels of wheat. Wilmington collected in a few days £2000.[3]

The possibility of armed resistance began to be discussed. The militia paraded in the different villages of Massachusetts.[4] When it was rumoured that Gage intended to employ his troops to enforce the laws at Worcester, the inhabitants prepared arms and ammunition, and threatened openly to fight in defence of their rights.[5] The inhabitants of Pepperell in an address to Boston declared themselves ready to appeal to arms. "Is not a glorious death," they asked, "in defence of our liberties, better than a short infamous life, and our memories to be had in detestation to the latest posterity?"[6] Of thirty-six mandamus counsellors appointed, twenty either declined to act, or were compelled to resign. One of them warned the people that the consequences of their proceedings would be rebellion, confiscation, and death; and they replied, "No consequences are so dreadful to a free people as that of being made slaves."[7] All civil proceedings were stopped. At Springfield, one thousand five hundred, or two thousand men occupied the court, set up a black flag, and threatened

---

[1] Bancroft, vol. vii., p. 82.
[2] Annual Register, vol. xviii., p. 15. Bancroft, vol. vii., p. 65.
[3] List of donations to Boston during the operation of the Port Bill. Massachusetts' "Historical Collection," 2d series, vol. ix., pp. 158-166. Bancroft, vol. vii., p. 73.
[4] Bancroft, vol. vii., p. 101.   [5] Annual Register, vol. xviii., p. 15.
[6] Bancroft, vol. vii., p. 99.   [7] Bancroft, vol. vii., pp. 104, 105.

death to any one who should enter. At Barrington, the people refused to allow the judges or their officers to enter the court, and upon the sheriff's commanding them to make way, they answered that they knew no court nor other establishment independent of the ancient laws and usages of their country. At Boston, the jurors unanimously refused to serve. "The old constitution being taken away by act of parliament, and the new one being rejected by the people, an end was put to all forms of law and government in the province of Massachusetts bay, and the people were reduced to a state of anarchy."[1]

The journey of the Massachusetts' deputies to the congress was a triumphal procession. Feasts were given in their honour; and when they entered or left a town, crowds went out to meet and escort them.[2] On the 5th of September the whole body of deputies met at Philadelphia.[3] They had not sat a week, or settled the preliminary question of the system of representation in congress, when news came which showed them that a crisis was close at hand. On the 1st of September Gage had seized the public store of powder at Boston, and stored it in the castle. The people rose in thousands—"not a mad mob"[4] or "a Boston rabble, but the freeholders and farmers of the country."[5] By the next day twenty thousand men were in motion. Confused reports of bloodshed flew about; but on receiving instructions from Boston that nothing was to be attempted at present, the insurgents dispersed.[6] The event, however, had shown the congress how much public spirit and organized power of resistance they could look for. Yet their proceedings were thoroughly temperate, proving that the desire for union was no empty profession. On the 17th of September they passed a declaratory resolution expressing their sympathy with the sufferings of Boston; their sense of the injustice of the enactments of Parliament; their

---

[1] Annual Register, vol. xviii., p. 17. Bancroft, vol. vii., pp. 110-113.
[2] Bancroft, vol. vii., pp. 106, 107. [3] Annual Register, vol. xviii., p. 23.
[4] Expression of Oliver, quoted by Bancroft, vol vii., p. 115.
[5] Gage in a letter to England. Bancroft, vol. vii., p. 115.
[6] Annual Register, vol. xviii., p. 18. Bancroft, vol. vii., pp. 114-116.

approbation of the past measures adopted by the citizens of Boston, and their desire that they would continue the same policy; together with a hope that the other colonies would still assist them. In subsequent resolutions they proposed that, if it should be found necessary for the people of Boston to move into the country, all the colonies should compensate them for the injuries sustained. They recommended the inhabitants of Massachusetts to submit to a suspension of the administration of justice, and they denounced any person in that colony who should accept any office from government as a public enemy. They wrote a letter to Gage expressing their regret that he should have taken up so hostile an attitude, and requesting him to discontinue his fortification, and to check the irregularities of his soldiers. They published a declaration of rights, in which they claim the full right of British subjects to fix their own taxes, but professed their willingness to allow England to regulate their trade. They protested against being deprived of the right of trial by their peers of the vicinage. They then drew up a non-importation, non-consumption, and non-exportation agreement in fourteen heads. In spite of the persistent refusal of the government to listen to any complaints from America, they drew up a petition to the king, a memorial to the people of Great Britain, an address to the colonists in general, and another to the people of Quebec.

To the natives of Quebec they pointed out the rights to which their new position as British subjects entitled them. They showed them that the Quebec Act makes the maintenance of their liberties depend on the arbitrary will of the English government, and they warned them that their own freedom depended on that of the other colonies. To anticipate any religious difficulty, they reminded them of the union of the Catholic and Protestant Cantons of Switzerland. They appealed to the countrymen of Montesquieu to join their political interests, as nature had joined their countries; to seize the opportunity of allying themselves with numerous and powerful neighbours, who, with open arms, were inviting them into fellowship, and not to hesitate whether they would have all the rest of North America their unalterable friends or their inveterate enemies.

In their address to the colonies they reviewed the unjust policy of England for the past eleven years. They professed, at the same time, an ardent hope that England would not push matters so far as to make separation inevitable, and expressed their confidence that the people of England, who would so soon be appealed to, would disavow the conduct of their rulers.[1]

There was unconscious irony in that appeal. Those resolutions had scarcely been passed, when England sent a parliament to Westminster, as thoroughly subservient to ministers, and as obstinately resolved to exercise its authority over the colonies as any that had gone before it. In corruption, it even surpassed its predecessors. One seat was occupied by a paid agent of the French king.[2] "If America could have saved for three or four years the money she spent in the fashions and fineries and fopperies of England, she might have bought the whole parliament, ministers and all."[3]

On the 30th of November, when a new parliament met, the speech from the throne set forth that a spirit of disobedience and resistance prevailed in the province of Massachusetts, stating at the same time that proper measures had been taken, and were then in progress, for maintaining the supreme authority of the legislature. When the address was moved, an amendment was proposed to the effect that the king should be requested to lay all the facts which bore on the case of America before the house. A debate ensued, in which the ministry was severely censured and reminded of the effects which they had predicted from the late acts against America; acts which, "instead of dividing the colonies, had joined them in a closeness of friendship and union which perhaps no other means in nature could have done." The division showed that the new house was of the same temper in

---

[1] This account of the proceedings of congress is taken from the Annual Register, vol. xviii., pp. 24-36.
[2] Bancroft, vol. vii., pp. 174, 175.   [3] Bancroft, vol. vii., p. 175.

American matters as its predecessor, inasmuch as the amendment was lost by a majority of one hundred and ninety-one. A debate also ensued in the Lords on the subject of the address, with a similar result. Nothing more was done with reference to America before the Christmas recess, though the production of the estimates gave Lord Sandwich an opportunity for insulting the Americans as a people "not disciplined nor capable of discipline, and formed of such materials, and so indisposed to action, that the numbers of which such boasts had been made, would only add to the facility of their defeat."

During the recess, the supporters of America were not idle. Meetings of American merchants were held in London and Bristol, and petitions agreed upon. The other great trading and manufacturing cities followed their example, and in January after parliament had assembled, petitions came in from London, Bristol, Glasgow, Norwich, Liverpool, Manchester, Birmingham, Wolverhampton, Dudley, and other places. A committee had been appointed to consider papers bearing upon America. To this committee they would naturally have been referred. The ministry, however, found a device which enabled them to keep to their policy of stifling complaints. They argued that, as the petitions were commercial and not political, and as the question was a political one, a separate committee should be appointed to consider them. This iniquitous device, whereby the petitions were "received with one hand, and thrown out of the window with the other,"[1] was carried by a majority of one hundred and ninety-seven against eighty-one. Three days afterwards, three agents, Franklin, Bolland, and Lee, stated that they had been authorised by the American Congress to present a petition, and requested to be heard on behalf of it. The supporters of America represented that the principal question before the house was the preservation of order, and that "the rejection of petitions was a principal cause of the present troubles," and "would infallibly end in universal rebellion, and not unnaturally, as those seem to

[1] Annual Register, vol. xviii., p. 53.

give up the right of government who refuse to hear the complaints of the subjects."[1] But the ministry were true to their policy of punishing first and judging afterwards, and the petition was refused. On the 3d of February, Lord North gave notice of his American policy. The principal points were, that the forces were to be increased, the New England fisheries to be cut off, and the colonies treated with gradations of severity according to their degrees of guilt. In other words, the government trusted to three means of subduing America, force, starvation, and internal disunion. He then moved for an address to the king, returning thanks for the communications of the American papers, declaring that the inhabitants of Massachusetts were in a state of rebellion, that it was necessary to maintain the authority of government in America, and that they were willing to listen to any grievances of his majesty's subjects, when laid before them in a proper manner; at the same time requesting his majesty to take effectual measures for enforcing obedience and pledging themselves to maintain his and their rights. This address met with strenuous opposition. Dunning contended that no rebellion existed in America, and that the disorders were due to the conduct of the government officials, whose designs were hostile equally to the liberties of the colonies and of the mother country. It was pointed out, that to accuse the Americans of rebellion, would be a sure step towards driving them to desperate measures. The idea of selecting Massachusetts as a special victim, was shown to be both unjust and impolitic. "The colonies were now compacted into one body. The proceeding of one was to become the proceeding of all. Every attempt to disunite them had been found to strengthen their union."[2] The address was, as a matter of course, carried. On the 6th, when the address was reported to the house, Lord John Cavendish re-opened the question. He deprecated driving the Americans to extremities, and thereby hurrying them into a civil war, which would inevitably bring a

[1] Annual Register, vol. xviii., p. 56.   [2] Annual Register, vol. xviii., p. 65.

foreign war along with it. "What," he asked, "was the prize to be gained by running all this risk and encountering all this danger? If we were successful we might subdue America, by which we gain nothing—America being to all wise intents and purposes our own already, and much more profitably so, than it could be in virtue of any conquest."[1] Wilkes denounced the address as "violent and mad." "Who can tell," he said, "whether the scabbard may not be thrown away by the Americans as well as by us, and should success attend them, whether in a few years the Americans may not celebrate the glorious era of the revolution of the year 1775, as we do that of 1688?"[2] The address, however, was carried by a great majority, and when taken up to the Lords with the proposal that they should join in it, it passed without any difficulty.

Meanwhile the opposition had received an addition of strength. Chatham had reappeared in parliament. On the 20th of January, he had brought forward a motion for the removal of the troops, as a preliminary step towards conciliation. In his speech he inveighed against the whole policy of the ministry. He charged them with having deceived the nation and held out unfounded hopes of tranquillity. He warned them to concede in time and of free grace what they would have to concede at length of necessity. He concluded with the prophetic words, "If the ministers thus persevere in misadvising and misleading the king, I will not say that they can alienate the affections of his subjects from his crown, but I will affirm that they will make the crown not worth his wearing. I will not say that the king is betrayed, but I will pronounce that the kingdom is undone."[3] The proposal to remove the troops was looked upon as dangerous by many of those who were inclined towards conciliation. Notwithstanding, they supported the motion as the first step towards a juster policy. The bill, however, was lost by a majority of sixty-eight to eighteen. Undeterred by this result, on the 1st of February, Chatham

[1] Annual Register, vol. xviii., p. 67.
[2] Bancroft, vol. vii., p. 225.
[4] Annual Register, vol. xviii., p. 48.

brought forward a scheme of conciliation. The principal points in the bill were, that a congress should be held in the ensuing month of May, to recognise the supreme legislative power of parliament, and to make a free grant to the king, his heirs, and successors, of a certain and perpetual revenue, subject to the disposition of parliament, and applicable to the alleviation of the national debt; that the late offensive acts should be suspended for a time, without being formally repealed; that the judges should be placed upon the same footing with those in England, and that all the privileges secured to the colonists by their charters and constitutions, should remain intact. It was a scheme which conceded all that America required, with the least possible humiliation to England, yet the authority of the proposer, the " clarum et venerabile nomen " of Chatham, his advanced age, his past services could not save the measure from the indignity, not merely of rejection, but of not being allowed to lie on the table of the house. Well might Franklin say, " hereditary legislators! there would be more propriety because less hazard of mischief in having, as in some universities of Germany, hereditary professors of mathematics." Well might it seem " the greatest of absurdities," that men should " claim sovereignty over three millions of virtuous, sensible people in America, when they appeared to have scarce discretion enough to govern a herd of swine."[1]

In that time of national shame, there is one figure on which an Englishman may look with satisfaction and pride. In the zenith of his career, when he was guiding the victorious arms of Britain in four continents, Chatham was never so truly great as when, with shattered health and fallen power, he was maintaining English liberties against the tyranny of England. If any think that patriotism is necessarily a narrowing or an exclusive spirit, let them look at Chatham. He loved England with

> " True love turned round on fixed poles,
> Love that endures not sordid ends
> For English natures, freemen, friends,
> His brethren and immortal souls."

---

[1] Franklin's Works, vol. v., p. 159.

He loved her because he saw in her the embodiment of great principles, because her past history had been a witness for freedom. And those principles which were dear to him in Englishmen, were not less dear to him when Englishmen had, by their own folly, arrayed them against themselves. He saw in the Americans the spirit of the heroes of ancient history,[1] the spirit, too, of the heroes of his own nation, the spirit of Pym and Hampden.[2] His last hours were saddened by the approaching "dismemberment of that ancient empire" which he had served so truly and loved so well; but hope may have revived as he remembered that, though England had been false to herself, there were men of English speech and English race who would not betray the inheritance that their fathers had won for them.

The next proceeding of the ministry was to bring in a bill for cutting off New England from the Newfoundland fisheries. The bill, as was pointed out, was not only unjust, but impolitic. By destroying the commerce of New England it would prevent the payment of English debts, and would turn the fishermen into recruits for the American army. It would drive the colonies to throw off their allegiance by showing them "that, if but a single branch of legislative power were left to England, it could distort that branch in such a manner that it should include all the purposes of an unlimited tyranny."[3] The opposition launched out into general invectives against the whole policy of the ministry. They pointed out how each measure of coercion had brought in its train another measure yet more severe, "till one by one parliament had ruined all its colonies and rooted up all its commerce, till the statute-book had become nothing but a black and bloody roll of proscriptions, and that wherever it was opened it would

---

[1] "They acted," he [Lord Chatham] said, "with so much temper, moderation, and wisdom, that he thought it the most honourable assembly of statesmen, since those of the ancient Greeks and Romans, in the most virtuous times." Franklin's Works, vol. v., p. 34.

[2] "These worthy New Englanders ever feel as Old Englanders ought to do." Expression of Chatham, quoted by Bancroft, vol. vi., p. 434.

[3] Annual Register, vol. xviii., p. 86.

present a title of destroying some trade, or ruining some province."[1] But notwithstanding that the opposition strove as throughout the session "to make amends for the smallness of their numbers by their zeal and activity,"[2] the bill was carried through all its stages.

But the temper of the house was to be more fully shown before the session was over. On the 20th of February, Lord North brought forward his scheme for conciliation. The plan was, that when a supply was required from any of the colonies, the colonial legislature should vote a certain sum, and *if this sum was approved of by the English government*, no taxation for purposes of revenue should be imposed. In other words, the colonies were to be allowed to determine the method of their own taxation, but to have no voice either in regulating the amount or directing the purposes to which it should be applied. As Franklin said, "It was similar to no mode of obtaining aids that ever existed except that of a highwayman who presents his pistol and hat at a coach window, demanding no specific sum, but if you will give all your money, or what he is pleased to think sufficient, he will civilly omit putting his own hand into your pockets; if not, there is his pistol."[3] Had the house known with how much scorn the colonists would reject the offer, they might have saved themselves some alarm. But the very word conciliation, when heard from a minister, produced a panic. "The courtiers looked at each other with amazement." "The treasury benches seemed to totter, and that ministerial phalanx which had been so irresistible, was ready to break and fall into irretrievable disorder."[4] To be likened to Hancock and Otis was all the reward that Lord North got for having for once allowed his humanity to lead him aside from the path of oppression.[5] His immediate supporters, however, were equal to the occasion. With a readiness which shows that parliamentary "cross-fishing" is not an invention of to-day, they

[1] Annual Register, vol. xviii., p. 87.
[2] Annual Register, vol. xviii., p. 85.
[3] Franklin's Works, vol. v., p. 87.
[4] Annual Register, vol. xviii., p. 97.
[5] Bancroft, vol. vii., p. 243.

represented that the present measures were not in any way inconsistent with the previous policy of government. As they pointed out, it reserved the right and provided for the substantial exercise of it. The compulsion of America was no longer a mere question of national honour, but was put upon its proper footing —revenue or no revenue. They held out the motion, in fact, as the opposition said, "to one side of the house as a measure of concession, and to the other as a strong assertion of authority," like the tea act, "which to this country was to be a duty of supply, and to the Americans a tax only of regulation."[1] Accordingly, the ministerial party, finding that the plan for conciliation had nothing conciliatory in it, returned to their accustomed docility, and carried it by a large majority.

Undeterred by the numerous proofs already given of the uncompromising spirit of parliament, Burke made one more attempt at conciliation. " If he could not give peace to his country, he would at least give it to his conscience." True to the principles he had always upheld, he refused to entertain the question of right. " The question was not whether parliament had a right to render its people miserable, but whether it was not their interest to make them happy." He warned them of the difficulty of the task which they were undertaking. " I am afraid," he said, " that the temper and character which prevail in our colonies are unalterable by any human art." " An Englishman is the unfittest person in the world to argue another Englishman into slavery." The enlistment of the negroes he looked on as a wild and dangerous project. He pointed out that the Americans were by their present state of anarchy being trained to be independent of English government. His scheme consisted of six resolutions, and altogether proposed a plan for placing the taxation of the colonies in their own hands. The first resolution declared that the colonies were not represented; the second declared that they had been subjected to taxes whereby they had been oftentimes " touched and grieved;" the third declared that no method had

[1] Annual Register, vol. xviii., p. 99.

hitherto been devised for representing the colonies in parliament; the fourth that each of the colonies had a representative body, with a power of taxation; the fifth that these bodies had at sundry times freely granted large subsidies; that their right to do so, and their "cheerfulness and sufficiency in the said grant, had been at sundry times acknowledged by parliament;" the sixth that it had been found by experience that taxation by the assemblies had been "more agreeable to the said colonies, and more beneficial and conducive to the public service than by parliament." Other resolutions followed, proposing the repeal of all the obnoxious acts, and an explanation and amendment of the statute of Henry VIII., entitled, "An act for the trial of treasons committed out of the king's dominions." Throughout his speech, Burke carefully eschewed any ground except that of expediency. Anticipating the possible argument that if taxation implied representation, legislation did so also, he pointed out that the colonies were devoted not to liberty in the abstract, but to "liberty according to English ideas, and on English principles," and that that liberty had always turned on the point of taxation. In conclusion, he met those slanders which had been cast on the loyalty and the spirit of the colonies, saying, "Your hold of the colonies is in the close affection which grows from common names, from kindred blood, from similar privileges, and equal protection. . . . . As long as you have the wisdom to keep the sovereign authority of this country as the sanctuary of liberty, the sacred temple consecrated to our common faith, wherever the chosen race and sons of England worship freedom, they will turn their faces towards you. The more they multiply, the more friends you will have; the more ardently they love liberty, the more perfect will be their obedience."[1]

In the ensuing debate, the ministry took new ground. They alleged that the raising of money by any authority except parliament was a violation of the bill of rights, a plea which the opposition met with the example of Ireland. Burke's proposal went

[1] Burke's Works, vol. iii., pp. 23-132.

the same way as every similar attempt, and was defeated by one hundred and ninety-two votes.

On the 10th of April, the citizens of London presented a petition to the king, deprecating the destruction of commerce, the prospect of bloodshed, the alienation of the colonies, and the establishment of military government. In answer to this, the king expressed his astonishment that any of his subjects should be capable of encouraging the rebellious disposition of the Americans.[1]

Such a brief account as I have given of the most important proceedings during the session of 1775, will suffice to illustrate the temper of the English parliament, and unhappily of the English people. Blind ignorance of the principles of government, utter indifference to the interests of the colonies, and an overweening contempt for the power of resistance—such were the influences by which the rulers of the British Empire were guided. Before that parliament rose, events were to show whether the Americans were, as Grant had told the House of Commons, "neither soldiers, nor ever capable of being made so; being naturally of a pusillanimous disposition, and utterly incapable of any sort or order of discipline,"[2] or whether they were "a brave, generous, and united people, the genuine descendants of a valiant and pious ancestry."[3] For six months after the dissolution of congress, no change took place in the relative position of parties in America. In New York the assembly had been won over to the side of government, but the mass of the inhabitants were faithful to the cause of freedom.[4] The provincial congress of Massachusetts had appointed a committee of safety to take possession of the military stores of the province, to make returns of the militia and minute men, and to muster so

---

[1] This account of the proceedings of the session is taken substantially from the Annual Register, vol. xviii., p. 36-120.

[2] Annual Register, vol. xviii., p. 66. Bancroft, vol. vii., p. 223.

[3] Chatham's Speech in Parliament, January 20, 1775. Bancroft, vol. vii., p. 197.

[4] Bancroft, vol. vii., pp. 210-212.

many of the militia as they judged necessary.[1] Another committee was appointed to draw up rules and regulations for the constitutional army. Meanwhile the soldiers and the citizens had become more and more odious to one another. On the 26th of February, Gage having learnt that some brass cannon had been deposited at Salem, sent a detachment of troops, under the command of a field officer, to seize the cannon and to bring them to Boston. When they arrived at Salem they failed to find the cannon. Believing, however, that they had only been removed that morning, they went further into the country in pursuit of them. Near Danvers, their passage across a river was barred by a number of countrymen who had taken up the drawbridge and refused to lower it. Meanwhile the cannon were being removed to a place of safety. The officer then attempted to get possession of a boat, but the people, seeing his design, scuttled it with their axes. Hostilities seemed imminent, but by the good offices of a clergyman who happened to be at hand, the two parties came to terms; the bridge was lowered; the troops marched across, and the officer having done all that was necessary for the point of military honour, marched back empty-handed.[2]

A fortnight after this, the anniversary of the massacre was kept, and a public meeting held, at which some forty British officers were present, listening to a harangue from Warren. After recalling the horrors of the massacre, he reminded them of the dangers with which they were surrounded, and of the necessity for courage, and, in conclusion, exhorted them, if the hour for resistance should come, "not to turn their faces from their foes, but undauntedly to press forward until tyranny should be trodden under foot." After the oration a motion was passed, amid the hisses of the English officers, for "appointing an orator for the ensuing year to commemorate the horrid massacre."[3]

Further symptoms of ill-feeling manifested themselves. A countryman bought a gun from a soldier. As soon as he had

---

[1] Bancroft, vol. vii., p. 228. [2] Annual Register, vol. xviii., p. 125.
[3] Bancroft, vol. vii., pp. 253-256.

paid for it, he was seized by some of the troops for having violated an act of parliament which forbade trading with soldiers, and was shut up all night in the guard-room. The next day he was tarred and feathered, and carted through the principal streets with a placard on his back, "American liberty, or a specimen of democracy," followed by the drums and fifes of the 27th regiment, by a guard of twenty men with fixed bayonets, and a mob of officers, among whom was an English lieutenant-colonel.[1]

During the winter Virginia had not been idle. In December, the Fairfax county committee, led by Washington, had followed the example of Maryland in forming the inhabitants into small militia companies, under officers of their own choice.[2] On the 20th of March the Virginian convention assembled at Richmond. Their tone was at first moderate. "Where," said the party of inaction, "are our stores, our soldiers, our generals, our money. We are defenceless, yet we talk of war against one of the most formidable nations in the world. It will be time enough to resort to measures of despair when every well-founded hope is vanished." But Henry saw the vanity of such delay, and bade them arm, in a speech which sounded the first war-note of American independence. "Are fleets and armies necessary to a work of love and reconciliation? Our petitions have been slighted, our remonstrances have produced additional violence and insult, our supplications have been disregarded, and we have been spurned with contempt from the foot of the throne. In vain after these things may we indulge in the fond hope of peace and reconciliation. There is no longer any room for hope. If we wish to be free—if we mean to preserve inviolate those inestimable privileges for which we have been so long contending—if we mean not basely to abandon the whole struggle in which we have been so long engaged, and which we have pledged ourselves never to abandon, until the glorious object of our content shall be obtained—we must fight. I repeat, sir, we must fight! An

---

[1] Bancroft, vol. vii., p. 256.   [2] Bancroft, vol. vii., p. 207.

appeal to arms, and to the God of Hosts, is all that is left us. They tell us, sir, that we are weak, unable to cope with so formidable an adversary. But when shall we be stronger? Will it be the next week or the next year? Will it be when we are totally disarmed, and a British guard shall be stationed in every house? Shall we gather strength by irresolution or inaction? Shall we acquire the means of effectual resistance by lying on our backs, hugging the delusive phantom of hope, until our enemies shall have bound us hand and foot? Sir, we are not weak, if we make a proper use of those means which the God of nature hath placed in our power. Three millions of people arrayed in the holy cause of liberty, and in such a country as that which we possess, are invincible by any force which the enemy can send against us. Besides, sir, we shall not fight our battle alone. There is a just God who presides over the destinies of nations who will raise up friends to fight our battles for us. The battle, sir, is not to the strong alone; it is to the vigilant, the active, the brave. Besides, sir, we have no election. If we were base enough to desire it, it is now too late to retire from the contest. There is no retreat but in submission and slavery. Our chains are forged. Their clankings may be heard on the plains of Boston. The war is inevitable, and let it come. I repeat, sir, let it come.

"It is vain, sir, to extenuate the matter. Gentlemen may say peace, peace, but there is no peace. The war has actually begun. The next gale that sweeps from the north will bring to our ears the clash of resounding arms. Our brethren are already in the field. Why stand we here idle? What is it the gentlemen wish? What would they have? Is life so dear, and peace so sweet, as to be purchased at the price of chains and slavery? Forbid it, Almighty God! I know not what course others may take, but as for me"—and his gesture told of the intensity of his feeling—" give me liberty, or give me death."

All doubt and delay vanished. A militia was organised Nicholas, in his enthusiasm, proposed to raise ten thousand regulars.[1] To meet the danger, Dunmore, following Gage's example, seized the powder at Williamsburgh, and threatened to raise and arm the negroes. "If," he said, "any insult is offered to me, or those who have obeyed my orders, I will declare freedom to the slaves, and lay the town in ashes." Such conduct added fuel to the flame. On the 29th of April, upwards of six hundred well-armed men were in readiness at Fredericksburgh.[2] Everything was ripe for resistance; and while they knew it not, the hour had come. At that very time the war of independence had begun.

Ever since George III. had found, in Lord North, a minister ready to be the servile dictator of a servile parliament, that result had been inevitable. England had pledged herself, if necessary, to subdue the continent of America; to subdue by arms, and to hold by force nearly three millions of people. The Americans, it is true, were imperfectly armed, but they had the command of supplies and the choice of position. In an aggressive war a half-drilled army of citizen soldiers would be overpowered by a third of their number of regular troops. But, in a purely defensive struggle, the disparity is vastly diminished. A war in which the object is not to advance a frontier, or even to drive an enemy out of a territory, but only to harass them while in it, and make their position ultimately untenable, is peculiarly favourable to the readiness and enterprise in which citizen soldiers excel, and does not test so highly the machine-like merits of regular tooops. We must remember, too, that the New England or Virginian yeomen were no mere machines tied to one routine of daily toil. The life of a settler in a young country is specially calculated to develop his versatility. The backwoodsman of Virginia or Massachusetts was no mere tiller

---

[1] I have taken this account of the proceedings of the convention, of Pa'rick Henry's speech and its results, from Wirt, pp. 133–143. Bancroft questions the historical authenticity of Henry's speech, vol. vii., p. 273, *note*. In any case it represents much of the substance of what was said, and is a good exposition of the views of the extreme party in America.

[2] Wirt, pp. 149, 150. Bancroft, vol. vii., pp. 275–277.

of soil, working from day to day in a mechanical groove of toil, that neither asks nor arouses thought. He was at once farmer, hunter, and craftsmen. He made his own cart, he broke and shod his own horses, he raised his log hut with timber that he himself had hewn. Their leaders were many of them men of the same stamp; yeomen, like Patrick Henry or Putnam, who lived the life and spoke the dialect of the people. As in the citizen armies of the ancient world, every man fought side by side with those he knew, his townsmen, his friends, often his kinsmen, and there was enough of local division to rouse emulation but not jealousy. Moreover they were rebels but in name; in reality their war was purely defensive, as purely defensive as ever was the war of an invaded people. Their task was not to destroy but to preserve. This is no mere matter of words. Instead of a people setting to work to destroy institutions which had become the engines of tyranny, or which they had outgrown, they were people fighting to preserve, always the spirit and often the form of institutions under which they had become a great nation. They were not assuming new rights but maintaining old. They were not overthrowing an existing system with the after-task of evolving a new and untried order out of chaos. They had a clear, definite goal before them, the nature of which every man who took up arms could understand. The rebellion did not cut them off from the past, it bound them more closely to it. They were fighting not for abstract rights but for English rights. They could look back with pride on Hampden and Russell, on Sidney and Somers, on the acknowledged heroes of English history to whom England was now false. They saw that their friends in England felt this. Clive and Effingham had refused to take up arms against their brethren. The people of Ireland were with them almost to a man.[1] If they conquered they would not be destroying England, or even injuring her; they would only be crushing an unjust system of imperialism,

[1] It is worthy of notice that Burke, Shelburne, Barré, and Conway, four of the most consistent friends of America, were all Irishmen.

under which the liberties of no British subject could be safe. Above all, the colonies were united. The readiness with which they had answered to Adam's call for committees of correspondence proved this beyond a doubt. So long as that spirit prevailed, America could not be conquered. The arms of England might be for the time victorious, but all history showed that it was impossible to govern by force a resolute and united people living in a country three thousand miles distant. The Americans were asserting and recovering freedom, if not for themselves, for their children, and their children's children.

Far other must have been the feelings of those in England whose sympathies with America could not make them forget that they were Englishmen. The new life which Pitt had breathed into the English service was extinct. That system of favouritism and jobbery which had sapped the strength of our army and navy, and against which Pitt had warred with temporary success, was as rife again as ever. Never had a government rushed blindfold into war in more complete ignorance of the character of their enemy, or disregard of resources. They were to fight in an unknown country, in dense woods where marching was difficult, and the conveyance of cannon impossible, against an army of backwoodsmen trained to the chase, and many of them experienced in Indian warfare. Or were they to call in the Indians as allies, and see the bodies of their fellow-countrymen mutilated by the scalping-knife of the savage? And if these difficulties were overcome, what was to be the fruit of success? To destroy a nation which it was our greatest glory to have founded, to overthrow liberties which it was our chief pride to have nurtured. What should we have left to govern but "the ruins of depopulated towns, uncultivated fields, old men, women, and children, whose relations had fallen in the national contest?"[1] Well might a nation, deliberately and of its own choice, entering on such a war, be the ridicule of the whole civilised world.[2] The

---

[1] The Critical Moment, p. 54.

[2] Horace Walpole, in a letter to Conway, written from Paris, September 8, 1775, says, "There is not a Frenchman that does not think us distracted." Walpole's Letters, vol. v., p. 430.

destruction of our empire was not the worst part. All far-seeing men perceived that if we were successful, the time was at hand when

> "That England that was wont to conquer others,
> Should make a shameful conquest of itself."

To such a pass had misgovernment brought England, that our only hope lay in the incapacity of her commanders, and the courage of her foes.[1]

For six months, nothing noticeable had happened at Boston, although, as I said before, the ill-feeling between the citizens and the soldiers had been aggravated by a variety of circumstances. But on the night of the 18th of April, Gage sent off a force of eight hundred men to seize the cannon and stores at Concord. The attempt was planned and executed with caution, but the colonists were on their guard. Before the troops had gone far, they saw, by the hoisting of lights and ringing of bells, that they were detected, and Smith, who was in command, sent back for a reinforcement. At five o'clock in the morning, they reached Lexington. There, on the village green, they found some sixty men drawn up in two ranks. One of the officers ordered them to disperse. They stood their ground. Another officer thereupon fired a pistol, which was followed by a general volley by which eight of the militia were killed, and several wounded. From Lexington the troops proceeded on their errand. By seven o'clock they reached Concord. They spiked two guns, destroyed some stores, and plundered private houses. The colonists who had gathered outside the town, over four hundred in number, at first stood on the defensive. After a short deliberation, they resolved to march into the town. As they reached the bridge,

[1] The danger to English liberty, which would have resulted from the success of our arms in America, was fully recognised by thinking men. Burke said, "That the establishment of such a power in America will utterly ruin our finances is the smallest part of our concern. It will become an apt, powerful, and certain engine for the destruction of our freedom here." Burke's Works, vol. iv., p. 192. Lord Chatham wrote, "England will have fallen upon her own sword." Buckle, vol. i., p. 438. I have quoted another remark made by Chatham of similar tenor elsewhere.

the English troops began to take up the planks. The provincials advanced. Then, as at Lexington, two or three stray shots were fired by the soldiers, followed by a general volley. The colonists returned the volley, and the troops retreated. The first blow had been struck. Concord bridge was in truth the opening scene of the American War of Independence. The usual result of unexpected defeat followed. The troops were utterly demoralised, and were driven back to Boston like sheep. Reinforcements kept pouring in to the help of the colonists, till the hills and walls that flanked the road swarmed with rebels. At last, about a mile beyond Lexington, the officers managed, by threats of death, to get the troops into some formation. At that moment, Percy arrived with a reinforcement, and formed a hollow square round the fugitives, who lay stretched on the ground, panting and exhausted. By this time, two-thirds of the whole English force was on the ground, yet their only safety was in retreat. As the news of the morning's events spread abroad, every town and village sent out its troop of militia. The soldiers under Percy retreated, burning and pillaging by the way, murdering helpless old men, and driving women out of their houses half naked. Just after sunset, they reached Boston, having lost two hundred and seventy-three men. But the loss was not to be measured by men. The presence of British troops had lost its terrors; its spell was broken from that time as effectually as was that of "the barbarian" at Marathon.[1]

On the night of the 19th of April, the English troops were besieged in Boston. Three days afterwards, the Massachusetts congress resolved to raise a New England army of thirty thousand men, itself to contribute thirteen thousand six hundred. From New Hampshire, from Connecticut, from Rhode Island, volunteers poured in, each with his gun and store of ammunition.[2] The con-

---

[1] Annual Register, vol. xviii., pp. 126-128. Bancroft, vol. vii., pp. 288-310. Depositions laid before Congress, published in the Journal of the Proceedings of Congress, printed by order of Congress, and reprinted by Almann in London, 1776, pp. 19-40.

[2] Bancroft, vol. vii., p. 317.

dition of the inhabitants of Boston was most pitiable. The city was besieged by both sea and land. The king's stores were the only means of subsistence in the town. At length Gage entered into a capitulation by which the inhabitants were to be at liberty to depart with their goods, on condition that they surrendered their arms. The arms were surrendered, but Gage's part of the contract was not fulfilled. Many of the inhabitants did obtain leave to depart, but only by leaving behind them their goods, and what was worse, their relations. Families were broken up, and the dearest connections separated; part were compelled to quit the town, part were retained against their will.[1]

The second attempt of the rebels was as successful as the first, and even bolder. A band of about one hundred Vermont backwoodsmen, aided by fifty of the Massachusetts militia, conceived the adventurous design of capturing Ticonderoga, a fortress guarded by more than a hundred pieces of cannon, and commanding the passage from Canada to New England. Its capture had cost the English eight millions of money, and several campaigns. On the 9th of May, at daybreak, Ethen Allen with eighty-three volunteers marched into the fort, overpowered the sentinels, and in ten minutes were masters of Ticonderoga. Crown Point surrendered with equal ease.[2]

The colonists exulting in their newly discovered strength, ventured on exploits from which more experienced soldiers might have shrunk. A party of Vermont volunteers manned a schooner on Lake Champlain, sailed into the harbour of St John's, and captured a British sloop, thirteen soldiers, and brass cannon. Boston was besieged so closely, that its only supplies were derived from the small islands in the bay. On one occasion a small party of provincials were engaged in clearing off and destroying the stock and forage on one of these islands. Two vessels and a party of marines were sent from Boston to check them. An engagement ensued in which the English were de-

---

[1] Annual Register, vol. xviii., p. 130.
[2] Annual Register, vol. xviii., p. 132. Bancroft, vol. vii., pp. 338-341.

feated, with a loss of twenty killed and fifty wounded, and compelled to desert one of the ships. The Americans, whose loss had been trifling, boarded the ship, removed the cannon from her, and set her on fire.[1]

Everywhere the national spirit of daring was effectually raised. When the news of Lexington reached New York, two sloops, which lay at the wharfs laden with supplies for the troops at Boston, were instantly unloaded. Even the Quakers of Pennsylvania took up arms. In Virginia, Patrick Henry was at the head of five thousand men.[2] Everywhere Lord North's conciliation scheme was received with contempt.[3] As before, the delegates of Massachusetts, on their way to the congress, were received everywhere as the representatives of national liberty.[4] The congress, consisting of the delegates of twelve colonies, met on May the 10th at Philadelphia. On the 13th, they were joined by a delegate from Georgia. An American historian has well represented how anomalous was the position occupied by that congress.[5] They had none of the powers of government; they had not even an authorised legal existence. They had not the bond of common race or common religion. There were Swedes and Dutch, Quakers and Calvinists. Nor was there any presiding will to bind together these incongruous atoms. They had no Cromwell to overrule their conflicting impulses, and mould them all to one common purpose; no William the Silent who could enter into the feelings of the whole nation, and in whom each man might find the representative of his own needs. The first question to be decided was the policy to be adopted by New York where British troops were expected. The orders were, that the citizens should observe a strictly defensive policy, and should suffer the troops to land, but not to erect fortifications. The same spirit of moderation induced them to make a last effort at reconciliation with the mother country. To avoid creating an

---

[1] Bancroft, vol. vii., pp. 362-364.
[2] Bancroft, vol. vii., pp. 328-334.
[3] Annual Register, vol. xviii., p. 130.
[4] Bancroft, vol. vii., p. 332.
[5] Bancroft, vol. vii., p. 355.

insuperable breach, the congress recommended Massachusetts not to establish a new government, but to entrust the executive to the elective council, until a governor of the king's appointment would consent to govern the colony according to the charter. At the same time, they expressed their contempt for Gage's government by electing Hancock, who, with Adams, had just been proclaimed a traitor and rebel, President of the Congress. On the 3d of June, committees were appointed to draw up a petition to the king, and addresses to the inhabitants of Great Britain, of Ireland, and of Jamaica. On the 12th of June, they passed a recommendation that Thursday, the 20th of July, should be set apart as a day of humiliation, fasting, and prayer. Meantime, though studious to avoid anything that would seem like aggression, they had been making provision for a defensive war. On the 26th of April, they had drawn up a formal address to the inhabitants of Great Britain, setting forth the circumstances of the affair at Concord, stating that the English troops had commenced hostilities, declaring their intention of resisting "the persecution and tyranny of a cruel ministry," while, at the same time, they expressed their hope that, "in a constitutional connection with the mother country, they might soon be altogether a free and happy people." On the 18th of May, notice was given to the congress that an attack from the province of Quebec might be expected. The frontier colonies were recommended to make preparations against such an attempt, and an address was sent to the Canadians, conceived in much the same spirit as that drawn up by the last congress. Resolves were passed on the 2d of June, that no bill of exchange or money order should be negotiated for any English officer or army agent, or any money supplied to them in any way; that no provisions should be supplied to the British army or navy in Massachusetts; and that no vessel employed in transporting British troops to any part of America should be furnished with stores or necessaries. Soon after this, a letter was laid before the congress from the congress of Massachusetts, inviting them "to assume the regulation and direction of the army then collecting from different colonies for the defence of the rights of America." At the same time, Adams received a private letter from Warren on behalf of the Massachusetts' congress, expressing a desire that the general congress should appoint a general.[1] The suggestion as to the army does not seem to have been formally adopted, but on the 10th of June, it was recommended to the conventions of various colonies that they should take measures to have gunpowder manufactured "for the use of the continent," and on the 14th, it was resolved that ten companies of riflemen should be raised in Pennsylvania, Maryland, and Virginia, and that they should be enlisted as soldiers in the "American continental army." On the 15th, in accordance with the suggestion of Warren, congress proceeded to the choice of a general, and unanimously elected George Washington.[2]

Washington was then in his forty-fourth year. He had, as we have already seen, shown heroic courage and considerable military skill in the valley of the Ohio. After the congress of 1774, Henry had said of him, "If you speak of solid information and sound judgment, Colonel Washington was the greatest man on that floor."[3] Washington was not one of those, many of them the greatest names in history, whose powers have suddenly burst forth when the occasion has called for them. The qualities to which he owed his greatness were the same which had already made him successful in a narrower sphere. He was a great statesman and a great general, not from any special aptitude for war or politics, but from his industry, patience, strength of will, and clearness of judgment. His peculiar merit, that through which he stands almost alone among the great, is his public spirit. Above all men, he united the highest capacity for action with the most perfect freedom from personal ambition. Among the heroes of ancient history, Epaminondas alone perhaps equals him; in the modern world he is without a rival.

[1] Bancroft, vol. vii., p. 389.
[2] Journal of Proceedings of Congress, pp. 3–38. [3] Wirt, p. 132.

On the 25th of May, Howe, Burgoyne, and Clinton had arrived at Boston, with a number of marines and drafts from other regiments to supply the vacancies, and were soon followed by several regiments from Ireland.[1] Notwithstanding this reinforcement, they did not venture on any attempt to break up the blockade. Hitherto, both parties had neglected the important point of Charlestown. That town, the parent of Boston, stood on a peninsula to the north of that occupied by the younger city, and about parallel to it. The peninsula is about a mile long, and at its widest rather more than half a mile broad, but grows narrower at the point where it joins the mainland. Its north-east termination is occupied by Bunker's Hill, an eminence about one hundred and ten feet high. On the 15th of June it became known that Gage intended to occupy this position, and the Americans resolved to anticipate him. After dusk, on the evening of June 16th, a brigade of a thousand men, without uniform, armed with fowling-pieces, with no bayonets, carrying their ammunition in horns and hunting pouches, marched towards Charlestown, under the command of William Prescott. The point to be occupied was a height called Breed's Hill. After twelve the work of fortification commenced, and before daylight a complete redoubt was thrown up with considerable intrenchments, and a breast-work that was in some parts cannon-proof. As soon as the attempt was discovered, a heavy cannonade was opened from the ships, and from Copps Hill in Boston. The Americans stood their ground with the firmness of old soldiers. About one o'clock Howe landed on the north side of the Isthmus with two thousand men. The defenders of the hill numbered about eight hundred,[2] and were exhausted with the laborious work of intrenching, and with lack of food and water. But Howe thought it better to send back for more troops. Before they arrived, reinforcements were sent from the American camp. The number of troops on Bunker's Hill

[1] Annual Register, vol. xviii., p. 132.
[2] Two hundred had been detached to fortify the summit of Bunker's Hill. But the attempt was not carried out.

was doubled, and their line of defence was completed as far as the north side of the Isthmus. At half-past two the British line advanced in two columns, under cover of a heavy fire of howitzers and cannon. Not a shot was returned till the troops were close to the redoubt, and then for several minutes a close and continuous fire was kept up along the whole extent of the line. Nearly every officer near Howe was killed, and for a few seconds he was left alone. For about ten minutes the British troops stood the fire of the provincials, then they wavered and fell back in confusion. A second time they attacked the line; but in spite of the efforts of their officers encouraging, threatening, and even urging them on with their swords, they were again beaten back. For a third time they rallied. They had an ally that they did not reckon on. The Americans' supply of powder had failed, and they had little more than enough for one volley left. They held out for some time fighting against the bayonets of the English with the butt-end of their guns till their stocks were broken. At last they gave way, retreating across Charlestown neck under the fire of a frigate and two floating batteries. The English were too exhausted to press them severely, and their total loss was less than two hundred killed, and a little more than three hundred wounded. The severest loss the Americans sustained was the death of Warren. He had come as a volunteer from the committee of safety at Cambridge to fall as the Hampden of American liberty. But the hopes of America did not rest on the insecure basis of individual courage or wisdom. Never was there a great struggle in which the leaders more completely represented the nation's will and executed her designs. When she called, citizens were found as ready to command as they were to obey; none shunned greatness, none sought it.

One lamentable result of the battle was the destruction of Charlestown. It was set on fire by the cannonading of the British troops, and being built of wood was utterly destroyed.

The English had lost two hundred and twenty-six killed and eight hundred and twenty wounded, among whom were thirteen officers. This was the first British victory in America. Gage, who never seems to have entertained the same contempt for the Americans as the majority of his countrymen, wrote home to Dartmouth—"The trials we have had show the rebels are not the despicable rabble too many have supposed them to be. The conquest of this country is not easy. You have to cope with vast numbers." "England has lost her colonies for ever," were Franklin's words, when he heard the news.[1]

The confidence of the English cabinet was at length shaken. Barrington declared that no augmentation of the forces was possible. The king alone remained firm. He would have twenty thousand men in America by next spring.

"Flectere si nequeo Superos, Acheronta movebo"

seemed to be his motto. If Englishmen would not murder and enslave their kinsmen in America, Hessians or Russians, or even Red Indians should. In America a spirit widely different prevailed. On the 6th of July a declaration was laid before congress and agreed to, setting forth the causes and the necessities of the war. It declared that the legislature of Great Britain, "stimulated by an inordinate passion for power, not only unjustifiable, but which they know to be peculiarly reprobated by the very constitution of that kingdom, and desperate of success in any mode of contest where regard should be had to truth, law, or right, have at length, deserting those, attempted to effect their cruel and impolitic purpose of enslaving these colonies by violence, and have thereby rendered it necessary for us to close with their last appeal from reason to arms." They set forth the happy results of the union as it had previously existed; the injustice of the enactments imposed by parliament; the rejection of their petitions; the unprovoked attacks made by the British troops at Lexington and Concord; the perfidy of Gage towards the inhabitants of Boston, and the fear of an invasion from Canada. Finally they declared that although "resolved to die freemen rather than live slaves," they had no intention of dissolving the union. "We have not," they

[1] Annual Register, vol. xviii., pp. 134-137. Bancroft, vol. vii., pp. 406-435.

said, "raised armies with ambitious designs of separating from Great Britain and establishing independent states. We fight not for glory or for conquest. We exhibit to mankind the remarkable spectacle of a people attacked by unprovoked enemies, without any imputation or even suspicion of offence."[1] On the 8th of July, the petition to the king, drawn up by Dickinson, was laid before the congress. Its tone was loyal and temperate, but somewhat indefinite. It expressed a general desire for reconciliation, but did not contain any explicit statement of grievances. But it mattered little what the petition contained. The only acceptable address which the colonies could have presented would have been summed up in two words, "We submit," and those words the colonists were determined the king should never hear. At the same time they sent an address to the inhabitants of Great Britain. They appealed to their love of freedom; they repeated their avowals of loyalty, and warned them of the hopelessness of war, reminding them that success, even if it were possible, would be useless. They sent a letter to the Lord Mayor and the Corporation of London, thanking them for their advocacy. These documents were sent with a letter of instructions to Penn and to the colony agents in London. Addresses were also drawn up to the people of Jamaica and Ireland, and on the 31st July a resolution was passed, formally condemning Lord North's conciliatory scheme. On the 30th of June, a committee was appointed to prepare "proper talks to the several tribes of Indians," and on the 13th of July they laid before the congress a "talk," representing the state of affairs between the colonies and the mother country, and likening themselves to a child, whose father had been persuaded by servants to load him with too heavy a pack.[2]

As a means of organising national resistance, the congress had been eminently successful. As an instrument for governing an empire and conducting a war, it seemed in danger of being a

[1] Journal of Congress, pp. 120–129.
[2] Journal of Congress, pp. 116, 130–149, 154–166, 172–182, 188–195.

failure. Hitherto it had been a deliberative and advisatory body, now it was called on to exercise legislative powers, without any strictly defined limits to its authority, or any recognised basis on which that authority should rest. Not only had the congress no power to pass laws, but it had no means of executing them. It was at war with the existing executive, yet unwilling to take the decisive step of creating an executive of its own. In the camp this weakness was especially felt. The rolls promised seventeen thousand men, but there were never more than fourteen thousand five hundred fit for duty. After all possible exertions, the supply of powder was insufficient. The troops, though undoubtedly brave, were utterly undisciplined, and the officers possessed no authority. Courts-martial had to be frequently held, and Washington's life was "one continued round of vexation and fatigue." [1] Nor was the brilliant promise of success opened by the capture of Ticonderoga fulfilled. On the 18th of May, as we have seen, congress had been apprised that danger was to be apprehended from Canada. On the 13th of May, a letter written by Arnold from Crown Point was laid before congress, informing them that there were four hundred regulars at St John's in readiness to cross the lake, and expecting to be joined by a number of Indians, with the design of retaking Crown Point and Ticonderoga. It was thereupon decided that reinforcements should be sent to the garrisons at both those places, and other preparations made for their defence. [2] The position of congress was a difficult one. To attack Canada was to abandon the position of unaggressive resistance which the colonists had hitherto occupied; to neglect it might be to allow the enemy to gain a fatal advantage. Carleton, the governor of Canada, had been furnished with special powers to embody and arm the Canadians, to employ them out of the country against the other colonists, and to deal summarily with all whom he might deem rebels. [3] Under these circumstances, to anticipate his attack seemed necessary as a measure of self-

---

[1] Bancroft, vol. viii., pp. 44, 45.   [2] Journal of Congress, pp. 64-66.
[3] Annual Register, vol. xix., pp. 2, 3.

defence. That such an attempt on their part would be successful, they had good grounds for believing. The generality of the inhabitants were discontented under their new government, and were, it was generally believed, disposed to identify their own interests with those of the rest of the colonies.[1] Accordingly, three thousand men were sent out under the command of Schuyler and Montgomery.[2] Schuyler was a man of considerable social influence, honest, laborious, and patriotic, but wanting in enterprise; a civilian in his tastes and habits, and utterly unfit to become a general at a month's notice.[3] He, however, fell sick, and the command devolved on his colleague. Montgomery was an Irishman who had served with distinction in the Seven Years' War. Thinking that his claims had been unfairly passed over, he changed the career of a soldier for a life of studious retirement on a New York farm. His marriage had connected him with the Livingstones, an influential and patriotic New York family. Like all the great champions of American liberty, he did not seek command, but was sought by it. He left his farm, his newly married wife, and his books, in obedience to "the will of an oppressed people, compelled to choose between liberty and slavery."[4] Early in September, Montgomery laid siege to St John's. The garrison numbered between six hundred and seven hundred men, of whom about five hundred were regulars. At first Montgomery's operations were impeded by want of powder. By a bold stroke he obtained possession of the small fort of Chambley, and captured one hundred and twenty barrels of powder. Schuyler, though incapacitated for active service, took care that reinforcements of troops and abundant supplies of provisions should be sent up. In the meantime, Carleton had been making efforts to relieve St John's. With a motley force, composed principally of Canadians, with a few regulars and some English volunteers, he marched from Montreal. He had arranged

---

[1] Annual Register, vol. xix., p. 3.
[2] Annual Register, vol. xix., p. 4.   [3] Bancroft, vol. viii., p. 29.
[4] Bancroft, vol. viii., p. 178. Annual Register, vol. xix., p. 15.

to effect a junction with M'Lean, a Scotch officer, who had been raising a regiment among his countrymen, many of whom had recently emigrated into Canada, and had not yet settled. But Montgomery had been beforehand with him, and sent detachments to prevent the junction. Carleton's force was easily repulsed, and M'Lean, finding the case hopeless, retreated to Quebec. On the 3d of November, St John's capitulated. The garrison laid down their arms, and were sent as prisoners into the provinces.[1]

The success of the American armies in Canada had not, however, been unbroken. Allen, the captor of Ticonderoga, had taken in hand another enterprise equally wild, but not, like his former one, justified by success. He had been sent to raise a force to join Montgomery, and had collected about one hundred and ten men. But instead of joining the army with them, he bethought him of capturing Montreal. While yet on his march, a mixed force of Indians and Canadians of about four times his own strength fell upon him. Most of his men made good their escape, but Allen himself with thirty-eight others was taken prisoner.[2]

From St John's, Montgomery proceeded to Montreal. The inhabitants at once offered to come to terms, which Montgomery refused. In answer, however, to their proposal, he pledged himself, if they surrendered, not to interfere with their civil and religious rights, and to protect their property. His terms satisfied the citizens, and on the 13th of November, Montreal surrendered.[3]

The English hopes in Canada now centred in Quebec. Before Montgomery could reach that fortress, it was threatened by another force. Arnold, in command of one thousand one hundred men, had started from the mouth of the Kennebec, and marched up the course of the stream. For thirty-one days, he and his troops travelled through a wilderness without seeing a human

[1] Annual Register, vol. xix., pp. 5–7.
[2] Annual Register, vol. xix., p. 5. Bancroft, vol. viii., pp. 183, 184.
[3] Annual Register, vol. xix., p. 7.

being. Woods, swamps, and precipices, all barred their path. Sometimes they could not travel more than four or five miles a day. Their supplies failed. They were reduced to eating their dogs. Their clothes were torn by the thickets through which they struggled. On the march, the force was diminished by the desertion of three companies. When they reached Canada, they were but two-thirds of their original number. Once in Canada, they were received everywhere with good will and hospitality. Arnold, following the example of Montgomery and Schuyler, published an address signed by Washington, inviting the Canadians to join them, and promising them safety and protection. In a little less than three weeks afterwards, Arnold was joined by Montgomery. In spite of the supplies of clothing which Montgomery had obtained at Montreal, his troops had suffered severely from the inclement weather. By this time the imminence of danger had united the hitherto discordant and discontented inhabitants of Quebec. Montgomery finding that the town was likely to hold out, and that both his supplies and artillery were insufficient for a siege, proposed to try a storming party. On the 16th of December a council of war was held, and an assault was determined on. On the last night of the old year, Montgomery led the storming party, consisting of three hundred New Yorkers. That they might know one another in the darkness, they had pieces of white paper on their caps inscribed, "Death or Liberty." There was a strong north-east wind. The hail drove in their eyes, and they slipped on the frozen snow. The first position to be won was guarded by a battery of two three-pounders. When the Americans were within fifty yards, a cannonade of grape shot swept the path, and Montgomery fell dead. The grape shot was followed up by a discharge of musketry, and the storming party retreated. On the north-west side, the attack had at first been successful. Arnold had been carried off wounded at the first battery, but Morgan, a brave Virginian, had taken his place, and after a fierce engagement of an hour, had carried the battery. But by the time they had reached the next barricade, the garrison had recovered their surprise, while the arms of the assailants were rendered almost useless by the storm. Retreat was impossible. On both sides they were exposed to heavy fire, and the troops who had opposed Montgomery were now disengaged. Taken in flank and rear, all hope of escape was gone, and at ten o'clock the next morning, they surrendered. Sixty men had fallen in the assault, and between three hundred and four hundred were taken prisoners.[1]

In the death of Montgomery the American cause sustained an irreparable loss. Congress honoured him with the expression of "their profound respect and high veneration," and directed a marble monument to his "glory." In parliament his memory was eulogised, and even his enemies could only charge him with having undone his country by his virtues. Barré, his countryman and once his companion in arms, wept as he dwelt on his greatness. Burke contrasted him with the English commanders in Boston, and Fox retorted on those who called him a rebel, by reminding them that the House of Commons itself owed its existence to a rebellion.[2]

For the next three months, Arnold continued the blockade. More than once he attempted to set fire to the town and the ships in the harbour, intending to attack the town in the confusion, but although considerable damage was done, no decisive advantage was gained. The appearance of small-pox in the besiegers' camp created, as it always did in America, a panic, like that caused by the plague in Europe. The discipline of the New England troops, always defective, became yet worse under this trial. Besides, Arnold was ill supported both by congress and by the inhabitants of Canada. Could Quebec only hold out till the ice broke up, and till ships could arrive from England, it would be safe. That succour came before the blockaders expected it. On the 6th of May, English ships appeared in the river. The

---
[1] Annual Register, vol. xix., pp. 8-15. Bancroft, vol. viii., pp. 190-212.
[2] Annual Register, vol. xix., p. 15. Bancroft, vol. viii., p. 212.

besiegers, utterly unprepared for such intervention, were thrown into confusion. Immediately Carleton ordered a sally. The Americans retreated precipitately, abandoning their artillery stores and scaling ladders. The governor, however, was too weak to pursue them, and only the sick and wounded became prisoners. Although Carleton had shown a lack of skill and readiness in protecting the frontier of Canada, his defence of Quebec fully retrieved his military fame. But what is still more to his honour, is his humanity to the "rebels." Many of the sick and wounded were scattered through the woods and villages, and were in danger of perishing through famine or disease. To save them from such a fate, he issued a proclamation giving orders that they should be sought for and relieved at the public expense, and that as soon as they were sufficiently recovered, they should be at liberty to return to their respective provinces.[1] Nor should it be forgotten that he had done his utmost to deprive an unnatural war of its worst features, by preventing incursions of Indians on the New England frontiers.[2]

In Virginia, Dunmore had shown a widely different spirit. Not content with following Gage's example of seizing the public store of powder, he set spring guns about the magazine.[3] Further outrages followed. Dreading, not unnaturally, though it would seem without foundation, the revenge of the people, he took up his quarters on board a man-of-war, and refused to land. The assembly, on their part, refused to transact business on board ship. Various messages passed between them, till at last the assembly, seeing that the governor was immovable, dissolved, and the legislation of Virginia was at an end.[4] The governor then commenced his campaign. His programme was to exhibit to the colonists the spectacle of an English nobleman, the ruler of an ancient and important colony, carrying on a guerilla warfare against his own subjects, plundering their plantations, burning

---

[1] Annual Register, vol. xix., pp. 145-153.   [2] Bancroft, vol. viii., p. 186.
[3] Wirt, pp. 168, 169. Annual Register, vol. xix., p. 21.
[4] Annual Register, vol. xix., pp. 21-26.

their houses, and raising their slaves against them. The emancipation of the negroes certainly seemed strange policy for a government, that only five years back had so resolutely opposed any approach to such a measure. Possibly Dunmore and the king argued that the crime of freeing a negro was compensated for by the merit of employing him to enslave a white man. On the governor's proclamation being issued, several hundreds of blacks and whites flocked to his standard. On the 9th of December, hostilities commenced. The colonists were entrenched in a position defended by a narrow causeway. Captain Fordyce, at the head of upwards of sixty grenadiers, attempted to carry the causeway. They were met by a heavy fire in front and on the left flank. Fordyce fell, and his troops, after a brave resistance, were beaten back, having lost fully half their number.[1] The loyalists took to their ships, and lay off the coast of Norfolk. On the 21st of December, a man-of-war and a brig from England arrived. They brought three thousand stands of arms, for which Dunmore had promised to provide negroes and Indians. A flag of truce was sent on shore to demand provisions for the ships, which were refused. The governor, after consulting Below, the captain of the man-of-war, resolved that the town should be bombarded. On the 1st of January 1776, a cannonade was opened. Parties of sailors landed under cover of the ship's guns, and set fire to the town, and by the evening Norfolk, the richest city in Virginia, was a heap of ashes.[2]

What, meanwhile, was the condition of things in England? How far had the report of Bunker's Hill dispelled those vain hopes with which the English parliament had rushed headlong into war? One would have supposed that the hardiest reviler of the Americans must have seen by this time how utterly unfounded were his anticipations. The disasters of the war were not confined to defeats by land. Supplies had been sent out in the most lavish manner during the autumn of 1775. Five thousand oxen

---

[1] Annual Register, vol. xix., p. 29. Bancroft, vol. viii., pp. 226, 227.
[2] Annual Register, vol. xix., pp. 29-31. Bancroft, vol. viii., pp. 228-230.

and fourteen thousand sheep, with a vast number of pigs, had been shipped alive. Beer, and vegetables, and vinegar had been sent out at a cost of £22,000. Half a million of specie was remitted. With the mismanagement which had throughout characterised the conduct of the war, the ships were sent out too late in the year for the voyage to be safe. Some were windbound on the English coast, others stopped by storms. The channel was strewn with dead bodies of sheep and pigs. Nor was the fate of the ships that reached America better. Some were driven ashore on the West Indies, or captured by American privateers. A small proportion arrived at Boston, and these, with their cargoes, rendered almost worthless by the length and severity of the voyage.[1] The Fishery Act, like all the other coercive measures adopted by England, had recoiled on her own head. It had cut off supplies from our own fisheries, and thrown the whole trade of Newfoundland into confusion.[2] The Duke of Grafton had the candour to confess, when resigning his office, that he had been led to sanction the government policy by gross misrepresentation and concealment of facts; that events had taught him wisdom, and that he now saw that the only plan to avert the most destructive and fatal consequences would be to place the Americans in the same position as they occupied in 1763.[3] The prospect of diminished taxation, which had led the country gentry to go heart and soul into the war, was lamentably reversed. On the 13th of November, Lord North moved that the land tax for the ensuing year should be five shillings in the pound.[4] Yet the country was willing to pay this price for the triumph of destroying its own colonies. It was even willing to go about hiring troops at an extortionate price from every petty prince in Germany to fight against its own fellow-subjects. One influence which tended to keep up this state of things was that of the public journals. The partisans of government studiously filled them not merely with attacks on the opposition, but with

[1] Annual Register, vol. xix., pp. 51, 52.
[2] Annual Register, vol. xix., p. 49.
[3] Annual Register, vol. xix., pp. 69, 70.
[4] Annual Register, vol. xix., p. 99.

charges as ludicrous as malignant. A number of peers and eminent commoners had been detected in treasonable correspondence, and the country might soon hope to see the Tower filled with persons of rank, and a full harvest of impeachments and punishments succeed. One incident that occurred in the autumn of 1775, trivial in itself, throws light on the deluded state of the public mind, and on the artifices which were used to maintain it. A London banker, of good position by birth, an American, was seized under a warrant from the Secretary of State, and thrown into the Tower, on the charge of having suborned some of the guards to seize the king's person, and keep him prisoner in the Tower till he could be removed. The whole history of the Popish Plot cannot show anything more extravagant. The only sufferer ultimately was the Secretary of State, who was mulcted in £1000 damages for false imprisonment, but the rumour at first excited universal "indignation and horror," and "absorbed all other considerations with respect to public affairs."[1]

The petition of congress presented by Penn met with the reception that might have been expected. Moderate and conciliatory as it was, it was decided that to entertain any proposals would be unbecoming the dignity of a great nation, and the petition was refused an answer. Even an examination of Penn before the Lords was strenuously resisted.[2] His evidence was unlikely to be tainted by any suspicion of bias towards the Americans. His interests, and those of his family, as proprietaries of Pennsylvania, all led him to wish for the preservation of the colonies as dependencies. In fact, he united the interests of an Englishman with the information of an American. Yet so determined were the ministry to stick to one fixed line of policy, and so resolved to hear nothing that could lead them to modify it, that they did not make the least attempt to get any information from him about the state of America.[3] On his examination, he assured the House that the colonies had no desire for inde-

[1] Annual Register, vol. xix., pp. 53-55.   [2] Annual Register, vol. xix., pp. 93, 94.
[3] Annual Register, vol. xix., p. 96.

pendence, but that, if necessary, they were ready and able to defend their liberties. In his own colony there were sixty thousand men capable of bearing arms, and that twenty thousand, mostly men of good fortune and character, had enrolled themselves as volunteers. They had the means and the requisite skill for manufacturing brass cannon and small arms. He warned them that the colonists had staked their last hope of peace on the petition, and that if repulsed, they would probably seek foreign alliances. At the conclusion of his examination the Duke of Richmond, who had proposed it, brought forward a measure for conciliation on the basis of the petition. After a fierce debate, the motion went the way of all its predecessors, and was lost by eighty-six to thirty-three.[1] Six days later Burke made a similar attempt in the Commons. Taking up his old ground of constitutional policy, he modelled his scheme on the statute of Edward III., *De tallagio non concedendo.* He deprecated the imputations cast upon the supporters of America as being deficient in patriotism, or disposed to regard sedition with leniency. He examined the three possible lines of policy open to England,—force, concession, or a combination of the two. The employment of force, he argued, was impracticable; the arrangements made for it could not be carried out; the moment our troops marched into the country, they would be cut off from supplies. A mixed policy would give no satisfaction to the Americans; it was useless to send out pardons to a people who would not accept them. Concession was the only line of conduct open to us. He pointed out that the settlement of the question of taxation was an indispensable preliminary to peace. He allowed that the necessity for surrendering any part of our legislative power was to be regretted, but that it was the inevitable consequence of our injudicious policy. A long debate followed, but the motion was lost by a majority of two-thirds in a house of three hundred and fifteen.[2] On the 20th the fight was renewed over the Prohibitory

---

[1] Annual Register, vol. xix., pp. 95-99.
[2] Annual Register, vol. xix., pp. 104-107. Burke's Works, vol. iii., pp. 23-132.

Bill of the ministry. The object of this bill was to cut off all trade and intercourse with the thirteen united colonies. It empowered the officers of the king's ships to capture all American goods and ships, whether in harbour or on the high seas, and to impress all Americans that should be taken prisoners. The goods so seized were to become the property of the captors. At the same time, it enabled the crown to appoint commissioners, who should have power to grant special exemptions from the conditions of the act to such colonies as should have returned to their allegiance. The opposition denounced the measure as "a cruel, indiscriminate, and perpetual declaration of war." They represented that it would compel the Americans to convert their merchant ships into privateers, and would thereby endanger our commerce in every quarter of the globe. They ridiculed the idea of holding out offers of pardon to men "who acknowledged no crime, and were conscious, not of doing, but of suffering wrong." The clause which vested the property of seizures in the captors was denounced as lowering our sailors to the level of pirates. One speaker proposed that the bill should be entitled, "A Bill for carrying more effectually into execution the resolves of Congress."[1] In the Upper House the bill met with equally severe treatment. To compel the captured Americans to serve on board our vessels, was described as "a refinement in tyranny, which, in a sentence worse than death, obliges the unhappy men who shall be made captives in this predatory war to bear arms against their families, kindred, friends, and country; and after being plundered themselves, to become accomplices in plundering their brethren." Mansfield, in replying to these charges, hardily avowed that the time for all considerations of justice was past; we were in the war, and must fight it out; and he quoted the speech of a Scotch officer in the army of Gustavus Adolphus, who, pointing to the enemy, said to his men, "See you those, lads? kill them, or they will kill you;"

[1] Annual Register, vol. xix., pp. 109-112.

an illustration the main defect of which was its total inapplicability.[1]

On the 20th of February, Fox brought forward a motion attacking the ministry, not for their policy, but for the inefficient and extravagant manner in which that policy had been carried out. The defence they set up is interesting, as illustrating, perhaps, more forcibly than anything which we have yet seen, the principles which they applied to the case of America. The failure of our arms was due, not to mismanagement or even misfortune, but to our clemency and desire for conciliation, of which the Americans had taken an unworthy and base advantage. The failure of the war, so far, would only show to the world "the lenity, forbearance, and temperate justice of our government, and the incorrigible turpitude of the colonists."[2] The defeat at Concord was, it seems, due to the conciliatory spirit shown by Gage and his troops. Truly, if to blockade the colonists' ports, to cut off their fisheries, to place them under martial law, and to let loose on them bands of negroes and Red Indians were measures of lenity and conciliation, while the serious business of coercion had yet to begin, the Americans had no need to justify their rebellion.

On the 4th of March, the aspect of American affairs reached its culminating point. The Duke of Grafton moved in the House of Lords that a proclamation should be issued, declaring that if the colonists should, within a certain time, present a petition, setting forth their grievances, hostility should be suspended, and their petition taken into consideration. He pointed out that to adhere to the principle of requiring unqualified submission was, in the present state of things, simply an open declaration of war. He also warned his hearers, that the Americans had already commenced negotiations with France, and that to drive them to extremities would probably involve us in a foreign war. The debate was long and fierce, and the ground taken up by the

---

[1] Annual Register, vol. xix., pp. 118, 119.
[2] Annual Register, vol. xix., p. 130.

ministerial party more decided than ever. The Declaration of Independence was the only thing needed to make America and England two belligerent powers.[1]

At that very time the English arms had sustained the severest blow that had yet befallen them. The army in Boston numbered eight thousand men. Their supplies from England had, as we have seen, failed, and a famine in the West Indies cut off their hope of relief from that quarter.[2] The American army, on the other hand, was well supplied both with provisions and clothing. But in the means of reducing a strictly garrisoned town they were miserably deficient. Their supply of powder was insufficient; their military chest was empty; many of the muskets had no bayonets, and their artillery was chiefly supplied from prizes captured by American cruisers.[3] The last year's army had served their time, and the fresh enlistments went on slowly. Congress starved the army in the matter of money and supplies, partly through irresolution and dread of action, to some extent excusable in a body whose position was so indefinite and anomalous, partly through a desire to conciliate the ship-builders by favouring the navy at the expense of the land force. Nevertheless, congress expected bricks without straw, and on the 22d of December they passed a resolution, and forwarded it to Washington, authorising him "to attack Boston in any manner that he might deem expedient." Hitherto he had never complained, but his answer was a dignified remonstrance.[4] Still, ill supplied as he was, having only a hundred barrels of powder, on the 4th of March he determined on a bold attempt. After dark, a heavy bombardment and cannonade commenced from the American lines, and was kept up on both sides till morning. When day broke, Howe was met by a sight which showed him that at one stroke his position had been rendered untenable. As if by magic strong works had been in a single night created on Dorchester

---

[1] Annual Register, vol. xix., pp. 139, 140. [2] Annual Register, vol. xix., p. 146.
[3] Bancroft, vol. viii., pp. 234, 291–293. [4] Bancroft, vol. viii., p. 234.

Heights. To leave the Americans there would be to give them the command of the harbour, and to cut off Boston from all supplies; to attempt to dislodge them might end in a second Bunker's Hill. A council of war was called, and the bolder advice prevailed. Two thousand four hundred men were embarked to attack the newly-raised entrenchments. Had they landed, Washington had four thousand men in readiness to attack the town. A storm, however, interfered, and by the time that it was possible to renew the attempt, the works had been so strengthened as to render success hopeless. Nothing was left but to evacuate the town. On the 16th of March the British troops set sail, and Washington entered Boston. An English army sent to conquer New England, not by arms, but by intimidation, had gained a single victory in which their loss had been double that of their enemy; they had been cooped up in Boston for eleven months, and had finally retreated precipitately, leaving their stores and artillery to the enemy. Within a week the long excluded inhabitants began to pour in, and Boston was once more a free and an inhabited city.[1] In the south, if no such substantial success had been achieved, an equally heroic spirit had been shown. In North Carolina, Martin, the governor, had raised the royal standard, and had collected a force consisting of highland emigrants and of the backwoods outlaws known as "Regulators." Clinton was expected to join them with a small detachment from Boston. The plan of the campaign was to take possession of the interior of the country, to unite all the Regulators, and, if possible, to raise the Indians. On the side of the Americans, Moore, with one thousand one hundred men, was encamped in a strong position at Rockfish, and Caswell, with about eight hundred men, was marching to join him. To anticipate this movement, Donald M'Donald, the commander of the Highlanders, marched to meet Caswell with one thousand five hundred men. On the 27th he came up with Caswell, who had established himself, with a force now increased to about one

[1] Bancroft, vol. viii., pp. 292-307.

thousand men, on the west side of a stream called Moore's Creek. The loyalists trusted in their superior numbers, and resolved on an attack. At one o'clock on the morning of the 27th they advanced. M'Donald was confined to his tent by sickness, and his place was supplied by Donald M'Leod, a man of high character and great courage. They found that Caswell had retreated across the creek and broken up the bridge, leaving only two logs. Led by M'Leod, they endeavoured to cross the bridge. The rebels opposed their passage. M'Leod fell mortally wounded, and after a few minutes the loyalists fled. The rebels captured thirteen waggons and fifteen thousand pounds in gold, besides a great number of prisoners, among whom were the husband and son of Flora M'Donald, the heroine of '45. The moral effect of the victory was of immense value. It was the Concord of the Carolinas. North Carolina, which had been looked upon as one of the weakest of the colonies, had proved herself capable of self-defence. Nor was it of less importance that the Highlanders and Regulators had been disposed of before the regular troops had arrived from England. [1]

In the beginning of May, the squadron under Sir Peter Parker and Lord Cornwallis arrived, having been delayed by bad weather on the voyage. Clinton's troops met them at Cape Fear. Early in June they anchored off Charlestown Bar, with the view of attacking the town. The first step was to secure possession of Sullivan's Island, about six miles to the east of Charlestown. This was to be bombarded by the fleet, and attacked by Clinton from a neighbouring island, Long Island, the intermediate creek being, it was supposed, fordable at low water. The Americans, in the meantime, were proceeding rapidly with the fortification of Sullivan's Island. Works were erected of palmetto branches, seven feet high, with sixteen feet of sand between them; and by the 28th of June, though not complete, they were sufficiently advanced to be tenable against artillery. On that day, at half-past one, the cannonade opened from the fleet and from Long

---

[1] Bancroft, vol. viii., pp. 283 290.

Island. The fleet anchored within three hundred and fifty yards of the fort. During the whole of the day the cannonade was kept up on both sides, the Americans firing slowly, from the scantiness of their supply of powder. The creek by which Clinton's troops were to have crossed over was found to be impassable, and they were unable to co-operate with the fleet, a circumstance which unquestionably saved Charlestown. At nine o'clock in the evening the cannonade ceased. The inhabitants of Charlestown remained in suspense till a boat arrived from Moultrie, the commander of the fort, with the news that the admiral had slipped his cable and dropped down to his previous moorings. The loss of the British fleet was two hundred and five killed and wounded. Of the defenders of the fort, only eleven had fallen, and twenty-eight were wounded. Well might the people of Charlestown crowd to Fort Moultrie next day to thank their deliverers. They had not only rescued Charlestown from the fate of Norfolk, they had saved Carolina, and possibly the whole of the southern colonies.[1]

Before this, it had become evident that to defer any longer the formation of an independent government was to keep up an unnecessary source of weakness. Already the voice of the nation had protested unmistakably against the longer continuance of anarchy. The first definite step towards such a change had been taken in 1775 by New Hampshire. On the 11th of October, their delegates had petitioned congress to allow them to establish a government, but congress having still hopes of the success of the petition, had deferred answering their appeal. When, however, the king's proclamation arrived, the majority of congress saw at last that independence was only a question of time. An answer was sent to the convention of New Hampshire, recommending it to form a government. Similar advice was sent the next day to South Carolina, and a little later to Virginia. Yet New Hampshire shrank from so decisive a step, and coupled the formation of their new government with a studious expression of their

[1] Bancroft, vol. viii., 294–314.

allegiance.¹ Virginia showed a bolder spirit. In January, the convention passed a motion, instructing their delegates to recommend congress, to throw their ports open to all nations, and thus to cast off the commercial supremacy of England.² But the mere establishment of independent state governments was not enough. An imperial government, also independent of England, was essential. To establish independence without confederation would be only doing half the work. In the words of Franklin, "We must all hang together, unless we would all hang separately."³ About this time, Franklin's scheme for a confederation was laid before congress. The scheme did not include, but it evidently implied independence. Franklin had been throughout a strenuous advocate of reconciliation, as long as reconciliation was possible, and his opinion ought to have convinced all that the time for separation had come. But the timid counsels of his colleague, Dickinson, overruled the motion, and the scheme of a confederation was not even formally considered.⁴ On the 16th of February, the question of opening the ports was formally laid before congress.⁵ In the next month, measures were taken which clearly showed that independence was at hand. A private agent was sent to France by the authority of the committee of secret correspondence, and the instructions of the commissioners sent to Canada contained a clause inviting the people of Canada to "set up such a form of government as will be most likely in their judgment to produce their happiness." The clause was objected to as implying independence, and gave rise to a debate, but was ultimately carried. At last, after seven weeks' deliberation, the congress resolved to emancipate the colonies from all commercial restrictions, and on the 6th of April the ports of America were thrown open to the world.⁶

On the 27th of March, South Carolina proceeded to construct a government. They asserted as their principle of action that

---

[1] Bancroft, vol. viii., p. 243.
[2] Bancroft, vol. viii., p. 247.
[3] Spark's "Life of Franklin," ed. 1856, p. 408.
[4] Life of Franklin, p. 397.
[5] Bancroft, vol. viii., p. 313.
[6] Bancroft, vol. viii., p. 323.

the good of the people is the origin and end of all government, and they set forth the misconduct of the king, the parliament, and the officers of the English government. At the same time, they introduced no change into the system of representation or the qualification of voters.[1] On the 4th of May, the assembly of Rhode Island passed an act, discharging the inhabitants of the colony from allegiance to the king, and at the same time authorised its delegates in congress to conclude a treaty with any independent power, for the security of the colonies.[2] On May the 6th, the assembly of Virginia met at Williamsburg. After a declaration that all pacific measures were useless, and that "they had no alternative left but an abject submission to the will of those overbearing tyrants, or a total separation from the crown and government of Great Britain," they passed two resolutions; the first, empowering their delegates at the convention to propose a declaration of independence and a confederation of the colonies; the second, appointing a committee to draw up a declaration of rights and a scheme of government for the colony. On the 12th of June, the declaration of rights was laid before the assembly, and on the 29th, a constitution was produced. The assembly then proceeded to elect a governor. The choice fell on Patrick Henry. Rightly was he, who had first foreseen independence and bidden his countrymen look the danger of it in the face, deemed worthy to be the first to govern the state which he had called into being.[3] All the colonies except Pennsylvania and Maryland followed the example of Virginia,[4] and when, on the 1st of July, the motion for independence was laid before congress, the delegates of nine colonies were pledged to vote in its favour. The delegates of Pennsylvania and Maryland were divided, those of South Carolina unanimously opposed independence. The New York delegates were all in favour of independence, and represented the opinion of the colony, but could not vote as their

---

[1] Bancroft, vol. viii., pp. 345-351.
[2] Bancroft, vol. viii., pp. 355, 356.
[3] Bancroft, vol. viii., pp. 434-437.
[4] Bancroft, vol. viii., pp. 385-387.

convention had not yet been duly elected.¹ When the question came forward for decision next day, Dickinson, who had opposed it on the first day with great earnestness, stayed away, as did one of his colleagues, and the vote of Pennsylvania was altered. Another delegate arrived from Delaware, whose vote turned the scale, and South Carolina, rather than stand alone, withdrew its opposition. New York alone was unable to vote, and on the 2d of July, by the decision of twelve colonies, without one adverse vote, it was resolved "that these united colonies are and of right ought to be free and independent states; that they are absolved from all allegiance to the British crown, and that all political connection between them and the state of Great Britain is, and ought to be, totally dissolved." Seldom was the irony of history more strikingly illustrated than when Hancock, a rebel specially selected for proscription by the English government, put the question to the vote, and declared the American colonies for ever independent.²

Thomas Jefferson of Virginia was selected to draw up the declaration which had been resolved upon. His pen had already served his country. In 1774, he had published, "A Summary View of the Rights of British America," setting forth the dangers which menaced the country, and encouraging the people in defence of their liberties.³ He had, as we have seen, signalised himself in his own colony by his opposition to slavery. "Wherever he was, there was found a soul devoted to the cause of liberty, power to defend and maintain it, and willingness to incur all its hazards."⁴ On the 4th of July the declaration was produced. It declared the abstract principles on which their secession was justified; it then drew up an indictment against the king in eighteen heads, setting forth the various ways in which he had proved himself "a tyrant unfit to be the ruler

---

[1] Bancroft, vol. viii., pp. 450–457. [2] Bancroft, vol. viii., p. 459.
[3] Speech by Daniel Webster, in commemoration of Adams and Jefferson. Published in Webster's Works, vol. i., p. 125.
[3] Webster, vol. i., p. 125.

of a free people." Finally, it declared that the united colonies were free and independent states; that the connection with Great Britain was, and ought to be totally dissolved, and that as free and independent states, they had full power to levy war, conclude peace, contract alliances, establish commerce, and to do all other acts and things which independent states may of right do."[1]

Unless I have told the story of American independence utterly amiss, but little comment is needed. Seldom in human events do the facts of history carry their own explanation so clearly with them. A people who had grown up gradually, almost unconsciously, under democratic institutions, at last saw those institutions subverted. To preserve the spirit of them, they changed their form. We must not be misled into the error of under-rating the importance of the American struggle by any idea of the insignificance of the issue at stake. We must not suppose that it was as an earnest and eloquent writer has called it, "a war for the vindication of the principle of representative taxation."[2] Its immediate origin, it is true, involved no vital interest, such as often has been at stake when nations have risen against their rulers. But "rebellions may fall out on small occasions, they do not spring from small causes," was said by the first and wisest of political philosophers. Taxation was, as Burke says, that by which the colonists felt the pulse of liberty, "and as they found that beat, they thought themselves sick or sound."[3]

The whole key to the American revolution lies in two facts; it was a democratic and a conservative revolution. It was the work of the people, and its end was to preserve, not to destroy or to construct afresh. The policy of an early father of new England, "In a revolution burn all, and build afresh," was far from being

---

[1] Annual Register, vol. xix., pp. 261-264.
[2] Lectures on Great Men. By the Rev. F. Myers.
[3] Burke's Works, vol. iii., p. 51.

that of his descendants. Throughout the whole war of Independence, the colonists had a fixed known end in view. More than that, they had already within themselves the means for effecting that end, and making it enduring, as far as what is human can endure. The future that they proposed to themselves was not independent of their past, it was a fuller development of it. There was no need for beginning with the year one, or for throwing aside, as worn out, anything that their ancestors had left them. And it was essentially a democratic revolution. Throughout, the movement came from the people. The very blunders made by the hesitation and timidity of congress were the mistakes of an assembly of delegates, not of representative statesmen. When the final step was taken, the congress was not the originator of it, but was little more than a mouthpiece giving expression to the declared wishes of the nation. From the first moment that the resistance to England began, in political foresight, in endurance, in enterprise, in everything except military skill, the nation as a whole was in advance of its greatest men. Not that, measured by the standard of moral worth, any national struggle ever had leaders more worthy of it than were Washington and Samuel Adams, to lead the contest for American freedom. Both were essentially men of the people, men who represented two sides of the national character in their highest form. Adams, a worthy descendant of Puritan ancestors, whose highest ambition was, in his own words, to see New England a Christian Sparta; Washington, the type of a high-minded Virginian gentleman, neither soldier or statesman by profession or choice, but ready to take either part, when his country called upon him. But they led the American people only because they so truly represented them, and embodied their principles. The spirit of resistance did not come from them; it found in them the fittest instruments in whom and by whom it might act. To those who regard the world as the battlefield of a few chosen spirits, whose mission is to trample upon the will of the many, and who would make history but the record of their achievements, the struggle for American independence may well seem blank and barren. But they who believe that all great things must be done by, and not for, those who are to enjoy them; who believe that individuals, be they ever so great, can at best only direct and strengthen the spirit of a nation, but can never originate it, will see, in the history of a people with dispassionate foresight choosing its own highest good, and with patient courage winning it, the noblest spectacle, because the most hopeful, that the world can show us. Judged by the standard which we too often apply to political events, no doubt the American war may fail to impress us as does the revolt of the Netherlands, or even as does the English rebellion. The wrong of the ruler was far less flagrant, the suffering and heroism of the ruled far less striking. An obstinate, ignorant, well-meaning king, with the faults and virtues of an average English squire, possessed by the insane idea that he was fit to govern a great empire, is dramatically a poor substitute for the ruler of all the Indies forcing the Inquisition on a Protestant nation. The departure of Bernard can ill stand as a historical picture beside the trial of Strafford. America had no Hampden, no William the Silent, to command our admiration; England had no Alva to rouse our hatred, no Falkland to move our pity. Yet, as a step in the progress of the human race, the American rebellion was in advance of any movement that had gone before it. In the Netherlands, a nation had been lashed into resistance by the most iniquitous cruelty that civilised man ever inflicted on his fellows. In England, a nation had risen under the leadership of a party in defence of its chartered rights. In America we see a people, pressed by no severe material suffering, deliberately declaring itself independent of a government which could no longer satisfy its needs, a people in a spirit of calm political foresight choosing present suffering for the sake of future greatness, rather than present ease at the cost of future slavery. The American Declaration of Independence was a witness to the world that freedom, resting not on institutions, but on the necessities of human nature, was no mere abstract idea, but a vital principle of national life, not a remnant of antiquity for pedants to admire, and orators to declaim over, but a substantial good for which the New England merchant and the Virginian yeoman were ready to go forth and die.

THE END.

RIVINGTONS, LONDON, OXFORD, AND CAMBRIDGE.

www.ingramcontent.com/pod-product-compliance
Lightning Source LLC
Chambersburg PA
CBHW021836230426
43669CB00008B/989